POST-SOVIET DYNAMICS OF CENTRAL ASIA

POST-SOVIET DYNAMICS OF CENTRAL ASIA

Dr. Surya Narain Yadav

JNANADA PRAKASHAN (P&D)
NEW DELHI

Published by :
JNANADA PRAKASHAN (P&D)
4837/2, 24, Ansari Road, Daryaganj
New Delhi-110002
Phone : 011-23272047
Mobile : 9212137080

Assisted by :
TEXT BOOK PROMOTION SOCIETY OF INDIA
4837/2, 24, Ansari Road, Daryaganj
New Delhi-110002
Phone : 011-23272047
Mobile : 9212137080

Edition: 2016

Post-Soviet Dynamics of Central Asia

ISBN 978-81-7139-372-5

Typesetting by :
Vardhman Computers
New Delhi-110017

Published by Mrs. S. Chowdhary for M/s. Jnanada Prakashan (P&D) Daryaganj, Ansari Road, New Delhi-110 002 and printed at Balaji Offset, Navin Shahdara, Delhi-110032.

PREFACE

Despite the disintegration of the Soviet Union in 1991, the presence and influence of Russia in the Central Asian Republics are very significant.

The book entitled "Post-Soviet Dynamics of Central Asia" systematically and thoroughly examines the prevailing social, economic, political as well as strategic situations in the former Soviet republics. The emergence of radical Islam in Central Asia has been one of the most disturbing developments in the post-Soviet era. In order to combat the forces of separatism, extremism and terrorism, China and Russia are playing a significant role within the framework of the Shanghai cooperation Organization

In view of the strategic significance of Central Asia, especially in terms of geography and energy, India is also evolving its strategy to play a major role in this region. In the post-Soviet era, China is gradually expanding its influence in Central Asia both within the bilateral and regional framework. However, Russia is equally maintaining its overall presence and influence in this region. The book is the original, the Post–Soviet political, Socio–economic and cultural milieu of Central Asia.

The author is fully convinced that this book would be an invaluable source of knowledge for the academician, researcher as well as policy-maker. The book is the original, most comprehensive and critical analysis of China–Africa economic, political and strategic involvement is the 21st century.

ACRONYMS

CGNPC	China Guangdong Nuclear Power Holding
CNOOC	China National Offshore Oil Corporation
CNPC	China National Petroleum Corporation
CPC	Caspian Pipeline Consortium
CTEAS	Chinese Theban Electric Apparatus Stock Company
ETUE	East Turkestan Union in Europe
FIOC	First International Oil Company
GPP	Gas Processing Plants
IMU	Islamic Movement of Uzbekistan
NCSP	North Caspian Sea Project
ONGC	Oil and Natural Gas Corporation
PDPA	People's Democratic Party of Afghanistan
SAFTA	South Asian Free Trade Area
SCO	Shanghai Cooperation Organisation
TAE	Transit Asia Europe
TAPI	Turkmenistan-Afghanistan-Pakistan-India
TRACECA	Transport Corridor Europe Caucasus Asia
UIM	Uzbekistan Islamic Movement
ULO	Uighur Liberation Organisation
UNMOT	UN Mission of Observers in Tajikistan
UTO	United Tajik Opposition
ZTE	Zhongxing Telecom Equipment Corporation

CONTENTS

1

INTRODUCING CENTRAL ASIA

Central Asia is a region of Asia from the Caspian Sea in the west to central China in the east, and from southern Russia in the north to northern India in the south. It is also sometimes *known as Middle Asia or Inner Asia,* and is within the scope of the wider Eurasian continent.

Various definitions of its exact composition exist and no one definition is universally accepted. Despite this uncertainty in defining borders, it does have some important overall characteristics. For one, Central Asia has historically been closely tied to its nomadic peoples and the Silk Road.[1] As a result it has acted as a crossroads for the movement of people, goods, and ideas between Europe, West Asia, South Asia, and East Asia.[2]

In the modern context, Central Asia consists of the five former Soviet republics of Kazakhstan, Kyrgyzstan, Tajikistan, Turkmenistan and Uzbekistan. Other areas are often included such as Mongolia, Afghanistan, northern-Pakistan, north-eastern Iran, north-western India, and western parts of the People's Republic of China such as Xinjiang. South-western and middle China such as Tibet Autonomous Region, Qinghai, Gansu and Inner Mongolia, and southern parts of Siberia may also be included in Central Asia.

During pre-Islamic and early Islamic times, Central Asia was a predominantely Iranian[3,4] region that included sedentary Sogdians, Chorasmians and semi-nomadic Scythians, Alans. The ancient sedentary population played an important role in the history of Central Asia. Tajiks, Pashtuns, Pamiris and other Iranian groups are still present in the region. After expansion by Turkic peoples, central Asia became also the homeland for many Turkic peoples, including the Uzbeks, Kazakhs, Kyrgyz, and Uyghurs, and Central Asia is sometimes referred to as Turkestan.

Evolution of the Concept of Central Asia

The idea of Central Asia as a distinct region of the world was introduced in 1843 by the geographer Alexander von Humboldt. The borders of Central Asia are subject to multiple definitions. Many text books still refer to this area as Turkestan, which was the name used prior to Stalin's rule.

The most limited definition was the official one of the Soviet Union that defined the "Middle Asia" as consisting solely of Uzbekistan, Turkmenistan, Tajikistan, and Kyrgyzstan, but did not include Kazakhstan, Afghanistan and Mongolia. This definition was also often used outside the USSR in this period. However, there lacks a meaningful distinction between the two in the English language; and so "Central Asia" is used for both Russian usages, thus, creating some confusion.

Soon after independence, the leaders of the five former Soviet Central Asian Republics met in Tashkent and declared that the definition of Central Asia should include Kazakhstan as well as the original four included by the Soviets. Since then, this has become the most common definition of Central Asia.

The UNESCO general history of Central Asia, written just before the collapse of the USSR, defines the region based on climate and uses far larger borders. According to it, Central Asia includes Mongolia, Tibet, northeast Iran (Golestan, North Khorasan, and Razavi provinces), Afghanistan, Northern Areas and the N.W.F.P. province of Pakistan, Kashmir and Ladakh districts of India, central-east Russia south of the Taiga, and the former Central Asian Soviet Republics (the five "Stans" of the former Soviet Union).

An alternative method is to define the region based on ethnicity, and in particular, areas populated by Eastern Turkic, Eastern Iranian, or Mongolian peoples. These areas include Xinjiang Uyghur Autonomous Region, the Turkic regions of southern Siberia, the five republics, and Afghan Turkestan. Afghanistan as a whole, the Northern Areas of Pakistan and the Kashmir Valley of India may also be included. The Tibetans and Ladakhi are also included. Insofar, the mentioned peoples are considered the "indigenous" peoples of the vast region.

There are several places that claim to be the geographic center of Asia, for example Kyzyl, the capital of the Tuvan Republic in the Russian Federation, and a village 200 miles (320 km) North of Urumqi, Xinjiang, China.[5]

Geography

Central Asia is an extremely large region of varied geography, including high passes and mountains (Tian Shan), vast deserts (Kara Kum, Kyzyl Kum, Taklamakan), and especially treeless, grassy steppes. The vast steppe areas of Central Asia are considered together with the steppes of Eastern Europe as a homogenous geographical zone known as the Euro-Asian Steppe.

Much of the land of Central Asia is too dry or too rugged for farming. The Gobi desert extends from the foot of the

Pamirs, 77° east, to the Great Khingan (Da Hinggan) Mountains, 116°–118° east.

Central Asia has the following geographic extremes:

- The world's northernmost desert (sand dunes), at Buurug Deliin Els, Mongolia, 50°18' north.
- The Northern Hemisphere's southernmost permafrost, at Erdenetsogt sum, Mongolia, 46°17' north.
- The world's shortest distance between non-frozen desert and permafrost: 770 km (480 mi).

A majority of the people earn a living by herding livestock. Industrial activity centers in the region's cities.

Major rivers of the region include the Amu Darya, the Syr Darya and the Hari River. Major bodies of water include the Aral Sea and Lake Balkhash, both of which are part of the huge west/central Asian endorheic basin that also includes the Caspian Sea.

Both of these bodies of water have shrunk significantly in recent decades due to diversion of water from rivers that feed them for irrigation and industrial purposes. Water is an extremely valuable resource in arid Central Asia, and can lead to rather significant international disputes.

Climate

Since Central Asia is not buffered by a large body of water, temperature fluctuations are more severe.

According to the Köppen climate classification system, Central Asia is part of the Palearctic ecozone. The largest biome in Central Asia is the Temperate grasslands, savannas, and shrublands biome. Central Asia also contains the Montane grasslands and shrublands, Deserts and xeric shrublands and Temperate coniferous forests biomes.

History

The history of Central Asia is defined by the area's climate and geography. The aridness of the region made agriculture difficult and its distance from the sea cut it off from much trade. Thus few major cities developed in the region, instead the area was for millennia dominated by the nomadic horse peoples of the steppe.

Relations between the steppe nomads and the settled people in and around Central Asia were long marked by conflict. The nomadic lifestyle was well suited to warfare and the steppe horse riders became some of the most militarily potent peoples in the world, limited only by their lack of internal unity. Any internal unity that was achieved, was most probably due to the influence of the Silk Road, which traveled along Central Asia. Periodically great leaders or changing conditions would organise several tribes into one force, and create an almost unstoppable power. These included the Hun invasion of Europe, the Wu Hu attacks on China and most notably the Mongol conquest of much of Eurasia.[6]

During pre-Islamic and early Islamic times, southern Central Asia was inhabited predominantly by speakers of Iranian languages.[3,7] Among the ancient sedentary Iranian peoples, the Sogdians and Chorasmians played an important role, while Iranian peoples such as Scythians and the later on Alans lived a nomadic or semi-nomadic lifestyle.

The main migration of Turkic peoples occurred between the 5th and 10th centuries, when they spread across most of Central Asia. During the 13th and 14th centuries, the Mongols conquered and ruled the largest contiguous empire in recorded history.

The dominance of the nomads ended in the 16th century, as firearms allowed settled peoples to gain control of the region. Russia, China, and other powers expanded into the region and had captured the bulk of Central Asia by the end of the nineteenth century. After the Russian Revolution the Central Asian regions were incorporated into the Soviet Union. Mongolia remained independent but became a Soviet satellite state. However Afghanistan remained independent of any influence by the Russian empire.

The Soviet areas of Central Asia saw much industrialisation and construction of infrastructure, but also the suppression of local cultures, hundreds of thousands of deaths from failed collectivisation programs, and a lasting legacy of ethnic tensions and environmental problems. Soviet authorities deported millions of people, including entire nationalities,[8] from western areas of the USSR to Central Asia and Siberia.[9]

With the collapse of the Soviet Union five countries gained independence. In nearly all the new states former Communist Party officials retained power as local strongmen. None of the new republics could be considered functional democracies in the early days of independence, although it appears Kyrgyzstan, Kazakhstan and Mongolia have made great strides. Other parts of Central Asia remain part of China or Russia.

Religions

Islam is the religion most common in the Central Asian Republics, Afghanistan, Xinjiang and the peripheral western regions, such as Bashkiria. Most Central Asian Muslims are Sunni, although there are sizeable Shia minorities in Afghanistan. Islam is also the most prevalent religion in Northern Pakistan and northwest-India.

Buddhism was prominent in Central Asia prior to the arrival of Islam, and the transmission of Buddhism along the Silk Road eventually brought the religion to China. Tibetan Buddhism is most common in Tibet, Mongolia, Ladakh and the southern Russian regions of Siberia, where Shamanism is also popular. Increasing Han Chinese migration westward since the establishment of the PRC has brought Confucianism and other beliefs into the region.

Nestorianism was the form of Christianity most practiced in the region in previous centuries, but now the largest denomination is the Russian Orthodox Church, with many members in Kazakhstan. The Bukharian Jews were once a sizable community in Uzbekistan and Tajikistan, but nearly all have emigrated since the Collapse of the Soviet Union and the revival of Islam in the region.

Arts

At the crossroads of Asia, shamanist practices live alongside Buddhism. Thus Yama, Lord of Death, was revered in Tibet as a spiritual guardian and judge. Mongolian Buddhism in particular influenced Tibetan Buddhism. The Qianlong Emperor of China in the 18th century was Tibetan Buddhist, and would sometimes travel from Beijing to other cities for personal religious worship.

Note the human skulls and severed heads that festoon Yama's crown and necklace, which give some concept of the size that Yama was expected to be when one faced him at one's death. This particular Dharmapala is painted wood, four feet high in total.

Central Asia also has an indigenous form of improvisational oral poetry which is over 1000 years old. It is principally practiced in Kyrgyzstan and Kazakhstan by *akyns,* lyrical improvisationists. They will engage in lyrical battles, the *aitysh* or the *alym sabak.* The tradition arose out of early bardic oral historians. They are usually accompanied by a stringed instrument—in Kyrgyzstan, a three-stringed *komuz* and in Kazakhstan a similar two-stringed instrument.

Some also learn to sing the *Manas*, Kyrgyzstan's epic poem (those who learn the *Manas* exclusively but do not improvise are called *manaschis*). During Soviet rule, *akyn* performance was co-opted by the authorities and subsequently declined in popularity. With the fall of the Soviet Union it has enjoyed a resurgence, although *akyns* still do use their art to campaign for political candidates. A 2005 Washington Post article proposed a similarity between the improvisational art of akyns and modern freestyle rap performed in the West.[10]

Demographics

By the most inclusive definition, more than 80 million people live in Central Asia, about 2 per cent of Asia's total population. Of the regions of Asia, only North Asia has fewer people. It has a population density of 9 people per km^2, vastly less than the 80.5 people per km^2 of the continent as a whole.

Languages

The languages of the majority of the inhabitants of the former Soviet Central Asian Republics come from the Turkic language group.[11] Turkmen, closely related to Turkish (they are both members of the Oghuz group of Turkic), is mainly spoken in Turkmenistan and into Afghanistan, Iran and Turkey. Kazakh, Kyrgyz and Tatar are related languages of the Kypchak group of Turkic languages, and are spoken throughout Kazakhstan, Kyrgyzstan and Tajikistan, and into Afghanistan, Xinjiang and Qinghai. Uzbek and Uyghur are spoken in Uzbekistan, Tajikistan, Afghanistan and Xinjiang.

Russian, as well as being spoken by around six million ethnic Russians and Ukrainians of Central Asia,[12] is a lingua franca throughout the former Soviet Central Asian Republics. Mandarin Chinese has an equally dominant presence in Inner Mongolia, Qinghai and Xinjiang.

The Turkic languages belong to the much larger, but controversial Altaic language family, which includes Mongolian. Mongolian is spoken throughout the region of Mongolia and into Inner Mongolia, Qinghai and Xinjiang.

East Iranian languages were once spoken throughout Central Asia, but the once prominent Sogdian, Khwarezmian, Bactrian and Scythian languages are now extinct. However, the East Iranian Pashto is still spoken in Afghanistan and northwestern Pakistan, and other minor East Iranian languages, such as Shughni, Munji, Ishkashimi, Sarikoli, Wakhi, Yaghnobi and Ossetian are also spoken in various places in Central Asia. Varieties of Persian are also spoken in the region, locally known as Dar (in Afghanistan), Tojik (by Tajiks in Tajikistan), and Bukhori (by the Bukharan Jews in Bukhara).

The Tibetan language is spoken by around six million people across the Tibetan Plateau and into Qinghai, Sichuan and Ladakh.

Dardic languages are predominant in the Northern areas of Pakistan and north-western India and spread into Ladakh and NWFP and include Shina, Kashmiri and Khowar.

Tocharian, an Indo-European language, was once spoken in Xinjiang and parts of Afghanistan, but is now extinct.

Geostrategy

Central Asia has long been a strategic location merely because of its proximity to several great powers on the Eurasian landmass. The region itself never held a dominant stationary population, nor was able to make use of natural resources.

Thus it has rarely throughout history become the seat of power for an empire or influential state. Central Asia has been divided, redivided, conquered out of existence, and fragmented time and time again. Central Asia has served more as the battleground for outside powers, than as a power in its own right.

Central Asia had both the advantage and disadvantage of a central location between four historical seats of power. From its central location, it has access to trade routes to and from all the regional powers. On the other hand, it has been continuously vulnerable to attack from all sides throughout its history, resulting in political fragmentation or outright power vacuum, as it is successively dominated.

- To the North, the steppe allowed for rapid mobility, first for nomadic horseback warriors like the Huns and Mongols, and later for Russian traders, eventually supported by railroads. As the Russian empire expanded to the East, it would also push down into Central Asia towards the sea, in a search for warm water ports. The Soviet bloc would reinforce dominance from the North, and attempt to project power as far south as Afghanistan.
- To the East, the demographic and cultural weight of Chinese empires continually pushed outward into Central Asia. Manchu Qing dynasty would conquer Uyghurstan/East Turkistan and Tibet. As part of the Sino-Soviet bloc, China would keep Tibet. However, with the Sino-Soviet split, China would project power into Central Asia, most notably in the case of Afghanistan, to counter Russian dominance of the region.
- To the Southeast, the demographic and cultural influence of India was felt in Central Asia, notably in Tibet, the Hindu Kush, and slightly beyond.

Several historical Indian dynasties, especially those seated along the Indus river would expand into Central Asia. India's ability to project power into Central Asia although has been limited due to the mountain ranges in Pakistan (and the country itself, which has somewhat advanced greater into the affairs of the overall region), as well as the cultural differences between Hindu India, and what would become a mostly Muslim Central Asia. From its base in India, the British Empire competed with the Russian Empire for influence in the region in the 19th and 20th centuries.

- To the Southwest, Western Asian powers have expanded into the Southern areas of Central Asia (usually, Uzbekistan, Afghanistan, and Pakistan). Several Persian empires would conquer and reconquer parts of Central Asia; Alexander the Great's Hellenic empire would extend into Central Asia; two Islamic empires would exert substantial influence throughout the region; and the modern state of Iran has projected influence throughout the region as well.

In the post-Cold War era, Central Asia is an ethnic cauldron, prone to instability and conflicts, without a sense of national identity, but rather a mess of historical cultural influences, tribal and clan loyalties, and religious fervor. Projecting influence into the area is no longer just Russia, but also Turkey, Iran, China, Pakistan, India and the United States:

- Russia continues to dominate political decision-making throughout the former SSRs, although as other countries move into the area Russia's influence has slowly waned, yet they are still the dominant power.

- China, already controlling Xinjiang and Tibet, projects significant power in the region, especially in energy/oil politics (for example, through the · Shanghai Cooperation Organisation).
- Turkey exerts considerable influence in the region on account of its ethnic and linguistic ties with the Turkic peoples of Central Asia and its involvement in the Baku-Tbilisi-Ceyhan oil pipeline. Political and economic relations are growing rapidly (e.g. Turkey recently eliminated visa requirements for citizens of the Central Asian Turkic republics).
- Iran, the seat of historical empires which controlled parts of Central Asia, has historical and cultural links to the region, and is vying to construct an oil pipeline from the Caspian Sea to the Persian Gulf.
- Pakistan, a nuclear-armed Islamic state helped to sustain Taliban rule in Afghanistan, and is termed capable of exercising influence. For some Central Asian nations, the shortest route to the ocean lies through Pakistan. Pakistan seeks Natural Gas from Central Asia, and supports the development of pipelines from its countries.
- And the United States with its military involvement in the region, and oil diplomacy, is also significantly involved in the region's politics.

War on Terror

In the context of the United States' War on Terror, Central Asia has once again become the center of geostrategic calculations. Pakistan's status has been upgraded by the U.S. government to Major non-NATO ally because of its central role in serving as a staging point for the invasion of Afghanistan, providing intelligence on Al-Qaeda operations in the region, and leading the hunt on Osama bin Laden, believed to still be in the region.

Afghanistan, which had served as a haven and source of support for Al-Qaeda, under the protection of Mullah Omar and the Taliban, was the target of a U.S. invasion in 2001, and ongoing reconstruction and drug-eradication efforts. U.S. military bases have also been established in Uzbekistan and Kyrgyzstan, causing both Russia and the People's Republic of China to voice their concern over a permanent U.S. military presence in the region.

Western observers and governments have claimed that Russia, China and the former Soviet republics have taken advantage of the War on Terror to increase oppression of certain ethnic groups, including minority separatist movements, as well as some religious groups. The U.S. government, which considers Russia and China strategic partners in the War on Terror, has largely turned a blind eye to these claims.

NOTES AND REFERENCES

1. Steppe Nomads and Central Asia.
2. Travelers on the Silk Road
3. Encyclopædia Iranica, "CENTRAL ASIA: The Islamic Period up to the Mongols", C. Edmund Bosworth: "In early Islamic times Persians tended to identify all the lands to the northeast of Khorasan and lying beyond the Oxus with the region of Turan, which in the Shahnama of Ferdowsi is regarded as the land allotted to Fereydun's son Tur. The denizens of Turan were held to include the Turks, in the first four centuries of Islam essentially those nomadising beyond the Jaxartes, and behind them the Chinese (see Kowalski; Minorsky, "Turan"). Turan thus became both an ethnic and a geographical term, but always containing ambiguities and contradictions, arising from the fact that all through Islamic times the lands immediately beyond the Oxus and along its lower reaches were the homes not of Turks but of Iranian peoples, such as the Sogdians and Khwarezmians."

4. C.E. Bosworth, "The Appearance of the Arabs in Central Asia under the Umayyads and the establishment of Islam", in *History of Civilisations of Central Asia,* Vol. IV: The Age of Achievement: AD 750 to the End of the Fifteenth Century, Part One: The Historical, Social and Economic Setting, edited by M. S. Asimov and C. E. Bosworth. Multiple History Series. Paris: Motilal Banarsidass Publ./UNESCO Publishing, 1999. excerpt from page 23: "Central Asia in the early seventh century, was ethnically, still largely an Iranian land whose people used various Middle Iranian languages."
5. 43°40′52"N 87°19′52"E Degree Confluence Project.
6. A Land Conquered by the Mongols.
7. C.E. Bosworth, "The Appearance of the Arabs in Central Asia under the Umayyads and the establishment of Islam", in *History of Civilisations of Central Asia,* Vol. IV: The Age of Achievement: AD 750 to the End of the Fifteenth Century, Part One: The Historical, Social and Economic Setting, edited by M. S. Asimov and C. E. Bosworth. Multiple History Series. Paris: UNESCO Publishing, 1998. excerpt from page 23: "Central Asia in the early seventh century, was ethnically, still largely an Iranian land whose people used various Middle Iranian languages.
8. Deported Nationalities.
9. Anne Applebaum – Gulag: A History Intro.
10. In Central Asia, a Revival of an Ancient Form of Rap - Art of Ad-Libbing Oral History Draws New Devotees in Post-Communist Era» by Peter Finn, Washington Post Foreign Service, Sunday, March 6, 2005, p. A20.
11. Ethnographic maps.
12. Robert Greenall, Russians left behind in Central Asia, BBC News, 23 November 2005.

2

ETHNICITY AND POLITICS IN CENTRAL ASIA

Role of Religion in the Central Asian Politics

Tajikistan, Kazakhstan, Uzbekistan, Kyrgyzstan and Turkmenistan in Central Asia are located in the central area of Eurasia, an area influenced by the three great religions. In history, this area was influenced by various cultures, especially Islamic and Christian. Today, the majority of the population in this region is local ethnic Muslims and Russian Orthodox.

The politics and economy of the five Central Asian countries have been stagnant, and even gone backward since their independence; the living standards of the citizens have lowered and various contradictions have been prominent. What poses the biggest threat to the regional stability is the increasingly intensified contradiction between the governments of these Central Asian countries which advocate the separation of religion from politics and the anti-government organisations which attempt to establish regimes combining religion with politics. Armed conflicts frequently occur.

The turbulence of Central Asia can be attributed to both the problems in their own development and the influence of the outside world. This article will start from the present ethnic and religious contradictions of Central Asia, and elaborate their threats to the security and stability of this region and the surrounding areas it.

Formation of the Multi-ethnic Groups and the Growth of Islamic Renaissance

The five Central Asian countries cover an area of 4 million square kilometers with a population of 55 million and 130 ethnic groups. The distribution of the ethnic groups in this region is quite special, with the same ethnic group usually scatted in different countries and regions. This can be attributed to historical reasons, but more to artificial reasons. In history, the formation of the native ethnic groups in Central Asia experienced constant movement and integration. In the 15th century, after the nomadic ethnic groups in Central Asia began to settle and take up agricultural production, the major ethnic groups such as the Kazaks, Uzbeks, Kyrgyzs and Turkman began to emerge. The Tajik, originating in the 10th century, have the longest history.

Today, on the vast land of Central Asia, not all the major ethnic groups reside in their own regions, but different ones mix together. For example, in Ferganskaya Dolina, where Uzbeks, Tajiks and Kirghizes reside there are frequent ethnic and religious contradictions and inter-ethnic conflicts. Certainly, the former Soviet Union's constant change of the border at will is another major reason for the scattering of the same ethnic group.

Another major ethnic group in this region is Russian. In the mid-19th century, Russians began to migrate to Central Asia. After waves of immigration such as the Czarist Russia's expansion toward Central Asia, Stolypin's land reform, Second World War and Khrushchev's construction of a new Central Asia, a large quantity of Russians migrated to Central Asia. By the end of the 1980s, more than 5 million Russians had migrated to Kazakhstan, 2 million to Uzbekistan, over 0.9 million to Kyrgyzstan, 0.38 million to Tajikistan, and more than 0.3 million to Turkmenistan.[1] Russians occupied a dominant place in the Central Asian society since the day they stepped onto the soil of Central Asia and discriminated against the local residents, regarded as backward and ignorant. After their independence, the local residents have become the masters of their own territory, while Russians have been included in the list of non-native ethnic groups being squeezed out.

Another obvious change on this area after independence is the rapid religious renaissance, especially of Islamic consciousness. Native ethnic groups have been under the influence of external forces and religions. They became Muslims under the powerful and prosperous rein of the Muslim world. Under the rule of Czarist Russia and the Soviet superpower, Islam was severely damaged and during the period of the former Soviet Union Islamic and Christian cultures were replaced by the Communist ideal. After the Soviet Union disintegrated, an ideological vacuum appeared in Central Asia.

However, Islam, which had had strong influence in this area, spread widely and filled the vacuum immediately. In Uzbekistan, the Islamic renaissance developed the most rapidly. According to the materials of its National Commission of Religious Affairs, up to the end of August 1999, this Republic had more than 1,700 registered religious organisations, among which 1,566 were Islamic 30 were Russian Orthodox. The number of mosques increased from 300 in 1989 to 6,000 in 1993. It has 9 secondary religious schools; there are Islamic colleges and an Islamic University in Tashkent; 90 per cent of Uzbeks claim to be Muslims.[2]

In Kyrgyzstan, where only scores of Muslims made the pilgrimage to Mecca in the early 1990s, the number had amounted to over 3,000 by 1998, 95 per cent of whom came from Ferganskaya Dolina. More than 1,200 mosques and about 30 religious organisations have appeared since its independence.[3]

In Kazakhstan, more than 5,000 mosques have been built within the past ten years. Many theological seminaries have come into being, and young men have been sent abroad to learn religious scriptures and done mission service after returning home.[4]

It is the same with Turkmenistan and Tajikistan. The Muslim world played a decisive role in the Islamic renaissance in Central Asia. Muslim countries such as Turkey, Iran, Pakistan and Saudi Arabia have provided most of the funds for the construction of the mosques and religious schools. In addition, many foreign missionaries have poured into Central Asia and some have brought Islamic extremist thinking into the region. Religious belief itself is not a threat, but religious propaganda may become the catalyst of the social contradictions when the social and economic situation is worsens.

Major Factors Leading to Ethnic and Religious Contradictions

Central Asian countries have not had effective economic development since their independence. The division between the rich and the poor has become serious, with the poor stratum constituting the majority of the population. In Uzbekistan, the monthly per capita income of most of the poor residents is only 2 to 9 dollars; things in Kyrgyzstan and Tajikistan are even worse. Under the circumstances, someone sedulously propagandizing radical ideas with the aid of religion would undoubtedly be pouring oil on the fire, and conflicts would be intensified.

At present, among all the contradictions and conflicts in Central Asia, the armed conflicts between the extremist forces who attempt to set up Islamic regimes combining religion with politics and the secular states which advocate separation of religion from politics are the most threatening. Furthermore, issues concerning territory, water resources, migrants have also developed into factors leading to conflicts between ethnic groups that cannot be neglected.

Rise of Islamic Extremist Forces

With the renaissance of Islamic consciousness in Central Asia, Islamic extremist forces began to enter Central Asia and generally grow stronger and stronger. They oppose the present political power by force, and attempt to establish Islamic republics in the region. The civil war of Tajikistan is a specific example. After its independence, the issue of the character of the state sparked fierce debates among the parties.

The government authorities advocated a democratic, law-ruled and secular republic, with separation of religion from politics and non-Islamisation as a fundamental national policy. Opposition organisations such as the Islamic Renaissance Party insisted on establishing an Islamic state combining politics with religion. The Islamic Renaissance Party also formed an alliance with the Democratic Party of Tajikistan, the Renaissance-People's Movement and the Pamir Movement, and built up their own military forces. Certainly, the conflicts between Tajikistan government authorities and the opposition have some elements of ethnic antagonism left over from history. The civil war was unceasing.

In 1997, the "General Agreement of Peace and Ethnic Reconciliation" was signed between the Tajikistan Government and the opposition under the mediation of the U.N., Russia and Iran. Tajikistan Islamic organisations obtained legitimate status and were accepted into the government. However, political power and national stability, influenced by hostile forces at home and abroad, are still week. There are signs that Tajik Islamic organisations are assisting other countries' Islamic organisations in subversive activities against their secular governments in Central Asia.

Influenced by the Tajik civil war, the Uzbekistan Islamic Movement (UIM) proposed to build an Islamic republic as well. They recruited soldiers and set up armed forces to oppose their government. In 1999, under the leadership of Dzhuma Namangani, who once fought side by side with the Tajik opposition alliance and the Afghan Taliban and the spiritual leader Takhir Yuldashev, the UIM had frequent armed conflicts with government forces in the southern parts of Uzbekistan and Kyrgyzstan.[5] They also adopted extreme measures carrying out a series of terrorist activities such as kidnapping, bombing, murder in Central Asia. Instead of negotiating with them as did Tajikistan, the Uzbekistan government authorities took up means of suppression to solve the problem of Islamic extremists.

In 1999, Kalimov's suppression made 1,500 Islamic refugees accept the protection offered by Tajikistan opposition alliance and become an effective power against the Uzbek authorities. As a result, Uzbekistan-Tajikistan relations cooled. Kalimov's suppression did not at all weaken the anti-government Islamic forces. They set up bases in areas where there exist territorial disputes and Ferganskaya Dolina, shared by Uzbekistan, Kyrgyzstan and Tajikistan where pro-Islam sentiments are very strong, recruited young men from poor areas and Islamic extremists abroad offered them military training in local areas or abroad. In 2000, they rallied again and waged larger-scale and longer-lasting armed conflicts with government forces. The armed conflicts escalating year-by-year pose a great threat to the security and stability of Central Asia.

Rise of Territorial Disputes

Territorial disputes between Central Asian countries have resulted from the former Soviet Union changing the border at will. When the Soviet Union was demarcating the borders of its republics, it gave very little consideration to the ethnic and political realities, and changed the borders of its republics at will many times. As a result, there are more than ten "disputed territories" over which two ethnic groups claim to have sovereignty at the same time. Another result of demarcating the borders at will is that a lot of residents of one republic reside in another. In 1924, the Soviet Union put several counties and townships, which had more Uzbeks, under the administration of Kazakhstan. Kallarpak Autonomous Region under the administration of Kazakhstan from 1925 to 1930 was incorporated into Uzbekistan. In July 1946, the Council of Ministers' of the Soviet Union passed a resolution, agreeing to rent out 151,600 hectares of land in Kazakhstan to Uzbekistan for ten years. Kazakhstan also rented 8,500 hectares of land from Uzbekistan. The period of rent was extended until April 1991.

In 1956 and 1963, Kazakhstan returned to Uzbekistan respectively Hunger Prairie and Bastanlykskij District in southern Kazakhstan and Kilov District, Mahktalar District and Zhedsa District in southern Kazakhstan went to Uzbekistan. In 1971, the latter three districts were returned to Kazakhstan except two state-owned farms, but these districts were full of Uzbeks.[6] At the beginning of 2000, Uzbekistan proceeded to demarcate its border unilaterally, leading to territorial disputes between the two countries.

Border disputes also exist between Uzbekistan and Kyrgyzstan, with 130 border sectors unsettled today. Tashkent is always pushing forward the border in its own favor in negotiations, increasing border outposts, strengthening border regulations, even laying mines along some sectors of the border. Uzbekistan also exerts pressure on Kyrgyzstan by threatening to cut off the energy supply, resulting in a rift in relations between the two countries.

The disputes between Uzbekistan and Tajikistan are more than where to draw the border. There are many Tajiks in Buhara and Samarkand, two large cities put under the administration of Uzbekistan in 1924. Tajiks regard the two cities as the centers of their own ancient national culture and believe that only when Buhara and Samarkand are returned to their motherland can Tajikistan be an integrated state.

However Tajikistan thinks that Uzbekistan has a plot for the Hujand region, where live a great number of Uzbeks In 1998, a force led by the former Tajikistan army colonel Mahamud Khodabertiev, who had been against Tajikistan Peace Agreement, went into this region from Uzbekistan and launched an abortive but bloody coup. Tajikistan thought that the forces of the rebellion were obviously approved by Uzbekistan authorities, thus putting the two countries on bad terms.

The border between Kyrgyzstan and Tajikistan is very odd with a lot of enclaves and frequent frictions between local ethnic groups. Though the territorial issue has not risen as the principal contradiction in Central Asia, territorial disputes have caused bloodshed. Local Uzbeks in the Osh Region in Ferganskaya Dolina think that this region has been their own territory since ancient times. Hence, they act arbitrarily in commercial and political fields, which often leads to conflicts with the Kyrghize, causing many deaths.

Water Resources: A New Focus of Ethnic Conflicts

Water resources are of special significance to Central Asian countries, whose agriculture and animal husbandry make up most of their economy. Water resources are not well distributed in this region. Kyrgyzstan and Tajikistan are the two countries with the most water resources. The southern part of Kazakhstan and Uzbekistan are short of water resources. During the era of the former Soviet Union, the use of water resources was based on a unified principle and financially supported by the central government. Now, water-using countries still follow the same principle of the former Soviet Union, but they do not make compensation to Kyrgyzstan and Tajikistan for the expenses necessary for maintaining normal operation of those water conservation facilities, thus causing disputes over the use of water resources.

In addition, water reserves in Central Asia are decreasing, which will directly threaten water use in middle and lower reaches. In recent years, Central Asian countries have experienced disastrous drought, resulting in total crop failures and shortages of food even in rich Uzbekistan.

The lack of water resources has also become the focus of ethnic contradictions and conflicts in the areas short of water. For example, in the Osh Region disputes over water occur between the local Tajiks and the Kyrghize every summer.

Tides of Migrants and Refugees

Russians began to be suppressed by local governments from the day of the independence of the Central Asian countries. They are discriminated in employment and excluded from all government organs. Semi-official newspapers make every effort to abuse them all of this caused unhappiness which moved quite many Russians to migrate to Russia. Though, the Russian Government has coordinated with Central Asian countries many times, and local governments have adopted a series of measures such as granting Russians turn nationality, nearly one million Russians have left Central Asia according to incomplete statistics and the tide has not stopped up to now. As Russians usually have higher cultural qualities and technical, capabilities their departure is undoubtedly a great loss of talent for these countries.

Another problem is the tide of refugees caused by wars. A large number of refugees have poured into Central Asia, not only adding many factors of instability, but also laying heavier burdens on the already poverty-stricken local governments. The civil war of Tajikistan made nearly one million refugees leave their hometowns and escape to adjacent countries, especially in Central Asia. Hundreds of thousands moved to Ferganskaya Dolina. A large number of refugees caused by Afghan civil war have also poured into Central Asia.[7] Leaders of Central Asian countries have expressed many times that they are powerless in solving the refugee problem for lack of funds. Today, Ferganskaya Dolina with a great many refugees has become a source of turbulence and a place of frequent ethnic and religious conflicts in Central Asia.

Threat of Ethnic and Religious Contradictions to Regional and Peripheral Security and Stability

After breaking away from the control of the former Soviet Union, Central Asian countries entered upon the difficult path of independence and founding their own states, though lacking in experience and separated economically from the former Soviet Union. The economy of Central Asian countries cannot escape this difficult situation and move to normal development because of both their inborn weakness and the Russian economic crisis. The worsening of the residents' social and economic situation and the authorities' lack of ability to supervise and control the situation have given greater prominence to both old and new contradictions.

At present, Islamic extremist forces whose goal is to overturn the governments of these countries are a realistic threat to the security and stability of this region and its periphery. The legitimate status of the religious parties in Tajikistan undoubtedly will become the example that religious groups and organisations in other Central Asian countries will follow. There are signs that Tajikistan religious forces are secretly supporting the Islamic anti-government movement in Central Asia, with which leaders of Uzbekistan and Kyrgyzstan have already expressed their dissatisfaction. Anti-government armed elements entered Uzbekistan and Kyrgyzstan through Tajikistan in 2000.

In fact, Islamic extremist forces in Central Asia are only a subdivision of global religious extremist forces. Today, a turbulent belt where ethnic and religious extremist forces make frequent trouble is coming into being from Southeast Asia, Kashmir, Afghanistan, Central Asia and Chechenia to Kosovo. Ethnic separatist forces, and international terrorist forces coexisting with religious extremist forces, have been generally acknowledged as three evil forces threatening global security. Central Asia has become an ideal region for their development due to its backward economy, weak security forces, chaotic ethnic situation and Islamic tradition.

In recent years, religious extremist forces in Central Asia have become stronger and stronger with the support of the three international evil forces, which have provided funds for establishing strongholds in Central Asia and Afghanistan and recruit and train armed elements. The composition of

Central Asian anti-government armed elements also develops from localisation to internationalisation: They include mercenaries from the Muslim world, Chechens from Russia and Muslim Uighurs. These mercenaries are sent to fight in Chechenia, and steal into Xinjiang, China to organise separatist activities besides fighting in Central Asia.

In 2000, armed conflicts broke out in Uzbekistan and the southern part of Kyrgyzstan with the internationalisation of the elements and the short distance from the spot of the conflicts to the locations of national administrative organs. This shows that Central Asian anti-government armed forces have become a threat to the government of the present Central Asian countries. If they are allowed to develop with no restriction, the stability and security in countries and regions surrounding Central Asia will be threatened.

The provocative actions of Central Asian Islamic armed elements have aroused the concern of Central Asian countries, Russia and China. In July 2000, the "Shanghai Five" Summit in Dushanbe, capital of Tajikistan consulted on coordination in such fields as cracking down on international terrorist activities, religious extremism, separatism, drug trafficking and illegal migration.

In August 2000, in Bishkek, capital of Kyrgyzstan, a regional summit was held, at which leaders of Uzbekistan, Kyrgyzstan and Tajikistan decided jointly to eliminate the Islamic extremists groomed by international terrorism. In September of the same year, a regional rapid response force was formed. However, if Central Asian countries can't solve the complex domestic economic and social problems, and have no ability to supervise and control the political situation, a turbulent situation will be unavoidable in this region. The impact will spread to the wanton activities of separatist forces in China and Russia.

NOTES AND REFERENCES

1. Xinhua News Agency, February 7, 1994.
2. M. Kafarlyn, "How to Fight a War against Religious Extremism", *Independence Newspaper*, October 2, 1999.
3. E. Kaptadiev, "Islam in Kyrgyzstan", *Kyrgyzstan TUZ Newspaper*, December 12, 1998.
4. U. Kasenov, *Security of Central Asia* (Alma-Ata Publishing House, 1998).
5. *James Defense Weekly*, September 1, 1999.
6. Wang Zhilai, *History of Central Asia* (Social Sciences Publishing House of China, 1980).
7. K. Bolot, "Southern Part of Kyrgyzstan Facing Another Threat," Eurasia website, October 10, 2000.

3

CENTRAL ASIAN STRATEGY FOR COMBATING INSURGENCY

Rise of Insurgency in the Post-Soviet Central Asia

A new politics of insurgency and counterinsurgency is reshaping the post-communist transition in the countries of Central Asia. For most of the 1990s, political developments in Central Asia focused on political consolidation. Organised opposition to the governments of the Central Asian states was primarily subterranean, with the exception of the United Tajik Opposition (UTO), fighting in Tajikistan. When the June 1997, peace accord brought Tajikistan's opposing factions into a single united government, the region's last major civil conflict appeared to be nearing a resolution.

Political conflict flared again in the fall of 1998, when a former commander in the Tajikistan civil war, Makhmud Khudaiberdiev, led a band of about 700 rebels into the city of Hujand in northern Tajikistan. Troops loyal to the Tajik government, outnumbering the rebels by four to one, soon recaptured the city. But, the incident dramatised the willingness of Central Asian political opposition groups to use force to overthrow an internationally recognised government.

Following the Hujand uprising, political insurgency in Central Asia became more threatening. As political extremism, terrorism, drug trafficking, and lawlessness grew more severe, the regions' governments adopted bolder counterinsurgency measures to neutralise separatists, terrorists, and bandits. The crackdown cast a wide net, ensnaring legitimate critics and many innocent citizens. As the Central Asian political spectrum became polarised, international human rights organisations criticised governments and opponents alike.

The goal of the Central Asian revolutionaries was to sweep away governments regarded as illegitimate remnants of the Soviet era and establish an Islamic caliphate uniting Muslim faithful throughout the region.[1] Their call to *jihad*—a Muslim holy war—was in large part an outgrowth of the Afghanistan and Tajikistan civil wars. But, the issues involved in the developing revolutionary program went far beyond the winners and losers in these two conflicts. What was at stake was a competition for hearts and minds throughout the Central Asian Islamic crescent, from Chechnya in the west to Xinjiang in the east.[2]

Central Asia was again becoming, in the phrase coined five decades ago by Owen Lattimore, the "pivot of Asia."[3] Its oil and mineral wealth were attracting the attention of the Great Powers in Asia as well as Europe and North America, not to mention the Minor Powers of the Gulf region and the Middle East. As Russia receded and China and India advanced, Central Asia was coming to be recognised as a new fulcrum of geopolitical change.[4]

While the Western powers appeared to have no vital interests at stake in the region in the traditional sense—at any rate no Western state was seriously contemplating sending troops to the region to protect its interests—the possibility that the insurgency might spread mayhem beyond the region's borders was undeniable.[5]

The terrorist attack on the United States on September 11, 2001, transformed the situation in Central Asia. Evidence quickly led back to Osama bin Laden's al Qaeda organisation and its protector, the Taliban government of the Islamic Emirate of Afghanistan. The actions of the American-led coalition against terrorism and its Taliban protectors are shaping a new security terrain not only for Afghanistan, but for all of West Asia.

The Afghanistan war and the post-conflict reconstruction will have profound effects on the former Soviet states of Central Asia. How can they most effectively combat terrorism and lawlessness without abandoning the pursuit of democratic government and relatively free and open markets? The answer to this question lies in the roots of Central Asia's political insurgency. How have counter insurgency programs affected regime opponents?

Central Asia: One Decade After Independence

The five Central Asian countries that emerged from the Soviet breakup—Kazakhstan, Kyrgyzstan, Tajikistan, Turkmenistan, and Uzbekistan—were products of the Soviet system. None of these "republics" had existed within its present borders as an independent state prior to the Soviet period. They were artificial creations, products of the Soviet Marxist theory of economic and political development for underdeveloped regions.[6]

Indeed, during the Soviet period these "socialist republics" were not sovereign at all, but regions managed by Moscow. All serious political decision-making took place in the Kremlin, far from the republics' capitals. Despite their common religious, cultural, and linguistic traditions, there was little republic-to-republic interaction.

Moreover, the Central Asian republics were physically separated from the Middle East, China, and the countries of West Asia by the Soviet Union's nearly impassible southern and eastern frontiers and by decades of northward- oriented infrastructure development.[7]

The Central Asian states were not prepared for independence in 1991. The local administrative systems were not configured for self-governance, revenue collection and self-financing, diplomacy, or national defense. These countries had no organised, powerful nationalist movements. There were no charismatic heroic leaders living in exile, waiting to be swept into power with a moral mandate to oust a corrupt, quasi-colonial political elite.

Independence came to the Central Asian countries much as had communist control decades before—imposed by external forces. At the dawn of independence, the opportunities for democratic progress were substantial. The initial reform trends were clearly oriented in the right direction. The Party leaders in the republics—transforming themselves into nationalist protectors of the interests of the newly independent states—advocated the establishment of secular, democratic, independent governments, market economic relations, and foreign relations based on international standards.[8]

Kazakhstan's Nursultan Nazarbaev, one of the region's foremost figures, for instance, declared that rejecting communism and adopting international standards was "merely common sense."[9]

The five new countries became members of major international organisations, including the United Nations, the World Bank, and the International Monetary Fund, and set about establishing national sovereignty and transforming their communist-era institutions.

Kazakhstan and Kyrgyzstan made notable progress in meeting international standards of good governance, eventually adopting tax laws and civil codes that were said to be among the best in the post-communist world. In December 1998, Kyrgyzstan became the first post-Soviet country to join the World Trade Organisation. Uzbekistan, despite its inability to liberalise prices and adjust its currency to international practice, strove energetically to develop a commercially oriented welfare state. Initially torn by war and internal divisions, Tajikistan moved in the direction of national reconciliation following the June 1997 peace accord. Even Turkmenistan, the least successful in making the psychological transition to an open, modern society, attempted to harmonise its laws with international practice.

To be sure, progress toward post-communist structural reform was uneven. While important elements of economic and structural reform were put in place, they were not always accompanied by progress in democratisation and the anticipated economic prosperity. After a decade of independence, all of the states of Central Asia were governed by "presidents."[10] But, none of them had been elected in genuinely free and fair elections with true political competition. None of the governments was judged by international monitoring organisations to have fully conformed to international standards. While all of the presidents had been elected to specific terms of office, electoral laws and constitutions had been changed and amended to virtually eliminate term limits.

All the countries had institutionalised this practice by establishing "presidential" systems, giving the leaders the power to rule by decree with the force of "constitutional law." In all the cases the leaders had come from the former Communist Party system or high rungs of the Soviet establishment. None of the governments had what could be described as an independent judiciary. None of the governments established a functioning legislature with true powers of the purse. Even in the most open and liberal of the countries, Kazakhstan and Kyrgyzstan, the parliaments had been routed by presidential decree.[11]

But, the imperfections of the domestic political and economic systems are not the source of Central Asia's revolutionary movements. The revolutionaries' ardor and preparation are rooted in the Afghanistan war, itself a product of the Soviet system.

Afghan Roots of Central Asian Insurgency

The Soviet Union inherited its Central Asian territories from the tsarist empire. The region's southern frontier, the border that separated the Soviet Union from Iran, Afghanistan, and China, was a product of the nineteenthcentury Great Power competition between Russia and Britain. Afghanistan lies to the south of the frontier, beyond the Panj (Amu Darya) River. Moscow's direct political influence in the region did not cross beyond the Panj until the People's Democratic Party of Afghanistan (PDPA), Afghanistan's Marxist party, overthrew the Daud government in April 1978. After the assassination of the PDPA's leader, Nur Muhammad Taraki, in September 1979, the Soviets invaded Afghanistan to establish a puppet government and secure the region against foreign influence.

Moscow sought to stabilise Afghanistan by carrying out socialist-style "progressive" reform. But the outcome was a far cry from what was expected or desired. The Soviet occupation provoked fierce internal opposition, galvanizing Afghanistan's regional and ethnic factions into a unified opposition. Harkening back to long-standing traditions of guerilla warfare against foreign invaders, Afghanistan's seven main factions united in *jihad* against the Soviet occupation. The mujahideen resistance fighters sought and received assistance from the outside world. The Western powers, led by the United States, were anxious to see Soviet territorial expansion rebuffed by an indigenous opposition.[12] Most of the foreign security assistance was funneled through Pakistan, particularly to opposition encampments filled with Afghan refugees in Pakistan's North-West Frontier province.

Afghanistan proved to be an intractable conflict for Moscow. It was an important factor in the wave of dissent that swept Soviet society in the 1980s, eventually leading to the union's disintegration. In 1986, after years of brutal but futile conflict, the Soviet Union resolved to quit Afghanistan. By the terms of the April 1988 Geneva accord, Mikhail Gorbachev agreed to withdraw all Soviet troops by February 15, 1989.[13] Although the Red Army pulled out, the Sovietinstalled government, led by Muhammad Najibullah since 1986, remained in power.[14]

Meanwhile, the most important factions of the mujahideen opposition banded together to form an Afghan Interim Government, intent on displacing the Najibullah government. But, it was three years before the mujahideen troops captured Kabul in April 1992. Najibullah was placed under house arrest and remained in the United Nations compound in downtown Kabul. Intense ideological and ethnic divisions between the leaders of the wartime coalition reemerged, and the commanders turned on one another in a contest for control of the government. The internecine conflict quickly turned back to the instruments of war.

In the wake of the devastating fratricidal conflict among the Afghanistan factions, a new force emerged. The Taliban, or "students," was born as a movement in the refugee camps and madressahs (religious schools) of Pakistan's North-West

Frontier province during the early 1990s. In 1994, the Taliban took up arms to cleanse Afghanistan of corruption and bring an end to the internal strife among the mujahideen warlords. Capturing the cities of Kandahar in November 1994, and Herat in September 1995, Taliban fighters pushed through southern and eastern Afghanistan, uniting the primarily Pashtu areas under strict Islamic rule. The Taliban captured Kabul in September 1996, murdering Najibullah,[15] ousting the coalition government of Burhanuddin Rabbani, and establishing the Taliban supreme leader, Mullah Mohammad Omar, in power. The leaders of the Taliban refused to negotiate or compromise with the regional warlords. Their declared goal was the establishment of the world's most purely Islamic state, returning the faithful to the precepts of true religion and banning such idolatries as television, music, cinema, and pictorial representations. They proclaimed a campaign against official corruption. Their attempts to eradicate crime were reinforced by the introduction of Islamic law, including public executions and amputations. They soon adopted strict regulations forbidding girls from attending school and women from working.

Opposition to Taliban rule remained active, however, in the northern and eastern parts of the country. Commander Abdul Rashid Dostam's National Islamic Movement, consisting mostly of ethnic Uzbeks, controlled several north-central provinces. Commander Ahmad Shah Masood controlled the primarily ethnic Tajik majority areas of the northeast.[16] The "Northern Alliance" thus, came to be composed of former mujahideen forces that had fought together against the Soviet invasion through the mid-1980s, struggled against one another after the Soviet withdrawal, and then were reunited in opposition to the Taliban.

The spread of Taliban control in Afghanistan spawned some very unusual alliances. The prospect of the Taliban gaining control of portions of northern Afghanistan was a major factor inducing the warring sides in the Tajikistan civil war to return to the negotiating table and, eventually, develop a plan for national reconciliation. The U.S. and Russian governments, formerly on opposing sides in the Afghanistan conflict, found themselves drawn together against the Taliban.[17] In October 1999, the United States and Russia jointly sponsored United Nations Security Council Resolution 1267, demanding that the Taliban authorities extradite Osama bin Laden.[18] When Kabul refused to cooperate, the UN imposed sanctions against Afghanistan in November 1999.

In December 2000, the United States and Russia sponsored Security Council Resolution 1333, imposing even more comprehensive sanctions.[19] The Taliban's refusal to comply resulted in the imposition of new UN sanctions in January 2001. During 1999 and 2000 the Taliban gradually extended its control northward, eventually ousting Ahmed Shah Masood's Tajik troops and capturing the city of Taloqan in September 2000.[20] With the defeat of the opposition around Toloqan and the fall of the northern Afghanistan provinces, the Taliban exercised authority throughout the country, except for parts of the Panshir Valley. The conflict entered a new phase when the Taliban sought to obtain diplomatic recognition as the legitimate government of Afghanistan.[21]

In April 2001, after a publicity tour through European capitals and an opportunity to address the European Parliament, the leading chieftain of the Northern Alliance, Shah Masood, returned to Afghanistan to rally the remaining anti-Taliban forces for a renewed joint military offensive. Masood recruited Ismail Khan, who had ruled in the western city of Herat; General Abdul Rashid Dostum, the former communist-era leader who later controlled northwestern Afghanistan and had recently returned from exile in Turkey; and Karim Khalili, head of the pro-Iranian Shi'ite Muslim group Hezb-i-Wahdat in northern Afghanistan.[22]

The assassination of Masood, just two days before the terrorist attack on the United States, greatly complicated the process of identifying a unifying figure for the post-Taliban political reorganisation of Afghanistan. Many factors, including essentially unpredictable political events in neighboring countries, will determine the shape of the post-Taliban coalition. It is significant, however, that in appointing an ambassador to the Northern Alliance in November 2001, the U.S. government conferred what amounts to diplomatic recognition of a post-conflict government.[23]

Afghanistan and the Tajikistan Civil War

Tajikistan lies to the north of Afghanistan, just across the Panj River. A picturesque though relatively underdeveloped corner of the former Soviet Union, it rapidly dropped from a lower-income country to one of the world's poorest states.[24] Tajikistan probably would have moved toward post-communist reform sooner if it had not succumbed to an internal contest for power in the first years of independence. The contest plunged the country into five years of civil war.[25] This resulted in a blockade of Tajikistan by its neighbors, further compressing the collapsing economy.

The modest level of civil normality in Tajikistan was largely the result of foreign peacekeeping forces. Tajikistan's economy grew to be based primarily on subsistence agriculture, foreign assistance from donor organisations, barter relations with neighbors, and the commercial export of a few commodities. As much as 80 per cent of Tajikistan's foreign-exchange earnings resulted from sales of three commodities: aluminum, cotton, and illegal drugs.

The events that precipitated the Tajikistan war took place in April and May 1992, but the underlying causes of the conflict were lodged in territorial and ethnic identities that pre-dated the Soviet period. Before the Soviet takeover, no single authority had ruled the peoples of Tajikistan's rugged mountains and fertile agricultural valleys. The Soviet government brought unified rule but never displaced traditional regional and clan-based loyalties. The territorial division of Central Asia during the Soviet period had long-enduring implications.[26] Democratisation and economic reform in the core regions of the Soviet Union in the late 1980s brought greater selfrule to the outlying regions. In Tajikistan, this was manifested primarily in a resurgence of local territorialism rather than Tajik national self-determination.

In the chaotic changes following the disintegration of Soviet power, a former first secretary of the Tajik Communist Party, Rakhmon Nabiev, assumed political control in 1991. The country was swept up in waves of escalating tension that resulted in armed groups vying for control in the streets of the capital. In September 1992, Nabiev, a native of the northern Leninabad region, was forced to resign at gunpoint. Dushanbe then fell under the control of a coalition led by Tajikistan's Islamic Renaissance Party.[27]

Nabiev returned to the northern province of the country. Civil war ensued, and Tajikistan was briefly divided into north and south. Then, aided by military assistance from Russia and Uzbekistan, a coalition of forces from the southern regions of Kurgan-Tyube and Kulyab and the northern industrial region in Leninabad oblast collaborated to recapture the capital and reunite the country. These combined forces attacked Dushanbe on October 24, 1992. Thousands of civilians and soldiers were killed, while thousands more fled the capital. This early, violent phase of the civil war was resolved in favor of a coalition based in the valley region centered on the city of Kulyab. The coalition selected as its leader a former Kulyab district Communist Party official, Emomali Rahmonov.

During the fighting in Tajikistan, the Russian 201st Motorised Rifle Division, already deployed in the country to guard the Soviet Union's southern border, was given a new domestic peacekeeping mission. Officially, Moscow was neutral. In practice, however, the peacekeepers favored the communist-era political elite. The Russian troops had to delicately balance the goals of peacekeeping and stability with Russia's long-term intention of maintaining a reliable outpost in the sensitive mountain passes of Inner Asia. Russia assumed primary responsibility for Tajik military operations, and its military presence gradually transformed the country into what Lena Jonson characterised as a "Russian protectorate."[28]

The fighters displaced by the recapture of the Tajik capital—the groups that eventually comprised the United Tajikistan Opposition—were scattered in the mountain areas to the north and east of the capital.[29] Large parts of the country remained under military control, because commanders who were victorious in the war divided the territory among themselves. In the wake of the war, normal political and governmental activities were suspended. The civil war divided Tajikistan on several dimensions simultaneously, splitting region against region, clan against clan, religion against religion, and internationalists against nationalists. Most important, the conflict divided the country into victors and vanquished. Many of the vanquished retained their weapons.

After the intense fighting in the autumn of 1992, Tajikistan followed a tortuous path of gradual normalisation. Some vanquished fighters fled to Afghanistan, Uzbekistan, or Iran. Others continued the conflict from small pockets in Tajikistan. Rebel groups continued to control certain regions of the countryside, particularly the Garm Valley. The country's urban areas were subject to continuous harassment and conflict. Hostage taking became an important mechanism for settling outstanding wartime disputes. Assassinations and contract killings became commonplace. The United Nations Mission of Observers in Tajikistan (1994–2000) established itself as the center of international donor activity.

At the insistence of the international organisations, the government and the leaders of the opposition entered into a dialogue on national reconciliation. On June 27, 1997, President Rahmonov and Said Abdullo Nuri, the putative leader of the United Tajik Opposition, signed the General Agreement on the Establishment of Peace and National Accord in Tajikistan.

The signing of the Agreement and the subsequent convening of the Commission on National Reconciliation launched a period of transition. According to the terms of the agreement, refugees were to return to their homes, UTO fighters were to be demobilised and their leaders were to be reintegrated into the governmental structures, the armed forces, police, and security service were to be reformed, and democratic processes in the country were to be reinvigorated. Despite numerous temporary setbacks, the peace process moved forward.

During 1999, more than 6,000 ex-fighters were registered and amnestied, and many were integrated into the Tajik armed forces and border guard. By late 1999 the reintegration quota of 30 per cent of the ministerial posts was satisfied by the appointment of UTO personnel. A September 1999 referendum provided a mandate for the Rahmonov government, and Rahmonov was re-elected to a sevenyear second term in November 1999. On March 27, 2000, a joint session of the two newly elected houses of parliament declared the peace process officially complete and dissolved the Commission on National Reconciliation.

A single post-conflict government was officially proclaimed. The peace process produced a coalition government devoted to post-conflict reconstruction yet consisting of representatives of factions that had been mortal enemies only a short time before.

In post-conflict reconstruction, the choices are few. The usual formula is a de facto separation of the warring parties brought about by exiling the vanquished. The exiles then either dissipate in foreign countries or gradually develop an opposition movement that threatens to return to the homeland. A more difficult formula was attempted in Tajikistan—victors and vanquished sit down at the negotiating table to develop a *modus operandi* within a single state, not denying the legitimacy of either side but not allowing hegemony by either. The Tajikistan model of reconciliation is truly a heroic one. It might have succeeded if not for the ongoing threat of intervention from Afghanistan.

Insurgency and Counter-insurgency in Uzbekistan

Uzbekistan is the linchpin of Central Asia. It is the most populous and in many respects most advanced of the Central Asian countries. Uzbekistan's strongman leader, Islam Karimov, has charted a highly nationalistic, independent political path while encouraging an Uzbek cultural renewal.[30] In ways reminiscent of Turkey's Kemal Ataturk, Karimov has engineered a determined national consolidation that subordinates government, economics, and culture—the entire spectrum of policy arenas—to the drive to "recover" Uzbekistan's natural heritage.

During the Soviet period, Uzbekistan's political elite was deeply entrenched in the system through extraordinarily strong, but nearly invisible, relationships of patronage, clan, and family. The formal political institutions sometimes functioned merely as representational, not representative, institutions. A political culture of authoritarianism pervaded the public bureaucracy. Polarisation between the regime and its ideological opponents drove the opposition into hiding or exile, and transformed much legitimate dissent into opposition. There was virtually no organised political opposition until the very last days of Soviet power. In the period 1990–92 a political opposition emerged from the intelligentsia and Party cadres that spanned a wide ideological spectrum, ranging from exponents of a constitutional framework and secular state in the European mold to advocates of a unified "Turkestan" or an Islamic caliphate.

After the attempted coup in Moscow in August 1991, the Soviet Union collapsed from the center outward. Once it was clear that Moscow could not re-impose its authority, and would not attempt to do so, Uzbek government and Party officials, led by Karimov, formed a new nationalist government. A crackdown on the local opposition movements swiftly followed. Virtually every variety of political opposition was treated in heavyhanded fashion by the government. Some of the regime's opponents re-educated themselves, eventually accepting the single vision of the Karimov state. Others went into exile in Moscow, Ankara, Teheran, or Washington, while still others went underground. Some members of the opposition went to Tajikistan, where ideological conflict was becoming the fuel that would sustain the Tajikistan civil war.

Independent Uzbekistan has emphasised economic progress as a precondition to political liberalisation. During the 1990s, the executive branch of government evolved toward complete domination of the country's political life. The electoral system, political competition, supremacy of law, civic development, judicial independence, and press freedom were broadly subordinated to its strategy for national economic development. On a rhetorical level, Uzbekistan's constitutional and legal framework provided for internationally accepted principles of civil rights and good governance. Yet, in reality Uzbekistan became a highly authoritarian state where fundamental human political freedoms were severely restricted. The government circumscribed the rights to speech, assembly, and religion.[31]

Many of newly independent Uzbekistan's young men had done their military service during the Soviet occupation of Afghanistan. When they returned home from Afghanistan, they were confronted by a society in flux. The communist paradigm had been discredited by the Afghanistan war and the inability of the Soviet system to deliver on its promises of prosperity in an era of quickly advancing globalisation. Some veterans saw the rigid transition from Soviet authority to Uzbek authority as offering little hope for improving their way of life. One movement that won adherents during the early period of independence was the Hizb-ut-Tahrir. This clandestine revolutionary group was identified early on as a threat to state stability. Uzbek authorities carried out a quiet but extensive campaign against the movement's "wahabbis" during the early 1990s. The Hizbi Tahrir had links to Hamas, to Egypt's Islamic Brotherhood, and to groups in Afghanistan, Algeria, Jordan, Iran, Iraq, Egypt, and Pakistan.

Armed opposition to the Karimov government was dangerous in tightly controlled post-independence Uzbekistan, but the war in Tajikistan offered both ideological and mercenary opportunities to Uzbek revolutionaries. Two natives of Uzbekistan's Fergana Valley who joined the United Tajik Opposition forces were Takhrir Yuldash (Takhrir Yuldashev) and Juma Namangani (Djuma Khodzhiev). Like many others in the Tajikistan conflict, Yuldash and Namangani fled to Afghanistan after the defeat of the UTO forces. While in Afghanistan, they gradually developed personal connections, financial sponsors, and a more systematic program for revolutionary action in Central Asia. In 1998, the two returned to Central Asia to establish the Islamic Movement of Uzbekistan (IMU) and declare war on the region's secular governments.

In February 1999, a series of terrorist bomb explosions in downtown Tashkent took sixteen lives and, according to Uzbek press accounts, narrowly missed President Karimov. The IMU claimed credit for the bombings. Karimov declared what amounted to a war against terrorism and appealed to major governments and international organisations for help. Many outside actors had difficulty distinguishing Karimov's campaign against extremists from his campaign against domestic opponents, however. Thus, at first he found little support outside Uzbekistan for what looked like an internal dispute. As summer thaw came to the mountain passes of Tajikistan in 1999, bands of insurgents claiming allegiance to IMU leader Juma Namangani descended from their mountain redoubts into staging areas in Kyrgyzstan in preparation for an attack on Uzbekistan's Fergana Valley.

As they moved down through the mountain passes of the Altaisky mountain range into the ill-defined border areas of Kyrgyzstan, the rebels captured a number of Kyrgyz villages, taking hostage both villagers and four Japanese geologists who happened to be traveling through the area at the time. Their kidnapping escalated the action into an international incident, focusing the attention of major world governments on the potential for instability in the region. After tense negotiations, the foreign hostages were released, reportedly for a ransom. Tajik government troops escorted the rebels across the border into Afghanistan. The IMU rebels returned the following summer, sweeping through Tajikistan and Kyrgyzstan en route to Uzbekistan. The rebels attacked and occupied villages in Kyrgyzstan. Some of them reportedly advanced to within 60 miles of Tashkent in August 2000 before being driven off by Uzbek security forces. In early 2001 reports circulated that the rebels had established a staging area in the inaccessible Tavildara region of central Tajikistan.[32] The Tajik government denied the reports, but the tone of the denials gave credence to the idea that some members of the former United Tajikistan Opposition sympathised with the rebels and were secretly aiding them. Throughout the spring and summer of 2001, Central Asian chancelleries were anxiously developing plans for a coordinated inter-state program to repulse widely expected terrorist attacks.

Meanwhile, Washington was becoming more receptive to pleas from the Uzbek government to support the anti-terrorist effort. In September 2000, the State Department officially condemned the IMU and identified it as a terrorist organisation.[33] But, at the same time, Secretary of State Madeleine Albright called for international cooperation to combat terrorism, with the reservation that the "United States will not support any and all measures taken in the name of fighting drugs and terrorism or restoring stability. One of the most dangerous temptations for a government facing violent threats is to respond in heavy-handed ways that violate the rights of innocent citizens."[34]

Albright argued that the best way to defeat terrorist threats was to increase law-enforcement capability while simultaneously promoting democracy and human rights. Albright's response was at least in part a recognition of the arguments of the International Crisis Group and other organisations, which maintained that the most effective way to combat insurrection in Central Asia was by expanding employment and educational opportunities and ensuring respect for the rule of law—a rule of law that would make governments themselves subject to the constraints of fair play and due process.[35]

Regional Cooperation to Combat Insurgency

The unrest in Central Asia has forged a consensus among the countries of the region and the regional Great Powers, based on recognition that they are all threatened by a syndrome of lawlessness that involves political opposition, radical religious doctrines, gun running and narcotics trafficking. As Kyrgyzstan's president, Askar Akaev, put it, the traffic in drugs and weapons has become "problem number one" for his country.[36] Similarly, Kazakhstan's president, Nursultan Nazarbaev, warned that drugs, terrorism, and competition over the region's scarce water resources were the main threats to stability in Central Asia.[37]

The Russian imbroglio in Chechnya and the related terrorist war against civilians in Russia was a major factor in Russia's effort to defuse *jihad* movements that it believed were intellectually and financially supported from Afghanistan. Moscow believed that the war in Chechnya, the terrorist acts in Russia and Uzbekistan, and the hostage taking in Kyrgyzstan all had links to Islamic extremism that led back to training camps in Afghanistan. Russia saw the Central Asian states as an imminent battleground in the contest between civilisation and lawlessness. During a visit to Astana, Kazakhstan, in March 2000 Defense Minister Igor Sergeev informed his Central Asian colleagues that, "the military-political situation in this region suggests that the Central Asian states are in the vanguard of the struggle against international terrorism and religious extremism."[38]

The consensus on the seriousness of the threat brought forth a new spirit of cooperation among the states of the region. The evolution of the Shanghai Cooperation Organisation is one result. Regional leaders began meeting in 1993 to discuss the normalisation of their West Asian borders. In April 1996, the presidents of China, Russia, Kazakhstan, Kyrgyzstan, and Tajikistan met in Shanghai to sign a package of fourteen agreements on border issues, including related economic and security measures. But the "Shanghai Accord," as the agreement came to be known, soon took on a broader mandate.[39] The Shanghai Five (China, Kazakhstan, Kyrgyzstan, Russia, and Tajikistan) invited Uzbekistan (which shares no border with China or Russia) to participate as an observer with the intention of extending their cooperation beyond border issues to include broad diplomatic initiatives including security cooperation against Taliban-inspired insurrectionism. The U.S. government also found it had grounds to spur the countries toward greater regional security cooperation.

Initially Washington was interested primarily in any nuclear weapons capability that the region had inherited from the Soviet Union. When the last of the special nuclear material was removed from Kazakhstan in early 1995, U.S. interest in Central Asian security arrangements flagged. Two things began to change the situation in the late 1990s. One was the actions of Osama bin Laden's terrorist group. The other was the emergence of Afghanistan as the world's major opium producer.

Following the attack on U.S. troops in Somalia in 1993, Washington began to suspect that Osama bin Laden's organisation was a major exporter of mayhem. After the bombing of the U.S. embassies in Dar es Salaam and Nairobi in 1998 killed 224 people, including twelve Americans, the U.S. government became convinced that bin Laden's al Qaeda group was at the root of numerous anti-American operations. When four members of al Qaeda went on trial in early 2001 in New York for the embassy bombings, Washington demanded the extradition of bin Laden to stand trial on terrorism charges. The Taliban, however, refused. In response, on August 20, 1998, Cruise missiles were launched at a training camp in Afghanistan believed to belong to al Qaeda.

American and Yemeni officials believe that bin Laden was behind the October 12, 2000, bombing of the Navy destroyer USS *Cole* that killed seventeen American sailors in the Yemeni port of Aden.

Afghanistan has been a leading producer of poppies for centuries. But, most of the production was for the domestic market and not for cash export of narcotics. The war and Soviet occupation disrupted opium production. After the Soviet withdrawal, poppy production for export began rising rapidly. According to the annual report of the UN's Office for Drug Control and Crime Prevention, in 1999 Afghanistan accounted for 42 per cent of global poppy cultivation and 79 per cent of global opium production.[40] The expansion of poppy cultivation in Afghanistan was particularly evident in the northern part of the country, which, the report noted, could result in the "preferred use of Central Asia as a transit zone for opium and heroin trafficking."[41] In the first years of opium expansion, production was earmarked for markets outside West and Central Asia, primarily in Europe and Russia. But true to the pattern of development of many Latin American countries, indigenous demand soon soared.[42]

Opium cultivation in Afghanistan may have been a contentious issue within the Taliban. Mullah Omar, the movement's spiritual leader, decreed a ban on opium in August 1997, and in 1999 ordered a one-third decrease in poppy cultivation.[43] On July 28, 2000, Mullah Omar decreed that the cultivation and trade in opium was forbidden. This prohibition was repeated in October 2000. The UN drug-monitoring program in Afghanistan reported in early 2001 that the Taliban's anti-drug measures appeared to be having an effect.[44]

International cooperation to combat terrorism and drug trafficking led Moscow and Washington to jointly sponsor UN Security Council Resolutions 1267 (October 1999) and

1333 (November 2000) calling for sanctions if the Taliban government failed to curb the export of drugs and terrorist activities. The UN resolutions constituted a new and ironic stage in international cooperation.[45] The United States and Russia, formerly rivals in the confrontation over Afghanistan, now stood together to counter the threat of terrorism and lawlessness that constituted the legacy of the Afghanistan war.

Future Prospects

As the experience of Central Asia over the last decade amply illustrates, efforts to fight insurgency may foster counterinsurgency measures nearly as damaging as the violence they seek to combat. Balancing civil rights with public order in contemporary Central Asia will not be easy. Whatever the ultimate arrangement in Afghanistan, whether partition or the establishment of a mandate territory under the trusteeship of an outside power or consortium, Uzbekistan's role will be critical. The Islamist rebels have defined Uzbekistan as the prize in the regional competition for hearts and minds. It is Uzbekistan that they have repeatedly attacked, for as the home to Samarkand, Bukhara, Khiva, and Kokand, they see it as the key to Central Asia. Their choice of targets is not accidental. The Uzbeks have a distinctive political culture, very different from that of their Kazakh, Kyrgyz, or Tajik cousins.

Traditions of tribal democracy and inter-tribal confederation were strong among the nomadic peoples of the mountains and the plains but not in the sedentary culture of Uzbekistan. Its leaders have always celebrated traditions of hierarchy and authoritarianism. Among the nomadic peoples of Central Asia's plains and mountains, it is considered gracious to discuss and deliberate, whereas among the oasis peoples of Uzbekistan, it is considered gracious to obey, impolite to disagree, treachery to oppose. The Uzbek government has met treachery with ruthlessness, impoliteness with subtle manipulation. During the early 1990s, Karimov succeeded in co-opting many proponents of the nascent opposition, the pre-independence nationalist Birlik (Unity) movement, isolating and hounding its leaders while simultaneously inviting talented young activists into his Soviet-based, but cosmetically reconstituted, "nationalist Uzbek" government. Guerilla warfare is, above all, a competition based on skill at deception. Karimov will be a formidable competitor in this realm. So far, he has succeeded in outmaneuvering his nationalist opponents. The difference now is that the groups carrying the banner of revolution are less nationalist than internationalist, and less movements than organised obsessions.

NOTES AND REFERENCES

1. The idea of the caliphate evokes the state established by the successors of the prophet Muhammad. In the early Islamic period the Muslim world was united under a single ruler, the caliph (or khalifa, literally, "successor").
2. June Teufel Dryer, "The PLA and Regionalism: Xinjiang," in *Chinese Regionalism: The Security Dimension*, ed. Andrew N.D. Wang and Richard H. Yang et al. (Boulder: Westview Press, 1994), pp. 249–76; Felix K. Chang, "China's Central Asian Power and Problems," *Orbis* 41, no. 3 (summer 1997): 401–25.
3. Owen Lattimore, *Pivot of Asia: Sinkiang and the Inner Asian Frontiers of China and Russia* (Boston: Little, Brown, 1950), p. 32.
4. Rajan Menon, "In the Shadow of the Bear: Security in Post-Soviet Central Asia," *International Security* 20, no. 1 (1995): 149–81.
5. *Global Trends 2015: A Dialogue About the Future with Non-government Experts* (Washington, DC: Central Intelligence Agency, 2001). See also Charles Fairbanks, C. Richard Nelson, S. Frederick Starr, and Kenneth Weisbrode, *The Strategic*

Assessment of Central Asia (Washington, DC: Central Asia and Caucasus Institute, January 2001)

6. This is not to say, however, that there is no historical basis for the claim of Central Asian nations to national self-determination and statehood. For an analysis of the ethnogenesis of the region, see Beatrice F. Manz, ed., *Central Asia in Historical Perspective* (Boulder: Westview Press, 1994).
7. William Fierman, ed., *Soviet Central Asia: The Failed Transformation* (Boulder: Westview Press, 1991); Denis Sinor, ed., *The Cambridge History of Early Inner Asia* (New York: Cambridge University Press, 1990); Ahmed Rashid, *The Resurgence of Central Asia: Islam or Nationalism?* (London: Oxford University Press, 1994); Dilip Hiro, *Between Marx and Muhammad: The Changing Face of Central Asia* (London: HarperCollins, 1994); Roald Z. Sagdeev and Susan Eisenhower, eds., *Central Asia: Conflict, Resolution and Change* (Washington, DC: Center for Political and Strategic Studies, 1995); Mehrdad Haghayeghi, *Islam & Politics in Central Asia* (New York: St. Martin's Press, 1995); Shireen T. Hunter, *Central Asia Since Independence* (Westport, CT: Praeger, 1996); R.D. McChesney, *Central Asia: Foundations of Change* (Princeton, NJ: Darwin Press, 1996); Gregory Gleason, *Central Asian States: Discovering Independence* (Boulder: Westview Press, 1997); Lena Jonson, *Russia in Central Asia: A New Web of Relations* (London: Royal Institute of International Affairs, 1998); Olivier Roy, *The New Central Asia: The Creation of Nations* (New York: New York University Press, 2000).
8. Soon after independence the leaders of all the countries of the Central Asian region could be described as assenting to the general principles of the international community: namely, the sovereign equality of states, non-interference in domestic affairs, territorial integrity of the state, the obligation to abide by international agreements, the peaceful settlement of disputes, and the obligation to engage in international cooperation as consistent with national interests.
9. Nazarbaev's speech to the Supreme Soviet of the Kazak Soviet Socialist Republic, December 10, 1991, "Vybor—Tsvilizovannoe Demokratichskoe Obshchestvo," *Pyatlet nezavisimosti* (Almaty, 1996), pp. 19–24.

10. Nursultan Nazarbaev, president of Kazakhstan, is a former first secretary of the Kazakh Communist Party. Islam Karimov, president of Uzbekistan, is a former first secretary of the Uzbek Communist Party. Saparmurad Niyazov, president of Turkmenistan, is a former first secretary of the Turkmen Communist Party. Emomàli Rahmonov, president of Tajikistan, is a former Kulyab district official of the Communist Party. His predecessor as president, Rakhmon Nabiev (who died under mysterious circumstances in May 1993), was a former first secretary of the Tajik Communist Party. Among the Central Asian presidents, only the president of Kyrgyzstan, Askar Akaev, does not belong to the former Party *nomenklatura*, although in some respects even Akaev, a physicist who trained in Leningrad and served briefly as the president of the Kyrgyzstan Academy of Sciences, can be considered a member of the Soviet-era elite.

11. Amnesty International's *Annual Report 2000* (New York: Amnesty International, 2000); Committee to Protect Journalists, *Attacks on the Press in 1999* (www.cpj.org/attacks99/frameset_att99/ rightframe_att99.html); Freedom House, *Freedom in the World, 1998–1999: The Annual Survey of Political Rights and Civil Liberties* (New York: Freedom House, 2000); *U.S. Department of State Country Reports on Human Rights Practices for 2000* (Washington, DC: Department of State, Bureau of Democracy, Human Rights, and Labor, February 2001).

12. The Soviet justification for the invasion included the claim that foreign powers were providing financial assistance to the opposition to the pro-Marxist government. Zbigniew Brzezinski, in an interview published in 1998, explained that the U.S. government had been providing assistance prior to the December 1979 date of the Soviet invasion. Vincent Jauvert, "Les Révélations d'un ancien conseiller de Carter: 'Oui, la CIA est entrée en Afghanistan avant les Russes,'" *Nouvel observateur* 1732 [Paris] (January 15–21, 1998). See the discussion in David N. Gibbs, "Afghanistan: The Soviet Invasion in Retrospect," *International Politics* 37, no. 2 (2000): 233–46.

13. Diego Cordovez and Selig S. Harrison, *Out of Afghanistan: The Inside Story of the Soviet Withdrawal* (New York: Oxford University Press, 1995).

14. *Washington Post* (September 2, 1989): A1; Henry S. Bradsher, *Afghanistan and the Soviet Union* (Durham, NC: Duke University Press, 1985); Zalmay Khalilzad, "Soviet American Cooperation in Afghanistan," in *Soviet-American Conflict Resolution in the Third World*, ed. Mark N. Katz (Washington, DC: U.S. Institute of Peace, 1991), pp. 67–94; Ralph H. Magnus and Eden Naby, *Afghanistan: Mullah, Marx, and Mujahid* (Boulder: Westview Press, 1998).
15. Najibullah had remained under the protection of the UN compound until invading Taliban troops captured, tortured, castrated, and hanged him from a lightpost in downtown Kabul in September 1996. See Ahmed Rashid, *Taliban: Militant Islam, Oil and Fundamentalism in Central Asia* (New Haven: Yale University Press, 2000), pp. 49–50.
16. Gulbuddin Hekmatyar leads the Hezb-e-Islami (Party of Islam); Ahmed Shah Masood led the Jumbesh-e Melli-ye Islami-ye Afghanistan.
17. As Ahmed Rashid noted, "By walking away from Afghanistan as early as it did, the USA faced within a few years dead diplomats, destroyed embassies, bombs in New York and cheap heroin on its streets as Afghanistan became a sanctuary for international terrorism and the drugs mafia." Rashid, *Resurgence of Central Asia or Taliban?*, p. 209.
18. UN Security Council Resolution 1267 of October 15, 1999, S/RES/ 1267 (1999).
19. UN Security Council Resolution 1333 of December 19, 2000, S/RES/1333 (2000).
20. Associated Press (September 7, 2000).
21. Shortly after the capture of Taloqan, President Niyazov of Turkmenistan dispatched a special envoy, Boris Shikhmuradov, to Islamabad to initiate a dialogue on political recognition for the Taliban government with Pakistani officials. Reuters (August 31, 2000).
22. Reuters (April 23, 2001).
23. James Dobbins, a State Department career foreign service officer, was nominated ambassador to the Northern Alliance on November 5, 2001.

24. "Republic of Tajikistan: Recent Economic Developments," International Monetary Fund Staff Country Report No. 00/27 (March 6, 2000) (www.imf.org/external/pubs/ft/scr/2000/cr0027.pdf).
25. Mohammad-Reza Djalili, Frédéric Grare, and Shirin Akiner, eds., *Tajikistan: The Trials of Independence* (New York: St. Martin's Press, 1997).
26. Tajik and Uzbek populations in Central Asia have historically been intertwined. At the time of the territorial division of Central Asia into republics, only about 300,000 of the total population of 1,100,000 ethnic Tajiks in Central Asia found themselves within the newly established state of Tajikistan. The gerrymandering of borders is "explained by the desire of the Uzbeks to have the historically important cities of Bukhara and Samarkand as part of Uzbekistan, despite the fact that for centuries the majority of the cities' population was Tajik. This was a matter of prestige rather than a political necessity, for, when the Russians conquered Central Asia in the second half of the nineteenth century, they made Tashkent the political, administrative, and cultural center of Russian Turkestan, replacing the cities of Bukhara and Samarkand, which had been regional centers for centuries." Sergei Gretsky, "Civil War in Tajikistan: Causes, Developments and Prospects for Peace," in *Central Asia: Conflict, Resolution and Change*, ed. Roald Z. Sagdeev and Susan Eisenhower (Washington, DC: Center for Political and Strategic Studies, 1995), pp. 217–48.
27. Outside military and financial assistance played a role in the consolidation of the opposition forces during this early period, but the newspaper accounts, particularly by Moscow journalists, indicating that Iran and other Islamic states bankrolled the IRP are not well founded. Virtually all the weapons and ordnance in the Tajikistan war was of Soviet manufacture.
28. Lena Jonson, *The Tajik War: A Challenge to Russian Policy* (London: Royal Institute of International Affairs, 1998).
29. The UTO was composed of three main groups: the Islamic Renaissance Party of Tajikistan, the Democratic Party of Tajikistan, and the Rastokhez national-revival movement. These groups were mostly defeated by Tajik government forces in

the spring of 1993, but isolated units continued fighting fı bases in Afghanistan and in areas in the southeast of country until 1997, when the UTO became the recogni opposition in the reconciliation plan. Some UTO figures, sı as Said Abdullo Nuri, continued to play a significant role post-war reconstruction politics.

30. Islam Karimov's justification of authoritarianism is presen in his Uzbekistan on the Threshold of the Twenty-first Centu Challenges to *Stability and Progress* (New York: St. Marti Press, 1998). Some scholars taken an optimistic view Uzbekistan's policies. Frederick Starr argued in the pages *Foreign Affairs* in early 1996 that Kazakhstan might have w accolades for its democratic rhetoric and for relinquishing Soviet-era nuclear weapons, but that Uzbekistan show greater promise of promoting enduring reform and stabilit in the region. Starr viewed Kazakhstan's prospects for reform as dimmed by its ethnic and territorial divisions, the absence of a strong scientific intelligentsia, the weakness of local administrative institutions, and an underdeveloped industrial base. He saw Uzbekistan as the most likely candidate for regional stabilizer to fend off Russian and Iranian stratagems in the region. And finally, Starr saw in Uzbekistan the first tentative indications of a model that could be adopted to move the other newly emergent societies of Central Asia toward international standards of governance and economic functioning. Starr asserted that despite Uzbekistan's "flirtations with Middle Eastern and Asian models of authoritarianism," the country was developing the groundwork for a civil society. S. Frederick Starr, "Making Eurasia Stable," *Foreign Affairs* 75, no. 1 (January/February 1996): 80–92.

31. U.S. Commission on Security and Cooperation in Europe, *Human Rights and Democratisation in Uzbekistan and Turkmenistan* (Washington, DC: Government Printing Office, 2000). See also "Straightening Out the Brains of One Hundred: Discriminatory Political Dismissals in Uzbekistan," *Helsinki Watch* 5, no. 7 (April 1993); *Christian Science Monitor* (May 24, 1994): 7.

32. *Nezavisimaia gazeta* reported on January 10, 2001 that IMU troops under the command of Juma Namangani, who had just months before been escorted out of Tajikistan as a result of the deal to release the hostages, had returned to Tajikistan and

were ensconced in the Tavildara valley east of Dushanbe. But on January 17, Sherali Khairullaev, who at the time was the Tajik defense minister, denied foreign news reports that Namangani and his rebels had returned to Tajikistan, saying that a special government commission dispatched two weeks earlier to the Tavildara region had established that no members of the banned Islamic Movement of Uzbekistan had taken refuge there. On January 30, the Moscow newspaper *Kommersant- Daily* reported that the Tajik Ministry for Emergency Situations, headed by former UTO field commander Mirzo Zieev, had flown some 250 members of the IMU and Juma Namangani out of the country. See *RFE/RL Newsline* (January 11, 17, and 31, 2001).

33. The State Department designated the IMU as a foreign terrorist organisation in September 2000. Press statement by Richard Boucher, U.S. Department of State (September 15, 2000) (secretary.state.gov/www/briefings/ statements/2000/ ps000915b.html).
34. Madeleine K. Albright, speech at the University of World Economy and Diplomacy in Tashkent, Uzbekistan (April 17, 2000) (secretary.state.gov/www/statements/2000/000417.html).
35. International Crisis Group Asia Report no.14, *Central Asia: Islamicist Mobilisation and Regional Security* (Brussels: ICG, March 2001). Also significant is the effort of the OSCE to promote responsible counter-terrorism legislation in Uzbekistan. The OSCE prepared draft legislation which the Uzbekistan government took into consideration in preparing its own counter-terrorism legislation in March 2001.
36. RFE/RL Newsline (December 15, 1998).
37. Reuters (February 25, 2000).
38. Interfax (March 29, 2000).
39. Gregory Gleason, "Policy Dimensions of West Asian Borders after the Shanghai Accord," *Asian Perspective* 25, no. 1 (2001): 107–31.
40. Research Section of the UN International Drug Control Program, Office for Drug Control and Crime Prevention, *Global Illicit Drug Trends, 2000* (2001), p. 31 (www.undcp.org/ global_illicit_drug_trends.html).

41. Research Section of the UN International Drug Control Program, Office for Drug Control and Crime Prevention, *Global Illicit Drug Trends,1999* (2000), p. 20 (www.undcp.org/ global_illicit_drug _trends.html).
42. *New York Times* (April 19, 2000): A1.
43. United Nations Office for Drug Control and Crime Prevention press release, "Afghanistan Opium Cultivation in 2000 Substantially Unchanged: Country Still the Largest Opium Producer in the World" (September 15, 2000).
44. *New York Times* (February 7, 2001): A3.
45. In late March 2000, George Tenet, director of the Central Intelligence Agency, visited the Central Asian capitals of Astana and Tashkent. Somewhat later, in early April 2000, Louis Freeh, director of the Federal Bureau of Investigation, visited Tashkent for discussions on cooperation in the fight against crime and terrorism. Secretary of State Madeleine Albright made an official visit to Central Asia on April 14–20, 2000, stopping in Astana and Tashkent. General Anthony Zinni, commander-in-chief of the U.S. Army's Central Command, visited the region in May 2000. The Department of State hosted a regional Central Asian Counter-Terrorism Conference on June 13–15, 2000, in Washington. The conference focused on means for strengthened counter-terrorism cooperation and efforts to combat other trans-border threats, underscoring the proposition that national strategies needed to be based on the rule of law and respect for human rights if they were to succeed. Stephen Sestanovich, former ambassador at large and special adviser to the secretary of state for the newly independent states, visited Central Asia in July 2000.

4

STRATEGIC SIGNIFICANCE OF XINJIANG FOR CENTRAL ASIA

China's Xinjiang Region: An Area of Strategic Importance for Central Asia

From the collapse of the Soviet Union until September 11, 2001, China was able to successfully use its security concerns within the Xinjiang Uighur Autonomous Region to build alliances with the newly formed states of Central Asia. Russia's domestic concerns and the U.S.'s focus on fostering democratic principles in the new states allowed China to form multilateral organisations favorable to its concerns and establish economic ties with its western neighboring states. These conditions were of great importance to Beijing's strategies for containing separatist movements within Xinjiang, but following the attacks of September 11, 2001, the U.S. reengaged Central Asia and overpowered the multilateral agreements that China had established.

China's attempts to adapt to the new environment were initially met with mixed results. Beijing tried to link the Xinjiang separatists to the U.S.'s "war on terrorism," but even after a Uighur militant group was placed on the official U.S. list of terrorist organisations, Washington was generally cool to China's claims. Recently, China has been moving to reestablish the economic and cooperative security ties that it previously established with Russia, Tajikistan, Kazakhstan, Kyrgyzstan and Uzbekistan in order to contain the Uighur militants, reinforce Beijing's claim over the Xinjiang region and to prevent a strategic "encircling" by the United States. Russia's situation in Chechnya has prevented Moscow from countering Beijing's efforts, and in the current environment it is likely that Moscow will welcome China's attempt to regain regional power from the U.S. Should China be successful in this strategy, it will have profound effects not only on the status of the Xinjiang region, but also on the geopolitical environment of Central Asia.

Historical Background of the Xinjiang Region

Between the 1700s and mid-1800s, China conquered most of the homeland of the Uighurs—a Turkic-speaking people who converted to Islam in the 1300s. China maintained weak control over the region now known as Xinjiang until the Chinese civil war, during which the Republic of East Turkestan was briefly established. In 1949, Chinese Communist troops established control over the region, and Han Chinese were resettled throughout Xinjiang to dilute the Uighur population and secure the region's cooperation with Beijing. Since 1949, the Han population in Xinjiang has increased from 7 per cent to over 40 per cent.

Uighur groups who were opposed to China's control were fragmented and lacked a charismatic leader to gain appeal for their cause in Western countries, while the Han Chinese largely settled in the northeastern area of Xinjiang, away from the heartland of the Uighur population. The situation was largely unchanged, if not stable, until the 1990s.

In late 1990, 22 people were killed in a small uprising in Baren, a town near Kashgar, led by Abdul Kasim, a leader of the Free Turkestan Movement. Beijing claimed that the weapons were supplied by Afghan mujahideen, and its reaction was swift and harsh.

After the Soviet Union collapsed in 1991, the Central Asian republics formed independent states; the Uighur separatists within Xinjiang drew inspiration from their neighbors' independence. Militant Uighur groups exploited the weak, central governments of the newly formed states and Xinjiang's porous border with Kazakhstan, Tajikistan, Kyrgyzstan and Afghanistan to establish training camps outside of China's reach.

China's Move Toward Central Asia's Dominance

By 1996, Russia was prosecuting its second war with Chechnya, Tajikistan was still suffering from its civil war and the Uzbek government of Islam Karimov was dealing with Islamic fundamentalists looking to establish an Islamic government in Uzbekistan. China feared that this instability would spread to Xinjiang, and Beijing launched a series of new crackdowns and a controversial "Strike Hard" campaign to reestablish order; 1,700 suspected "terrorists" were arrested.

In April 1996, China looked to engage its western neighbors by creating the "Shanghai Five" —involving China, Russia, Tajikistan, Kazakhstan and Kyrgyzstan—to serve as a bulwark against Islamic fundamentalist subversion. Soon the signatory states began cooperating to end the "three evil forces" —terrorism, separatism and extremism.

China's new aggression was answered with a backlash from the Uighur separatists—in May 1996, a high ranking official to the Xinjiang Peoples Political Consultative

Conference was assassinated and there were a number of bombings on China's railroad lines linked to Uighur groups. When Afghanistan fell to the Taliban in September 1996, some Uighur groups fought on the side of the Taliban. China charged the Taliban and al-Qaeda with funding, arming and training Uighurs within Afghanistan. This was followed by more attacks within Xinjiang against Chinese interests. By late 1998, China feared that violence in Xinjiang was spiraling out of control, and Beijing moved to increase its regional influence in Central Asia.

China's move towards greater regional dominance was met with little resistance from the U.S. and with tacit cooperation from Russia. In the summer of 2000, Secretary of State Madeline Albright visited Central Asia, and offered a mere $16 million in assistance to the Central Asian states for help in the establishment of democracy and pluralistic societies. Tajikistan, Kazakhstan, Kyrgyzstan and Uzbekistan viewed this as a sign of disinterest because their priorities were focused on funding for security issues. China's anxiety over the Xinjiang region was more in line with the interests of the Central Asian states, and Beijing was able to use this convergence of concerns to increase its regional profile.

In June 2001, Uzbekistan was admitted to the "Shanghai Five," which then evolved into a permanent group called the Shanghai Cooperation Organisation (SCO). The coalition worked to prevent Kazakh and Uighur separatists from using Asian states as a safety zone to plot separatist activities, and it established an anti-terrorist center in Bishkek, Kyrgyzstan where the member states could better coordinate their efforts. During this time, China's relationship with Washington was becoming strained as the two states drifted towards becoming "strategic competitors."

Tensions were building over the new administration of George W. Bush's plans for a national missile defense system,

U.S. arms sales to Taiwan, the EP-3 spy plane collision, Chinese missile exports to Pakistan and frequent complaints about China's record on religious freedoms. Washington, and the Western powers, viewed China's claims that Uighur groups were tied to international terrorist organisations as propaganda and an excuse to persecute political dissidents.

American Post-9/11 Central Asian Strategy

After September 11, 2001, Washington's priorities quickly changed in Central Asia, as fighting Islamic terrorist networks tied to al-Qaeda became a top priority. The U.S. established bilateral agreements with the member states of the SCO, which greatly undermined the organisation's relevance and China's ties to the countries. The newly created SCO anti-terrorist center in Bishkek was not used by the U.S. and the bilateral agreements did not encourage cooperation among the S.C.O. members. Beijing began to worry that its "strategic competitor" was pursuing a long-term strategy to contain or encircle China's activities on its western border.

In this new environment, China tried to link its efforts to suppress the Uighur separatists to Washington's "war on terrorism" as a means of engaging the Bush administration with the hopes of maintaining its prominent role in Central Asia. On October 12, 2001, a Chinese foreign ministry spokesman said, "We hope that our fight against the East Turkestan [Xinjiang] forces will become part of the international effort against terrorism." Washington dismissed the ties between Uighur separatists and al-Qaeda in an effort to isolate China's interests from those of the other S.C.O. members. In October 2001, President Bush said that China should not attempt to use the "war on terrorism" as an "excuse to persecute minorities."

However, since the U.S. reengagement of the region, Beijing and Washington have established closer ties, largely for economic reasons, and the Bush administration gradually allowed its interests to shift towards those of China in return for cooperation on intelligence and anti-terror initiatives. Some analysts believe that Beijing is cooperating to gain concessions on Taiwan, Tibet and the Xinjiang region. One example that the U.S. was willing to go along with Beijing's concerns was the August 26, 2002 announcement that the East Turkestan Islamic Movement would be added to the U.S. list of terrorist groups.

Chinese Strategy to Counter the Americans

This new relationship with China has increased the importance for Washington to distinguish between violent militant groups and peaceful independence movements. It is in Washington's interests to root out those groups that have a history of cooperation with terrorist organisations outside of China's borders, but it is also important that peaceful independence movements are given tacit backing from Washington. This maintains pressure on China for concessions on human rights issues important to Washington, as well as weakening China's control of its periphery regions — a strategic importance should a conflict occur between the two states in the long term.

Beijing has received Washington's cooperation in dismantling groups such as the United Revolutionary Front of Eastern Turkestan, which took up arms against China in 1997; the Wolves of Lop Nor, which has claimed responsibility for train bombings and assassinations in China and received training in Kazakhstan; and the Uighur Liberation Organisation, where the group's dispersion throughout Central Asia has allowed it to assassinate Uighurs viewed to be cooperating with the government of China. However, other groups, such as the East Turkestan National Congress and the Regional Uighur Organisation, have received tacit and financial support from Washington. The Uighur American Association was the recipient of a grant from the U.S. government-funded National Endowment for Democracy—a first for a Uighur exile group.

Conclusion

Since 2003, China has been actively working to reestablish the importance of the S.C.O. and has expanded economic ties with the Central Asian states, while the U.S. has shifted resources out of Central Asia and into Iraq. In October 2003, China and Pakistan held joint naval exercises off the coast of Shanghai, China's first naval exercise with any foreign country. Kazakhstan and China began negotiating trade agreements to supply natural gas to China via a pipeline through Xinjiang. China has also increased its funding for the anti-terrorist center in Bishkek as an effort to decrease the importance of bilateral agreements with the United States in shaping the member states' foreign policies. This August, China and Pakistan held joint military exercises code-named Youyi-2004. The operations focused on counter-terrorism and were held in the southern section of Xinjiang near Kashgar, the region with the highest population of Uighurs in Xinjiang.

While China moves to assert its power in Central Asia by growing closer to its neighboring states, the U.S. has largely focused its relationship with China on issues in the Taiwan Straits and the Korean peninsula. Russia's concerns in Chechnya will drive its approach to the region, but, with limited recourses and domestic concerns taking a priority in Putin's response, Moscow is likely to be content with the existing structure of the Shanghai Cooperation Organisation, and allow China to consolidate its influence in the region. This environment provides China with an opportunity that it will not let pass to rout the U.S.'s encirclement on its western border. Washington will be reassessing the deployment of its diplomatic and military resources in Central Asia after the elections in Afghanistan; the size of the withdrawal of resources will signal how serious Washington is in controlling events in Central Asia and how concerned it is with the situation in Xinjiang.

NOTES AND REFERENCES

Akiner, Shirin, ed. *Central Asia: 130 Years of Russian Dominance, an Historical Overview.* Durham: Duke University Press, 1994.

Akiner, Shirin, ed. *Economic and Political Trends in Central Asia.* New York: Routledge & Kegan Paul, 1992.

Andreyev, Nikolai. "Central Asia: From Marx to Mohammed," *New Times International* [Moscow], No. 39, 1992, 19-22.

Andreyev, Nikolai. "What Future for Uzbekistan, Kirgizia, Turkmenia?" *Current Digest of the Post-Soviet Press,* 44, July 22, 1992, 8-11.

Baldick, Julian. *Imaginary Muslims: The Uwaysi Sufis of Central Asia.* Irvington: New York University Press, 1994.

Banuazizi, Ali, and Myron Weiner (eds.), *The New Geopolitics of Central Asia and Its Borderlands,* I. B. Tauris, London and New York, 1994.

Banuazizi, Ali, and Myron Weiner, eds. *The New Geopolitics of Central Asia and Its Borderlands.* Bloomington: Indiana University Press, 1994.

Baumann, Robert F. *Russian-Soviet Unconventional Wars in the Caucasus, Central Asia, and Afghanistan.* Fort Leavenworth, Kansas: Combat Studies Institute, 1993.

Blandy, C. W., *Oil is Not the Only Stake,* Conflict Studies Research Center, Report S28, Camberley, Surrey, February 1997.

Blank, Stephen J., *Energy, Economics, and Security in Central Asia: Russia and Its Rivals,* Strategic Studies Institute, U.S. Army War College, Carlisle Barracks, PA, 1995.

Bourdeaux, Michael, ed. *The Politics of Religion in Russia and the New States of Eurasia.* Armonk, New York: M.E. Sharpe, 1995.

Bremmer, Ian, and Ray Taras (eds.), *Nations and Politics in the Soviet Successor States,* Cambridge University Press, New York, 1992.

Brown, Bess A., "Security Concerns of the Central Asian States," in Jed C. Snyder (ed.), *After Empire: The Emerging Geopolitics of Central Asia*, NDU Press, Washington, DC, 1995.

Brown, Bess. "Central Asia: The First Year of Unexpected Statehood," *RFE/RL Research Report* [Munich], 2, No. 1, January 1, 1993, 25-36.

Clark, Susan L. *Security in Russia and Eurasia: The New National Militaries and Emerging Defense Policies*. Boulder, Colorado: Westview Press, 1995.

Clark, Susan, "The Central Asian States: Defining Security Priorities and Developing Military Forces," in Michael Mandelbaum (ed.), *Central Asia and the World*, Council on Foreign Relations, New York, 1994.

Coker, C. (2007): "Strangers at the Gates: Africa, the challenge of China and the Eclipse of the West", *Estratégia e Segurança na África Austral*, FLAD e IPRI-UNL, Julho 2007. www.ipri.pt/publicacoes/working_paper/pdf/2-coker.pdf

Council of the European Union (2007): *The Africa-EU Strategic Partnership . Joint Africa-EU Strategy and its First Action Plan (2008-2010)*, December 2007.

Davies, P. (2007): *China and the End of Poverty in Africa – toward Mutual Benefit?*

Dawisha, Karen, and Bruce Parrott. *Russia and the New States of Eurasia: The Politics of Upheaval*. Port Chester, New York: Cambridge University Press, 1994.

Diller, Daniel C., ed. *Russia and the Independent States*. Washington: Congressional Quarterly, 1993.

Doolotaliyev, S. "Some Issues in the Development of the Sary-Dzhaz Mining Industrial Center, Kirghiz SSR," *Sovetskaya Geografiya*, 30, May 1989, 371-4.

Eickelman, Dale F., ed. *Russia's Muslim Frontiers: New Directions in Cross-Cultural Analysis*. Bloomington: Indiana University Press, 1993.

Ellison, Herbert J., and Bruce A. Acker, "Azerbaijan: U.S. Policy Options," National Bureau of Asian Research Briefing, June 1997, pp. 1–9.

Emerson, Sarah A., "The Relevance of Caspian Oil for the World," paper prepared for the Fourth Annual Energy Conference on

Caspian Resources, The Emirates Center for Strategic Studies and Research, October 1998.

Evans, John L. *Russia and the Khanates of Central Asia to 1865*. New York: Associated Faculty Press, 1982.

Ferdinand, Peter. *The New States of Central Asia and Their Neighbors*. New York: Council on Foreign Relations Press, 1994.

Fierman, William, ed. *Soviet Central Asia: The Failed Transformation*. Boulder, Colorado: Westview Press, 1991.

Finberg, Jared, "GUAM's Potential Outside of the CIS," *Weekly Defense Monitor*, Center for Defense Information, May 24–31, 1997.

Furtado, Charles F., and Henry R. Huttenback, eds. "The Ex-Soviet Nationalities Without Gorbachev," *Nationalities Papers*, 20, Fall 1992, 1-124.

Gleason, Gregory. "The Political Economy of Dependency under Socialism: The Asian Republics in the USSR," *Studies in Comparative Communism*, 24, December 1991, 335-53.

Grimm, S. (2008): *Africa-China-Europe trilateral co-operation: Is Europe naïve?* Opinion, EDC2020, Nov.08.

Gross, Jo-Ann, ed. *Muslims in Central Asia: Expressions of Identity and Change*. Durham: Duke University Press, 1992.

Holstag, J. (2006): "The European Union and China: The Great Disillusion". *European Foreign Affairs Review*, Vol 11(4). www.ec-an.eu/node/149

Humphrey, J. (2007): *Research in Europe and Africa-China Relationships*. A Report for the Rockefeller Foundation, Institute of Development Studies, Brighton, UK.

Kaiser, Robert J. *The Geography of Nationalism in Russia and the USSR*. Princeton: Princeton University Press, 1994.

5

CHINA'S STRATEGY FOR COMBATING CROSS-BORDER TERRORISM IN CENTRAL ASIA

This study provides an overview of the Muslim separatist movement in China's northwestern Xinjiang Uighur Autonomous Region, China's attempts to stifle activities which it considers terrorism, and implications for U.S. policy. Some analysts suggest that the U.S.-led campaign against terrorism may make it difficult to pressure the Chinese government on human rights and religious freedoms, particularly as they relate to Uighur Muslims in Xinjiang.

China also has reportedly stepped up its suppression of Uighur Muslims following the attacks in the United States on September 11, 2001. A policy question for the United States is how to balance the anti-terrorist campaign with traditional concerns over human rights in China's western region, and how to react should Beijing use the threat of terrorism to abrogate rights of autonomy in Xinjiang as provided for in China's constitution.

Background

Over one hundred years after Qing Dynasty troops gained control over East Turkestan,[1] currently known as Xinjiang Uighur Autonomous Region, some ethnic Uighurs in Xinjiang continue to aspire to reestablish sovereignty over their homeland. Uighurs did briefly establish the Republic of East Turkestan during the Chinese civil war (1945-1949), but self-rule came to an abrupt end when Communist troops entered Xinjiang in 1949. The Chinese government immediately began to consolidate its control over Xinjiang by sending retired ethnic Han Chinese soldiers into Xinjiang to form new units called "Production and Construction" Corps (Bingtuan).[2] The Chinese government has continued to resettle the Xinjiang area with ethnic Han Chinese migrants and with other ethnic minority groups. This has exacerbated tensions with the Uighurs, who have witnessed the Han population in Xinjiang, once a mere 6 to 7 per cent, balloon to approximately 40 to 45 per cent of Xinjiang's total population.[3]

Fearing continued cultural marginalisation and religious persecution, Uighurs have become increasingly virulent in their protests against Chinese rule in Xinjiang. As a result of these protests and increased violence, in April 1996 the PRC government launched a series of new crackdowns and a controversial "Strike Hard" (Yan Da) campaign to reestablish order in Xinjiang. This has resulted in a number of Uighur leaders being killed, jailed, or driven into exile.[4]

The collapse of the Soviet Union in 1991 and the establishment of independent states by the former Soviet Central Asian republics, encouraged some Uighurs in their aspirations to reestablish an independent homeland. According to some analysts familiar with the region, many Uighurs in Xinjiang felt that having their own state "cuts to the core of their ethnic identity and ultimate survival as a culture."[5] Furthermore, other minorities in Xinjiang, the

Kazakhs, Kyrgyz, Tajiks, Uzbeks, and Mongols, all can look to sovereign states that border China, as pillars of "cultural and ethnic pride."[6] However, with no real chance to see their own dream of an independent homeland become a reality because of the PRC government's strong determination to retain control of Xinjiang at all cost, a number of underground separatist groups began to spring up throughout Xinjiang and the Uighur diaspora.[7]

The PRC's Xinjiang fears were compounded by a number of significant events going on in Russia, Afghanistan, and Central Asia beginning in 1996. The Russians were prosecuting a second war in the break-away republic of Chechnya. Tajikistan was still suffering from the effects of its civil war. And the Uzbek government, led by President Islam Karimov, was dealing with an increasing threat from Islamic fundamentalists looking to establish a radical Islamic state in Uzbekistan. China feared that all of these events, which involved "Islamic fundamentalist" elements, would spread to Xinjiang and radicalise the Uighur groups in Xinjiang. However, the one event that would prove the most problematic to China and the entire Central Asian region was the fall of Kabul, Afghanistan to the Taliban militia in September 1996.[8]

The Taliban movement has been accused by leaders in Beijing and secular leaders throughout Central Asia of spreading its radical views of Islam into many parts of Central and South Asia, leading in some cases to a rise of "Islamic fundamentalist" groups and activity, including bombing, assassinations, and other acts of terror and subversion. In particular, China and the Central Asian states over the years have charged that the Taliban and their close associate, Osama bin Laden, have been funding, arming, and training a number of Uighurs, Kyrgyz, Kazakhs, and Uzbeks in camps located inside Afghanistan.[9]

In 1996, China, Russia, Tajikistan, Kazakhstan, and Kyrgyzstan formed a group known as the "Shanghai-Five" to serve as a bulwark against the spread of Islamic fundamentalist subversion. It was initially designed to be an informal grouping to discuss ways to resolve old border disputes and fortify common borders against terrorist and separatist activity.

However, the group's members soon decided they needed to cooperate more thoroughly to deal with what they called the "three evil forces"–terrorism, separatism, and extremism.[10] In the summer of 2001, the Shanghai-Five admitted Uzbekistan into the organisation and established a permanent regional group called the Shanghai Cooperation Organisation (SCO). The new organisation approved two joint communiques that stressed its intentions to cooperate on combating terrorism and to establish an anti-terrorist center in Bishkek, Kyrgyzstan.

However, the terrorist attacks against the United States on September 11, 2001 appear to have caused an unintended halt to a number of the SCO plans, at least for the near term. Shortly after the September attacks, the United States made counter terrorism its number one priority. Some China and Central Asian analysts indicate that now that the United States is taking on global terrorism, particularly in the Central Asian region, the Shanghai Cooperation Organisation is beginning to feel a bit "overshadowed" and marginalised.[11] Surprisingly to some, Russia, Tajikistan, Uzbekistan, Kazakhstan, and Kyrgyzstan are all providing robust support for the U.S.-led counter-terrorism effort. Analysts say that with the United States now "monopolising" the agenda on anti-terrorism in the region, the Chinese are starting to fear that a major component of their Central Asian geopolitical strategy is being gradually neutralised.[12]

Implications for American Foreign Policy

The attacks on September 11, 2001 and the U.S.-led retaliation in Afghanistan has wide-ranging policy implications for America's China policy in the short term, and may cause a number of policy shifts and challenges in the long term. One of the most difficult challenges is how the United States will balance its need to create a broadbased multi-state coalition to fight against terrorism with traditional American obligations to protect and defend religious freedoms and human rights. According to a number of analysts, China, Russia, and the Central Asian states, in exchange for lending support and cooperation to the U.S. in the fight against global terrorism, may want "support for their campaigns against groups they view as terrorists," and a reduction in the level of criticism over what the United States views as human rights abuses.[13]

This may anger religious and human rights activists, who may view it as capitulation of American values and principles. Although it may be important to review and reformulate those policies to make it easier to fulfill the requirements and goals of a multi-state coalition, some policy-makers argue that an equally important consideration for U.S. policymakers pursuing the campaign against terrorism is ensuring that the terrorism campaign does not give a blank check to authoritarian regimes pursuing their own domestic agendas of civil, political, and religious repression. There is also the question of whether the U.S.-led campaign against international terrorism should apply to groups seeking religious and political rights in authoritarian countries.

On the one hand, it may appear that some Uighurs' ties with extremist groups could justify a crackdown by Beijing similar to that occurring in other countries. On the other hand, the political unrest by some Uighurs could be a logical response to suppression of their constitutional rights and the settlement of traditional Uighur lands by ethnic Chinese. The policy dilemma for the United States, therefore is the degree to which it may decline to react to possible human rights violations against Uighurs in Xinjiang in return for Chinese cooperation in the campaign against terrorism.

In the months leading up to the events of September 11, 2001, the United States and China seemed headed toward becoming "strategic competitors"or even adversaries. Before September 11, 2001, Sino-U.S. relations were plagued by a number of controversial issues such as national missile defense, U.S. weapons sales to Taiwan, the EP-3 spy plane collision, Chinese missile exports to Pakistan and elsewhere, and continued criticisms over China's violations of human rights and religious freedoms. But the tragedy of September 11, 2001, seemed to have pushed Sino-US relations in a different direction. The Chinese began to stress a common interest in combating terrorism, and U.S. policy makers began building a broad-based multinational coalition against terrorism that would include the PRC. Some see the anti-terrorism campaign as a new potential framework for a more constructive and cooperative relationship.

Despite this new cooperative environment and concessions that some in the foreign policy establishment consider as necessary to form the multi-state coalition against terrorism, the Bush Administration has also shown a willingness to stress the values and principles of human rights and religious freedoms, particularly with regard to China. Although the United States has lifted some sanctions against nations that are cooperating in the war on terrorism (e.g., Pakistan), neither the Bush Administration nor Congress, which has oversight authority on the waiving of sanctions placed on the PRC, has shown an inclination toward extending a waiver of any existing sanctions placed on the PRC.[14]

China reportedly expects the United States to moderate criticisms over the PRC's handling of Uighur separatism in Xinjiang. However, at the APEC Summit in Shanghai, in October 2001, President Bush made a statement that was interpreted as a strong reminder that the U.S. does not approve of China's policies toward ethnic minorities and does not intend to forgo its responsibilities to support human rights and religious freedoms. Bush stated that the Chinese should not attempt to use the war on terrorism as an "excuse to persecute minorities."[15] China nevertheless, insists that there are a number of Uighur groups that are actively involved in cross border "terrorism" and that it has the right to combat what it views as "terrorism" within and around its borders.

Also China and the SCO are being overshadowed by the U.S. presence and leadership in Central Asia at the moment, but Beijing may attempt to reassert its influence as a power broker in the region when the fighting in Afghanistan has died down by revitalising the SCO mechanism. However, the terrorist attacks on September 11, 2001 and the U.S.-led retaliation has caused a range of geopolitical realignments among nations in Central Asia, most notably among the member states of the Shanghai Cooperation Organisation. After the attacks on the United States, a number of SCO members immediately pledged full support and cooperation to the United States.

This apparent geopolitical realignment, combined with the possibility of long-term U.S. troop deployment in Central Asia, may raise concerns among the military and political elites in Beijing that the United States is engaged in a strategy of long term "containment"or "encirclement" of China on both its eastern and western borders. Analysts caution that the PRC has not lost its resolve to extend its sphere of influence into Central Asia nor has it abandoned its geopolitical strategy of using the SCO as its primary vehicle to achieve this goal. This could mean an increase in the possibilities for competition between China and the United States over influence in Central Asia.

Genesis and Composition of Uighur Movement

By the 14th century, ethnic Uighurs, a Turkic-speaking people from Central Asia were fully converted followers of Islam. They lived in ancient cities of great wealth and learning like Tashkent, in modern day Uzbekistan, and Kashgar in modern day Xinjiang, Western China. However, between the mid-1700's and the mid-1800's China conquered most of the Uighur homeland. The ethnic Manchu of Northern China[16] and Czarist Russian empires annexed the entire region of Central Asia by the late 1800's. Turkic-speaking peoples from West and East Turkestan were eventually brought under the sovereignty of these two empires.

Although the Uighurs reestablished East Turkestan just after World War II, Chinese Communist forces reincorporated East Turkestan into China at the end of the Chinese civil war, and East Turkestan became known as the Xinjiang Uighur Autonomous Region. The name was supposed to reflect the large degree of autonomy granted by the PRC to Uighurs in the constitution. However, some Uighurs allege that the name is only symbolic and that little autonomy and rights are enjoyed by Uighurs presently.

In 1991, Central Asian Muslims such as the Kazakhs, Uzbeks, Tajiks, Turkmen, and Krgyz,–ethnic groups of the former Soviet republics–finally won their independence and set up sovereign states. For the first time in several hundred years they governed their own independent homelands. Although the Uighurs did not gain independence like their Central Asian cousins, some saw the sovereignty gains of the newly independent states of Cental Asia as a source of inspiration for their own struggle and as a safety zone from which to organise an independence movement. Analysts note that the Xinjiang Uighur Autonomous Region shares a relatively porous border with Kazakhstan, Tajikistan, Kyrgyzstan, Pakistan, and Afghanistan,[17] and according to a number of reports these states have increasingly become a source of ideology, information gathering, arms procurement, and training for some Uighur groups in their struggle against PRC rule.[18]

Although the Uighur opposition to Chinese rule has existed in many forms throughout history, it has become more violent in recent years. Although some Uighurs have been trying to attain independence for a number of years, they have remained largely out of the view of mainstream media and have gained relatively little support from the international community. Some analysts argue that this is because the Uighur community lacks a single charismatic leader like Tibet's Dalai Lama, and because the Uighur resistance groups are largely fractured and disorganised, and lack the ability to gain the full attention of key states such as Britain and the United States.[19]

Other analysts and human rights activists argue that the reason that the Uighur resistance movement has trouble gaining robust support and international attention is because it lacks a well funded lobby effort such as that of Tibet and Taiwan for advocating its cause in the West. These analysts point out that Uighurs are generally extremely poor and geographically isolated in a corner of the world that is largely forgotten and overwhelmingly populated by Muslims.[20] Analysts also argue that Beijing has kept international attention away from the Uighur resistance movement by severely restricting access to Xinjiang Uighur Autonomous Region.[21] According to these analysts, the PRC did not want to cast any light on the "brutal tactics" that police have used to stamp out the resistance to Chinese rule.[22]

However, the events of September 11, 2001 have turned the attention of many analysts and journalists to the Uighur struggle. In particular, there appears to be interest in a number of reports about alleged links between some Uighur groups and the radical Islamic elements in Central Asia. Specifically, analysts have focused on the allegations that linkages exist between Osama bin Laden's Al-Qaeda network and some Uighur groups throughout Central Asia. In a November 2001 briefing, PRC Foreign Ministry spokesman Zhu Bangzao, listed more than 10 separate organisations based in Central Asia, Afghanistan, and Xinjiang that he accused of "conducting terrorist violence" in Xinjiang and other parts of China.[23]

Armed Uighur Groups Alleged to be Active in Xinjiang

A number of armed Uighur groups are believed to be active in the opposition to what they view as Chinese "occupation" of East Turkestan. Some of these groups advocate total separation from China and have resorted to violence against the PRC over the last several years. In late 1990, the level of violence in Xinjiang began to increase when a small uprising erupted in Baren, a town near Kashgar.[24] The PRC government cracked down swiftly and harshly, and local security forces were given wide ranging power to root out any element that "harms national unity" and "the solidarity of ethnic groups or social stability."[25] The Baren uprising, reportedly led by Abdul Kasim, laid the foundation for an underground armed struggle against the Chinese in Xinjiang.

In 1995, PRC security forces reportedly found a stowaway clutch of some 4,000 sticks of dynamite, 600 guns with ammunition, and 3,000kg of explosives.[26]

In April 1996, Chinese security forces arrested more than 1,700 suspected "terrorists." One month later a high ranking official of the Xinjiang Peoples Political Consultative Conference[27] was assassinated, and a number of bombings occurred along Chinese railroad lines.[28] Uighur armed resistance groups allegedly detonated three time bombs on buses in Urumqi on the day of Deng Xiaoping's funeral. By late 1998, China became concerned that the violence in Xinjiang was spiraling out of control. Beijing began to pressure the Central Asian states to assist with efforts to identify groups and leaders throughout the Diaspora. Beijing also insisted that any Xinjiang Uighur found outside Xinjiang be extradited to the PRC, and that all outside sources of assistance and shelter for the Xinjiang-based Uighur movement be cut off.

The PRC has accused a number of Xinjiang based Uighur groups of committing "terrorist" acts in Xinjiang and other parts of China and Central Asia. In light of the global anti-terror campaign, some western journalists have begun to focus more attention on these groups. They include:

United Revolutionary Front of Eastern Turkistan– led by 77 year old Yusupbek Mukhlisi, also known as Modan Mukhlisi. This group claims to have more than thirty armed units working in and around Xinjiang, including expert bomb makers. Mukhlisi fled China in 1960, and for more than thirty years he advocated peaceful resistence to what he calls "Chinese rule" over East Turkestan.[29]

However, this relatively moderate policy was disavowed in March 1997 when the United National Revolutionary Front of East Turkestan and two other Kazakhstan-based Uighur groups issued a joint declaration stating that they were "taking up arms against Chinese oppression."[30] In a recent article published in the *Japan Times*, Mukhlisi boasts of having a "well developed" movement in Xinjiang and says that he has "twenty-two million Uighurs" ready to conduct armed struggle against the Chinese. He claims to have "ties to several groups" across the border in Kazakhstan.[31]

Organisation for the Liberation of Uighurstan– led by Ashir Vakhidi. This group is said to be internally divided over many personal and political issues. Reportedly these divisions include disagreement over whether to use East Turkestan or Uighurstan as the name of a Uighur sovereign state.[32] However, the group is committed to armed struggle against Chinese "occupation" of the "Uighur homeland."

Wolves of Lop Nor– this group has not publicly listed its leader, but it is reported to have claimed responsibility for a number of bombings on trains and for several assassinations in Xinjiang. According to reports, this group released a statement to Taiwan radio stating that all of its attacks are in response to "suppression of proindependence activism" of Uighurs in Xinjiang by Chinese government forces. Additionally, following a Beijing bombing, this group revealed that the attack had been planned by Uighur exiles in Kazakhstan and that more events would be planned. Although there have been no incidents or threats against Chinese nuclear facilities, some China watchers point out that the city of Lop Nor in Xinjiang Uighur Autonomous Region, home of the "Wolves," is also the site of one of China's largest nuclear test sites.[33]

Xinjiang Liberation Organisation and Uighur Liberation Organisation (ULO)–reportedly active in Uzbekistan and Kyrgyzstan. According to some reports, they are responsible for the assassinations of Uighurs who they viewed as "collaborators" with the PRC and Central Asian governments.[34] There are also reports that Uighurs from this group are dispersed throughout the region;[35] and that the countries of Tajikistan, China, Uzbekistan, Afghanistan, and the Russian republic of Chechnya are home to ULO members.[36]

Home of East Turkistan Youth–(branded as Xinjiang's Hamas) is a radical group thought to be committed to armed struggle against the Chinese in Xinjiang. This group reportedly has over 2,000 members and allegedly has undergone explosives training in camps inside Afghanistan.[37]

Free Turkistan Movement– led by Uighur and reported "Islamic fundamentalist" Abdul Kasim, this group led an uprising in April 1990 in the Xinjiang town of Baren. Although figures vary, PRC officials report 22 people were killed in the incident. The Baren incident touched off harsh crackdowns on religious activity throughout Xinjiang. Additionally, Chinese officials claim that the weapons used in the Baren incident came from Afghan Mujahadeen.[38]

Other Extremist Groups and the Uighur Opposition

Xinjiang Uighur Autonomous Region is home to an estimated 10 million Uighurs. According to some reports there are an additional 500,000 Uighurs in "Western Turkestan," which includes Uzbekistan, Kazakhstan, Tajikistan and Turkmenistan, and another estimated 150,000 Uighurs in Pakistan, Saudi Arabia, Afghanistan, Western Europe, Turkey, and the United States.[39] According to the figures and information listed above, the Uighur Diaspora is surprisingly large and spread throughout several countries. Chinese government officials and a number of Western sources suggest that some of the groups in the Uighur Diaspora are linked to extremist elements in the countries in which they reside. PRC officials allege that these include links to Osama bin Laden's terrorist network.

On June 9, 2000, a Bishkek journalist named Aleksandr Knyazev, stated what the Chinese government has believed for several years, that "it is widely known" that "Uighurs are fighting on the Taliban side" in the war in Afghanistan.[40] Knyazev named several well known groups, such as the Hizb-ut-Tahrir Party and the Islamic Movement of Uzbekistan as having trained and recruited Uighurs. He also stated that he had the opportunity to meet and interview a Uighur captured by the Anti-Taliban forces in Northern Afghanistan; the captured Uighur came from the small town of Aksu in Xinjiang. According to comments made by the Uighur captive, he had received his training in a camp near the Pakistani town of Peshwar.[41]

In another report, the Russian special envoy to Pakistan in September 2000, pointed out that he had identified five camps in Pakistan used to train terrorists, and that there is proof of Chechens, Uzbeks, Tajiks, and Uighurs from China being trained in those camps.[42] According to other reports, some Uighur resistance groups have ties to other groups listed below. This listing, however, does not imply that the groups have significant, or even recognizable, influence on Uighurs living in China.

Tableeghi Jamaat—a Pakistani Islamic missionary organisation that China believes has supplied Uighurs with arms and recruited Uighurs to train and fight in Afghanistan. In 1998, Krygyz authorities broke up a faction of this group led by a Chinese-born Uighur called 'Kasarli,' showing that China and the Central Asian states were beginning to cooperate on cracking down on the violent groups in Central Asia and Xinjiang.[43] This group has also caused some difficulty in the Chinese-Pakistani relationship over the last couple of years. According to reports that appeared in the ITAR-TASS Russian news agency and Reuters news service in February of 1997, the Chinese government accused this group, and indirectly the Pakistani government, of distributing religious materials in Xinjiang and with being "actively involved" in violence and unrest in Xinjiang.

Hizb-ut-Tahrir (Islamic Revival)– has a number of cells throughout Central Asia. According to some reports, the goal of this group is to create a "Caliphate" or independent state within the territory that includes parts of China's Xinjiang, Uzbekistan, Tajikistan, and Kyrgyzstan.[44]

Committee for Eastern Turkistan– based in Alma-Ata, Kazakhstan, this group was originally formed by Uighur Guerillas who fought against the Peoples Liberation Army from 1944-1949.[45]

Jamaat-i-Islami– is Pakistan's largest Islamic political party, and is led by Qazi Hussain Ahmad. Several reports indicate that a number of Uighurs, some say hundreds, have been recruited by Jamaat-i-Islami and trained by the Afghan Mujahadeen.[46]

Islamic Movement of Uzbekistan (IMU)– military wing is led by Juma Namangani, who has been recently identified as a top Lieutenant to bin Laden and is accused by many Central Asian states and China of actively recruiting and training a number of Uighurs in the IMU's paramilitary centers in the city of Mazar-e-Sharif, Northern Afghanistan. In addition to being linked to the Taliban and Al-Qaeda, the IMU has also been linked to Hizb-ut-Tahrir. The IMU was one of three groups, in addition to the Taliban and Al-Qaeda, named in U.S. President George Bush's address before a joint session of Congress on September 20, 2001. Although not independently confirmed, Namangani was reportedly killed in late November 2001, during a battle with the anti Taliban forces to retain control over Mazar-e-Sharif.

Osama bin Laden's Al-Qaeda Organisation– reports suggest that some 6,000 to 7,000 foreign fighters and guerillas are in Afghanistan. These mercenaries reportedly include some who are Pakistani, Kyrgyz, Arab, Uzbek, Tajik, Chechen, and also reportedly includes Uighurs from Xinjiang and other parts of the Uighur Diaspora. Allegedly, most of these foreign mercenaries were funded and trained by Osama bin- Laden's Al-Qaeda organisation in Afghanistan.

Non-Violent Uighur Groups and Associations

A number of Uighur groups and individuals advocate only a modicum of autonomy from the PRC. They also claim to want the PRC to only honor its promises of autonomy for minorities as presented in the Chinese Constitution. Some other Uighur groups within Xinjiang and abroad seek independence from the PRC, but seek it through non-violent political activities. For example, there are "Uighur oppositionin- exile" groups in countries such as the United States, Germany, and Turkey. They belong to groups such as the Uyghur American Association and the East Turkestan National Congress, which is a federation of a number of Uighur associations. Some of these non-violent groups, such as the Regional Uighur Organisation, also are based in Central Asia.[47]

In addition to these groups and associations, Uighur news groups and media sources are dedicated to reporting on the situation of Uighurs in Xinjiang. For example, the East Turkestan Information Bulletin, published by the East Turkestan Union in Europe (ETUE), a Munich based organisation, says that its mission is to "disseminate objective current information on the people, culture and civilisation of Eastern Turkestan and to provide a forum for discussion on a wide range of topics and complex issues."[48] According to some analysts, most of these groups and associations have "consistently advocated peaceful means" to gain their independence from the PRC.

Human Rights Issues in Xinjiang

Although for a number of years the PRC government has claimed that some Uighur groups are linked to terrorist groups in Central Asia, until recently the allegations were viewed by many in the West as mere "propaganda"or as an excuse to persecute political dissidents in Xinjiang. According to some analysts and rights activists, one reason that Chinese allegations against Uighurs are so highly disregarded by many in the West is that Beijing is prone to group all Uighurs into the "terrorist" category. Since September 11, however, there has been an increase in the number of reports by outside sources about Uighur violence in Xinjiang, and some of the reports make claims similar to those that have been made by the PRC over the past five years.

However, since the terrorist attacks on the United States, a number of international Uighur groups and activists have been concerned that as the U.S. prosecutes the war on terrorism, the Uighur cause will be viewed in a new unfavorable light by the international community. Uighur activists fear that Chinese complaints about terrorism are becoming more accepted in the west. In a recent interview with the *Washington Post*, imprisoned Uighur businesswoman Rebiya Kadeer's son expressed his concerns that the U.S. will "weaken" its support for human rights among China's minority populations, "especially the Turkic speaking, Uighur Muslims" of Xinjiang.[49]

According to Turdi Ghoja of the Uyghur American Association, the PRC is taking "advantage of the global war on terrorism" to indulge in "killing, torturing, and imprisoning" Uighurs in Xinjiang "without causing too much criticism from the international community."[50] Recently, U.N.

High Commissioner for Human Rights Mary Robinson in a meeting with PRC leaders, stressed that the war on terrorism "must not infringe on the human rights of China's Muslims." Robinson told PRC officials that since the September 11 attacks, her office has seen a rise in allegations of "summary executions, imprisonment, and torture" of Uighurs, which is considered a serious violation of the principles embodied in the United Nations Covenant on Civil and Political Rights and the Universal Declaration of Human Rights. China is a signatory of both documents.[51]

Additionally, China has drawn criticism from a number of Uighurs and human rights advocates because it "consistently fails" to live up to its own constitutional provisions governing autonomous regions.[52] For example, Amnesty International cites several instances of Uighurs being detained "merely for being relatives or friends of political prisoners or fugitives," or they say Uighurs could be detained and held without charge for a number of months, just for rousing suspicions that they are involved in acts deemed harmful to the national security of the state.[53] Chinese Vice Premier Qian Qichen denies these allegations and insists that "China strictly distinguishes the separatists from the rest of the 10 million Chinese Muslims in the Xinjiang region."[54]

Shanghai Cooperation Organisation

On June 15, 2001, in Shanghai, the heads of states of China, Russia, Kazakhstan, Kyrgyzstan, Tajikistan, and Uzbekistan, formerly known as the "Shanghai Five" and later the "Shanghai Forum," released a joint-press communique describing what they called their intention to "raise the Shanghai Five to a higher level" and "build a regional organisation of multilateral cooperation covering various fields."[55] This joint communique announced that the new regional organisation would be called the Shanghai Cooperation Organisation (SCO). The establishment of the SCO, largely spearheaded by the Chinese, is seen by many observers as part of a security strategy to prevent Kazakh or Uyghur separatists from using Central Asian states as a safety zone to plot separatist activities in Xinjiang. It is also seen by some analysts as an organisation that the Chinese have used to spread their sphere of influence, both economic and geopolitical, throughout Central Asia.

SCO and the Aftermath of September 11

In the days and weeks after the terrorist attacks on the U.S. in September 2001, China has reportedly become increasingly concerned that its strategy for expanding its presence and influence in the Central Asian region through the SCO mechanism is in jeopardy.56 They point out that the U.S. efforts to build and lead an international coalition against terrorism, particularly in Central Asia, have been swift and effective.

The U.S. appears to have completely seized the initiative from the newly formed SCO regional grouping, and has provided SCO members with an unanticipated alternative for addressing the issue of regional terrorism.[57] Indeed, the willingness and level at which a number of SCO member states have offered their support and cooperation to the United States is disturbing to a number of Beijing's elites. Several western diplomats and Asia specialists note that many in Beijing are deeply concerned that Washington could so quickly project its power into Central Asia and even develop close working relations with China's closest ally in the region, Pakistan.[58]

The New Great Game

The PRC's reported plans to expand its influence throughout Central Asia may be put on hold because of rapidly unfolding events in the region. However, prior to September 2001, it appeared that China was well on its way to establishing a powerful presence in Central Asia. According to some western analysts, by the Spring of 2000, China and Russia both seemed poised to take advantage of what was viewed by the Central Asian states as U.S. indifference toward the region. As an example of the latter, analysts point to former Secretary of State Madeleine Albright's "whirl-wind" tour of the region in 2000. In an unsuccessful attempt to address the pleas from the governments of Uzbekistan, Kazakhstan, and Kyrgyzstan for security assistance, the U.S. offered a mere $16 million dollars of combined assistance for all three states.[59] They reportedly considered Washington's $16 million dollar offer a "declaration of disinterest" in the region and its security concerns.[60] Analysts argue that this sent an immediate signal to China that the time was ripe to capitalise on Washington's perceived "ambivalence" toward the region.

Although the United States had delivered around $1.5 billion in aid to the region between 1992 and 1998, this assistance was accompanied by pressure on the Central Asian states to establish pluralistic and democratic societies. On the other hand, the Central Asian states were more concerned about security and consolidation of their secular governments in the wake of increased "Islamic fundamentalism" than they were with democracy and pluralism in their societies.[61] China, which was much less concerned about democracy and pluralism, saw an opportunity. For example, China provided military and technical aid to Uzbekistan, Kazakhstan, and Kyrgyzstan. China also increased trade and economic ties with most of its western neighbors, hoping to ensure access to valuable Central Asian oil and natural gas resources.[62]

Additionally, Beijing was using the SCO to develop closer ties to Moscow than it had enjoyed at any other time since the Sino-Soviet split in the late 1960's. Most of these relationships were further enhanced by the signing of the Declaration of the Establishment of the Shanghai Cooperation Organisation, the Shanghai Covenant on the Suppression of Terrorism, Separatism, and Extremism, and the Sino-Russian Friendship Pact, signed this past summer in Moscow.[63]

An important component of this process was the development of a potential Sino-Russian counter-weight to closer ties between Russia and the United States. This potentially significant gain for China was undermined by the geopolitical and policy shifts following the September 11 attacks. At the same time, many in China believe that heightened U.S. awareness of possible threats posed by Islamic fundamentalist groups could serve Chinese interests.[64]

However, since September 11, the eagerness of some member states to assist the United States bilaterally in the war on terrorism raises a number of questions about the future of the SCO and China's plans for spreading its influence and presence in the region. For example, Uzbekistan, Kazakhstan, and Kyrgyzstan, all key members of the SCO and recipients of Chinese security and technical assistance, have offered their broad support to the U.S. efforts to fight global terrorism, and each state appears to have pushed its own domestic interests and agenda over those of the SCO.[65]

Bilateral versus Multilateral Cooperation

The absence of the SCO as a regional player in the war against terrorism has surprised a number of China watchers, who believed that the Shanghai Cooperation Organisation had, on paper at least, a number of options that it could have offered the United States to assist in the war on terrorism. Some analysts argue that the SCO had been involved in the fight against "terrorism" and what it calls the "three-evils forces" in the Central Asian region since 1996 and could have used this collective experience and its new antiterrorist center in Bishkek, Kyrgyzstan to offer multilateral regional support to the war on terrorism. Instead, it appears as though the multilateral SCO option has been put on hold as each state is offering bilateral support to Washington and possibly looking to gain military and security aid along with other support.

NOTES AND REFERENCES

1. Qing Dynasty troops after encountering strong resistance to Uighur fighters established its rule in 1884 and renamed East Turkestan, Xinjiang, which means "new frontier" or "new territory".
2. Human Rights Watch Report, *Xinjiang, China's Restive Northwest*, 1998.
3. People's Republic of China, Year 2000 Census.
4. Uyghuramerican.org media reports, "Central Asia: Uighurs Say States Yield To Chinese," by Jean-Christopher Peuch.
5. Asia Week Inside Story China: Beijing vs. Islam, by Michael Winchester, [http://www.asiaweek.com/asiaweek/97/1024/is1.html].
6. *Ibid.*
7. The Scotsman, Uighurs warn of return to terror, by Damien McElroy, May 31, 2000.
8. BBC News Report: *Who Are the Taleban*, December 20, 2000.
9. BBC Monitoring Central Asia, "Central Asians, Uighurs training in Pakistan, Afghanistan for "subversive" acts," July, 11, 2000.
10. Institute for Peace and Conflict Studies article No. 521, Shanghai Five: Emerging Foreign Policy Dimensions, by P.A. Mathew, July 15, 2001.
11. Wall Street Journal, "Chinese Goals Take A Backseat As U.S. Rises To The Fore In Asia," by Andrew Higgins and Charles Hutzler, October 19, 2001.

12. *Ibid.*
13. South China Morning Post, "Beijing Moscow support Afghan coalition government." October 11, 2001.
14. There are a number of existing sanctions contained in Section 902 of P.L. 101-246, put in place after the Tiananmen crackdown, which ban the sale and export of a number of items to China, such as criminal detection and crowd control instruments, munitions including helicopters and helicopter parts, and satellites for launch by Chinese launch vehicles. Shortly after the September 11 attacks, several media reports hinted that in exchange for Chinese support and cooperation in the war on terrorism, some of these sanctions would be eased or dropped.
15. *The Washington Post,* "China Vows To Help in Terror Fight," by Mike Allen and Philip P. Pan, October 19, 2001.
16. The Manchu ethnic group launched the Qing Dynasty (1644-1911) after overthrowing the ethnic Han Chinese of the Ming Dynasty. It was the Manchus that first incorporated Uighur areas in Central Asia and later brutally repressed a rebellion in the late 1800's.
17. Xinjiang Autonomous Region shares a 5,000km border with the five states mentioned above, roughly 1,500km of the border has Turkic-speaking peoples on both sides.
18. Center for Computational Science at the University of Kentucky, "Uighurs' Independence is Important to the Survival of Their People," by Gwynne Dyer, [http://www.ccs.uky.edu/~rakhim/doc_files/gwyne_dyer.html].
19. Dialog.com, "International Data Reference on Terrorist, Guerilla and Insurgent Groups- Asia, Indo China and the Pacific Rim," May 1999, [http://www.dialog.com/info/home/australia/fastways/terrorism_in_china.html].
20. *Christian Science Monitor,* "Roots of a Race Riot," by Robert Marquand, July 18, 2001.
21. *The Wall Street Journal,* "China Provides Extensive Briefing On Separatists in Xinjiang," by Charles Hutzler, November 15, 2001.
22. *Ibid.*
23. *Ibid.*

24. Laogai Research Foundation Special Report, *The World Bank and Chinese Military: Ignorance– Incompetence– or Cover Up?,"* April 4, 1996.
25. Dialog.com, "International Data Reference on Terrorist, Guerilla and Insurgent Groups– Asia, Indo China and Pacific Rim, May 1999, [www.dialog.com/info/home/australia/fastways/terrorism_in_china.html].
26. *Ibid.*
27. The Political Consultative Conference an entity controlled by the Communist Party that is made up of minority or non-Communist political parties. It has no real power and serves no real political purpose such as being an opposition party to the Chinese Communist Party. There are National Peoples Consultative Conference and several Provincial Political Consultative Conferences in China.
28. Dialog.com, "International Data Reference on Terrorist, Guerilla and Insurgent Groups– Asia, Indo China and Pacific Rim, May 1999, [www.dialog.com/info/home/australia/fastways/terrorism_in_china.html].
29. Radio Free Europe and Radio Liberty Online, "Kazakhstan: Exiled Uighurs Step Up Fight Against Beijing, by Jeremy Bransten, 14 October 1997, [http:www.rferl.org/nca/features/1997/10/F.RU.971014135113.html].
30. *Ibid.*
31. The Japan Times Online, "Fighting for independence in the shadow of a Goliath," by Russell Working, November 6, 2001.
32. Dialogue.com, "International Data Reference on Terrorist, Guerilla and Insurgent Groups- Asia, Indo China and the Pacific Rim, May 1999.
33. *Ibid.*
34. Stratfor.com, "Chinese Cleanup Targets Uighurs," May 16, 2001.
35. These reports from Strategic Forcasting Service, an analylitical new service, are attributed to Aziz Soltobaev, on the staff of the American University of Kyrgyzstan.
36. Stratfor.com, "Chinese Cleanup Targets Uighurs," May 16, 2001, [http://www.stratfor.com/asia/commentary/0105162140.html].

37. Federation of American Scientist: Intelligence Resource Program, " Uighur Militants: Committee for Eastern Turkistan."
38. The Pioneer, "China Tries to quell the Xinjiang uprising, by Aditya Bhagat, February 27, 1997.
39. Federation of American Scientist: Intelligence Resource Program, "Uighur militants: Committee for Eastern Turkistan."
40. BBC Monitoring Central Asia, "Central Asians, Uighurs training in Pakistan, Afghanistan for "subversive" acts," July 11, 2000.
41. *Ibid.*
42. BBC Monitoring South Asia, "Putin envoy says Afghan Taliban training Uighurs, Chechens, Central Asians," September 27, 2000.
43. Dialogue.com, "International Data Reference on Terrorist, Guerilla and Insurgent Groups- Asia, Indo China and the Pacific Rim, May 1999.
44. Uyghuramerican.org, "Central Asia: Uighurs Say States Yield To Chinese," by Jean- Christophe Peuch, March 29, 2001.
45. Federation of American Scientists: Intelligence Resource Program, "Uighur militants Committee for East Turkistan."
46. The Pioneer, "China tries to quell the Xinjiang uprising," by Aditya Bhagat, February 27, 1997.
47. Human Rights Watch Backgrounder, China: Human Rights Concerns in Xinjiang, October 11, 2001.
48. East Turkestan Information Bulletin, [http://www.caccp.org/et/etib3_5.html#1].
49. Washington Post, "Uighur Activist Back U.S. but Worry Their Cause Will Suffer," by John Pomfret, October 13, 2001.
50. National Review Online's Guest Comment, "Meanwhile, In China: On Persecution of Muslims, Christians, and the Falun Gong," by Ann Noonan (Laogai Research Foundation), November 9, 2001.
51. Los Angeles Times, "U.N. Voices Concern Over Rise in Alleged Abuse of Chinese Muslims," by Anthony Kuhn, November 10, 2001.
52. Chinese Constitution *Section VI: Sections 112-122 The Origins of Self Government of National and Autonomous Areas* and *Chapter*

Two: The Fundamental Rights and Duties of Citizens, with particular emphasis being placed on Articles 35, 36, and 37.

53. Amnesty International On-line,"Peoples Republic of China Uighurs arbitrarily detained and tortured," February 4,1999.
54. *Ibid.*
55. *BBC Monitoring Asia Pacific,* "China: Press communique of Shanghai summit," June 16, 2001.
56. Wall Street Journal, "China Worries That Rising U.S. Influence In Central Asia Could Harm Its Interests," by Charles Hutzler, September 24, 2001.
57. *Ibid.*
58. The Christian Science Monitor, "China's new balancing act," by Robert Marquard, November 8, 2001.
59. *Ibid.*
60. The Wall Street Journal Europe, "Shanghai Five: The 'Great Game' Returns," August 23, 2001.
61. *Ibid.*
62. Central Asian Caucus: Analyst, "Did Putin Shanghai Bush?," by Robert M. Cutler, July 4, 2001.
63. The Christian Science Monitor, "China's new balancing act," by Robert Marquand, November 8, 2001.
64. On December 6, 2001, while meeting with terrorism officials in Beijing, Francis X. Taylor, the U.S. State Department's top counter terrorism official, noted that some Chinese Muslims had fought for Al-Qaeda in Afghanistan. However, Taylor stressed that Washington did not support the PRC's insistence that Muslim separatists in China's northwest are a part of a global fundamentalist terror threat.
65. The Wall Street Journal Europe, "Shanghai Five: 'Great Game' Returns, by Ilan Berman, August 23, 2001.

6

RUSSIAN STRATEGY TOWARDS TAJIKISTAN

Social, Economic and Political Conditions of the Post-Soviet Tajikistan

Tajikistan is a small country located at what might be described as the geophysical center of the Asian landmass. Bordered to the south by Afghanistan, to the east by China's Xinjiang province, and to the west and north by other countries that emerged from what was once was called Soviet Central Asia, Tajikistan lies at the interstices of several cultures, languages, religions, and zones of commerce.[1]

Since the disintegration of the USSR in 1991, Tajikistan has experienced wrenching economic dislocations, civil war, and post-war political, economic, and social decay. In a short period of time Tajikistan went from the status of a middle-income country to one of the poorest countries in the world.[2] Yet, during this same period, Russia maintained a substantial, continuous, and expensive military and diplomatic presence in Tajikistan.What accounts for the endurance of Russia's commitment to Tajikistan?

Tajikistan is not an immediate neighbor of Russia, that is, it does not share a common border. Nor does it share a common border with any state that is an immediate neighbor of Russia, with the exception of China. Tajikistan is culturally far removed from Russia. Tajikistan, a country in which the predominant native language is Tajik, a variant of Farsi, has more cultural ties to the Middle East and West Asia than to Moscow and Europe.

Tajikistan has little of commercial value to Russia.[3] The country has virtually no oil or gas production. Tajikistan is rich in metal mineral resources and has vast hydroelectric potential, but mineral resources are plentiful in Russia and Tajikistan's hydroelectric energy is too far away to transport cost-effectively.[4] Tajikistan's largest commodity export, aluminum, competes with Russian domestic enterprises rather than offering complementary commercial possibilities.[5]

There was a sizable contingent of ethnic Russians in Tajikistan during the Soviet period, but the Russian population of Tajikistan—excluding soldiers and diplomats—dropped by 65 per cent in the first 5 years of independence.[6] Moreover, Russia elsewhere has demonstrated it has little enthusiasm for defending the rights of ethnic Russians in the "near abroad," certainly not to the extent of maintaining troops for their protection.[7] These and other factors might suggest that the Russian government, following the collapse of the USSR and the pain of post-collapse economic contraction, easily could have concluded that it was not in Russia's national interest to maintain an expensive and logistically challenging commitment to Tajikistan. Russia, some might have argued, has little to gain and much to lose from continued interaction with Tajikistan.

Yet, Russia's commitment to Tajikistan over the past decade may be described as unwavering. During this period, Russia maintained as many as 25,000 troops in Tajikistan.

Russia was by far the largest financial supporter of Tajikistan, having extended the country loans of more than $200 million as early as 1993. Russia increased that level of assistance throughout the decade, with assistance eventually amounting to more that $288 million in 1998.[8] In November 1999, Tajikistan President Imomali Rahmonov announced that Russia was and will continue to be Tajikistan's most important "strategic partner".[9] This study analyses Russia's engagement in Tajikistan, surveying Russia's commitment to Tajikistan in terms of its psychological, tactical, and strategic dimensions. The essence of Russia's commitment to Tajikistan can be summed up in the observation that Tajikistan is crucial for Russian policy makers because it is situated, to use Owen Lattimore's apt phrase, at the "pivot of Asia".[10] To appreciate Russia's role in Tajikistan, it is useful to look back to the historical roots of Russia's presence in the Central Asian region.

Russia's Presence in Central Asia

Tajikistan is home to the Pamirs, a unique high mountain complex located in the heart of Asia. The eastern region of Tajikistan is sometimes referred to as the Pamir Knot, as it is the central hub from which the five great ranges of Asia extend: the Himalaya, extending southeast; the Karakoram, extending southeast; the Hindu Kush, extending southwest; the Tian Shan, extending northeast; and the Kunlun Shan, extending east.

For the past several hundred years, political control of the territories of Central Asia was divided among three competing powers: the Persian Safavis, who were in control of much of modern-day Iran; the various Uzbek Khanates occupying the lands between the Oxus (now, Syr Darya) and Jakartes (now, Amu Darya) rivers; and the Indian Moghul Dynasty that was forged under Babar in 1530 and remained in authority until 1857 with the onset of British influence. The contemporary borders and spheres of influence in Central Asia are a legacy of the European great power competition of the 19th century.[11] As the British influence on Central Asia increased from the South, Russian territorial expansion into Central Asia increased from the north. Russia took possession of much of the Uzbek lands and the British occupied the previous position of the Indian Moghuls.

The area to the east of Tajikistan, or Eastern Turkestan, came under the control of the Qing dynasty in 1759 and, with the exception of some local liberation movements, China retained its control over the area for a century. Russian troops, advancing eastward, captured the city of Vernyi (now Almaty) in 1855. Russia then pushed yet further east, coming into confrontation with China over control of Eastern Turkestan. In 1860 the Treaty of Beijing established the frontier between China and Russia, but Russia, anxious to gain control of the fertile Ili River Valley, drove further east, reaching the headwaters of the Ili River Valley in 1871.

Meanwhile, Britain was expanding its influence in the subcontinent, having taken control of India in the late 1850s. As Russian territorial expansion into Central Asia increased from the north, British expansion increased from the south. Alarmed that Russia was making headway in capturing "inland China," Britain offered support to the Chinese to assist them in rebuffing Russian advances. China recaptured Eastern Turkestan and renamed the area New Territories, or *Xinjiang*. In 1891, after Tsarist forces gained the advantage on the British at the battle of Bozai Gombaz in the southern Pamirs, Russian and British negotiators established the new buffer state of Afghanistan.

The border of what the British in India regarded as the "northern territories" was drawn at the western flowing

Pyandzh and Amu Darya rivers, leaving a narrow swath of territory, the Vakhan Corridor, between the two empires as a buffer zone. The agreement implied that the Russians could claim control of Gorno-Badakhshan, thereby establishing the Pamir Knot as within Russian control. This was done despite the fact that China, which had at least as much claim to Gorno-Badakhshan as did Russia, was not party to the agreement. Excluded from the agreement, China has never consented to the legitimacy of this border, maintaining that frontier between Tajikistan and Xinjiang was established on the basis of an "unequal treaty".[12]

After the collapse of the Tsarist empire following World War I and the Bolshevik takeover, the Russians returned to Central Asia to establish communist rule. In 1918 the northernmost areas of Central Asia were included within the boundaries of the Russian Soviet Federated Socialist Republic. The First Congress of Soviets in 1922 adopted a Treaty of Union that recognised the Turkestan Autonomous Soviet Republic as an autonomous entity within the Russian Soviet Federated Socialist Republic. After communist political consolidation in Central Asia, a land reform was carried out in Central Asia in 1924 that also established new administrative boundaries, creating four socialist republics in Central Asia. The Tajik Autonomous Oblast initially was included in the Uzbek Soviet Socialist Republic. Five years later Tajikistan was transformed into a Soviet Socialist Republic, a status that Kazakhstan and Kyrgyzstan gained only in 1936.

During the Soviet period, Tajikistan lagged behind the all-union norm and even behind other national republics in terms of measures of social and economic development. But it was not an unusual or unruly republic by comparative standards. Soviet power in Tajikistan, as in all the other national republics, was often more apparent than real; it was based on a subtle political contract. According to this contract, the locals agreed not to challenge key formal Soviet precepts regarding the party, political leadership, ideology, and religion, but in turn the Russians agreed not to challenge key informal processes and procedures by which the locals conducted their own affairs in accordance with their culture and preferences. When the USSR began to disintegrate in 1990 and 1991, the transition from the formal to informal levels of power was swift. The Russian population fled the republic as the political situation deteriorated. The Soviet military, however, remained.

Civil War in Tajikistan

In mid-1991, the prospects for postcommunist democratic change in Tajikistan looked comparatively bright. Tajikistan's heritage of ancient traditions of Persian civility mixed well with the egalitarian values of the Soviet period. Tajikistan's multinational population was well educated, with a high level of scientific and technical expertise. Tajikistan was well endowed with mineral resources and had abundant food resources. Sovietera Tajikistan had the highest per capita rate of hydroelectric generation in the world. Given the conditions in 1990 and 1991, Tajikistan was a country that, like its northern neighbor, Kyrgyzstan, easily could have set out on a course of peaceful, democratic, socially responsible market-oriented reform.

Yet, just beneath the surface of the USSR's "friendship of nations," old resentments had resisted the homogenising forces of the USSR's proletarian internationalism. Prior to the Soviet takeover of Tajikistan, no single authority had ruled the peoples of Tajikistan's rugged mountains and fertile agricultural valleys. When the Soviets established control, they brought the country under a single government but never fully succeeded in disestablishing traditional regional and clan-based loyalties. During the Soviet period, Islamic organisations, with the exception of the proregime officially sanctioned, ideologically docile organisations, were prohibited. Tajikistan's physical infrastructure was integrated into the larger Soviet infrastructure of communication, transportation, and energy in such a way that made Tajikistan dependent on external actions. Moreover, Tajikistan was on the border of Afghanistan, a country that by 1991 had known only war for over a decade and had nurtured a generation of barbarised and poorly educated armed insurrectionists.

As political change swept Moscow in Summer 1991 it reverberated through the outlying republics. In August 1991 Tajikistan leader Kahar Makhamov was forced to resign as president. Rakhmon Nabiev, a former Tajikistan communist party first secretary and a strong defender of continued close ties with Moscow, gained control in the November 1991 presidential election. But in spring 1992 Tajikistan was caught in a wave of escalating tension that brought armed groups into the streets of Dushanbe, the capital. In September 1992 members of the Islamic Renaissance Party forced Nabiev to resign, claimed control of the capital, and established a government.[13]

Armed opposition to the takeover was organised by a coalition of forces from the southern regions of Kurgan-Tyube and Kulyab and the northern Leninobod region. These forces attacked and recaptured the capital in the early morning hours of October 24, 1992. Sporadic but intense fighting continued until December. Thousands of civilians and soldiers were killed and 100,000 persons fled to neighboring countries; as many as 600,000 Tajikistan citizens fled their homes as internal refugees.[14] This early violent phase of the civil war was resolved in favor of a political coalition based in the city of Kulyab. It is this group, under the leadership of Imomali Rahmonov, that rules the country today.

After the conflict, the fighters defeated by the ruling coalition—the groups that eventually gained the name "the United Tajikistan Opposition" (UTO)—scattered to the mountain areas to the north and east of the capital. Large areas of the country remained under military control, as the victorious commanders divided territory among themselves. Although political control was well established in the capital and in the northern city of Hujand as early as 1993, some outlying regions and the eastern part of the country, in particular the Garm region and the Gorno-Badakhshan region, remained in the control of local leaders and military chieftains rather than under the control of the Dushanbe government for much of the period between 1993 and 1997.

During the first period of the Tajikistan hostilities, the Russian government's official position was one of neutrality. When fighting broke out, the Soviet 201st Motorised Rifle Division, already deployed in Tajikistan, officially undertook a neutral peacekeepingmission. In reality, however, Russia supported the Rahmonov coalition and used its presence in Tajikistan to influence the course of events. Other countries did the same. Neighboring Uzbekistan provided both material and moral support to the Rahmonov coalition. At the same time, numerous press reports stated or implied that the opposition forces were receiving financial and technical support from abroad, in particular from Iran and other Muslim countries.

The level and usefulness of outside support provided by all the Muslim countries have been shrouded by the events of the war. There is a preponderance of evidence, however, that outside support from Islamic countries did not play a key role. In contrast, the Russian government's support clearly had a direct impact on the outcome of the civil war and the consolidation of power under the Rahmonov government.

Although the war interrupted the transition from communist to postcommunist rule in Tajikistan, the transition went relatively smoothly in the neighboring states of Kyrgyzstan, Turkmenistan, and Uzbekistan and in Kazakhstan. To be sure, the goal of establishing democratic, market-oriented societies was not pursued with the same enthusiasm and the same efficacy in each of these countries. But open conflict was avoided. Tajikistan, accordingly, stood out as a demonstration of what could go wrong. A consensus emerged among the leadership of the Central Asian states to take steps, independently or within multilateral organisations, to counter the "Tajik disease." Following urgent appeals from President Islam Karimov of neighboring Uzbekistan, the newly established Commonwealth of Independent States undertook to establish a multilateral peace keeping operation in Tajikistan.

Russia and the Tajikistan Civil War

Meanwhile, domestic politics within Russia was driving a substantial revision of Russian foreign policy goals and objectives. The collapse of the Soviet Union was not the product of the actions of renegade national republics, as many outside observers had anticipated. Rather, the Soviet collapse was a product of the unwillingness of key Russian politicians to continue paying the "cost of empire."

The evidence for this is clear. A withdrawal from commitments outside core Russian territories was seen as a way of reinvigorating Russia. The Russian government acceded to the idea of retreating to the borders of the Russian Soviet Federation Socialist Republic, despite the fact that large areas of what could be regarded as historically Russian territory were relinquished to neighboring republics, particularly Kazakhstan and Ukraine.[15]

Ironically, Russia opted to withdraw from the Soviet Union even while Central Asia's leaders were opposing the dissolution of the USSR. The chaotic events of the August 1991 coup attempt in Moscow changed this situation dramatically, however. After the coup attempt, the Central Asian countries reoriented quickly, assuming separate and independent trajectories.

This introduced a moment of decision for Russia's foreign policy makers. Should Russia's influence in the post-Soviet world be identified with the boundaries of the old USSR or should new spheres of influence be drawn? Russian political officials soon found themselves defending the principle that, despite the national independence of the Central Asian republics, Russia's special sphere of influence in the Asian region after the Soviet breakup should continue to coincide with the borders of the former USSR.

Russian Foreign Minister Andrei Kozyrev early on emphasised that the first priority of Russian diplomacy was the formation of the Commonwealth of Independent States, an organisation that he thought would entitle Russia to continue exerting a dominant influence throughout Eurasia generally, but particularly in Central Asia, where the states were seen as being dependent on Russia economically and militarily.[16]

The Russian Duma and the Kazakhstan parliament both approved Russian peacekeeping forces for Tajikistan in April 1993.[17] The Russian parliament presented an alternative to the Yeltsin administration's proposals for troop deployment to Tajikistan. But, the alternative plan did not question the concept of the defense of Tajikistan, only that further deployments should be conditioned on the willingness of other states to send troops as well.[18] Even after the Tajikistan civil war had escalated the costs of Russia's commitment to

Tajikistan, Foreign Minister Kozyrev continued to argue forcefully that Tajikistan should remain under Russian protection.[19]

As the Tajikistan war unfolded, the Russians were balancing goals of peacekeeping and stability with Russian's long-term interest in maintaining an outpost in the sensitive mountains passes of Central Asia. Russia publicly represented that it could achieve this by maintaining neutrality throughout the war. Members of the Tajik opposition, however, did not regard the Russian influence as neutral. Russian soldiers became a weather vane for conflict. One bloody confrontation at a border station in July 1993 left 24 Russian border guards dead and 18 wounded. In the wake of the political fallout over this incident, a Russian presidential decree reprimanded the Russian Security Minister and dismissed the head of Border Troops.[20] Afterward, the Russian government began giving more support to the idea of maintaining domestic political stability in Tajikistan. Russia assumed primary responsibility for Tajik military operations. Russia's military presence gradually turned the country into what Lena Jonson characterised as a "Russian protectorate".[21]

Appeals also were made for intervention by the United Nations. The United Nations sent a team in October 1994 to assess the possibility of establishing an observer mission in Tajikistan. Shortly afterward, the UN Mission of Observers in Tajikistan (UNMOT) was established in Dushanbe, with military observers detached to key regions throughout the country. The UN, the Russian military, and many international donor organisations began applying diplomatic pressure to encourage the newly established Tajikistan government to develop a program of national reconciliation. Under the auspices of the UN, negotiations were begun between the government and opposition representatives. The negotiations eventually came to be known as the inter-Tajik talks.

In the context of these negotiations, President Rahmonov and Said Abdullah Nuri, Chairman of the UTO, concluded a protocol on principles for achieving national reconciliation in August 1995 and in December 1996, the leaders signed a ceasefire agreement. In June 1997 the leaders signed a peace accord that provided a detailed program and time frame for reduction in war-fighting capacities, reintegration, and political reconciliation. Confidence-buildingmeasures were designed to lead in increments toward the surrender of arms by Tajikistan's hard-to-regiment irregular militias. A military protocol was adopted that provided for the designation of 10 assembly areas for UTO fighters, the registration of fighters, the registration of weapons, and medical examination of fighters.

In the inter-Tajik talks, the negotiating parties in Tajikistan may have been brought to the negotiating table less by calculations of potential mutual benefit than by calculations of potential individual loss. Both sides in the negotiations were united in the negotiations by the fact that they viewed events that were unfolding in Afghanistan as a common threat. In 1995, the Taliban, a group of radical Afghan Muslims that had coalesced in the rugged and notorious refugee camps of Peshawar, Pakistan, succeeded in mounting a military offensive for political control in Afghanistan. With Pakistani backing, the Taliban captured southern and eastern Afghanistan and, in September 1996, captured the capital, Kabul. The Taliban's zealotry and ruthlessness forged a consensus among Iran, Russia, Uzbekistan, and both the competing factions in Tajikistan. All these parties, divided as they might be on other issues, agreed that the spread of Taliban ideology and methods into Central Asia was an outcome to be avoided at all costs.

The 1997 Peace Accord included provisions relating to the parliamentary elections of 2000 and the subsequent dissolution of the National ReconciliationCouncil as a milestone of political reintegration. In February and March 2000, parliamentary elections were held in Tajikistan and, in accordance with the Peace Accord, the National Reconciliation Council was dissolved. In June 2000 UNMOT withdrew from Tajikistan after a 6-year stay.

Looking South to Afghanistan

The Soviet Union occupied Afghanistan in late 1979 after a local insurrection threatened to establish a government unfriendly to Moscow. After 10 years of futile conflict, the Soviet military withdrew from Afghanistan, although neither a military nor political settlement had been reached to resolve key issues of the decade-long occupation. For nearly a decade following the Soviet withdrawal, Afghanistan remained politically divided. Political control was fragmented among regionally and ethnically based war-era military chieftains.

In 1995, the Taliban organised a campaign to wrest political control from Afghanistan's postwar Kabul-based government that was under the leadership of Burhanuddin Rabbani. The Taliban . ghters pushed through southern and eastern Afghanistan, uniting the primarily ethnic Pashtu areas under strict Islamic rule. The Taliban succeeded in capturing Kabul in September 1996 and ousting the Rabbani government. Opposition to the Taliban remained active, however, particularly in the northern and eastern part of the country. Commander Abdul Rashid Dostam's National Islamic Movement, consisting heavily of ethnic Uzbeks, controlled several north-central provinces. Commander Ahmad Shah Masood controlled the ethnic Tajik majority areas of the northeast

Given the illegitimate conditions under which the Taliban gained power and established political control, the UN and other international organisations were unwilling to recognise the Taliban as the legitimate government of Afghanistan. The UN and many states deferred decision on diplomatic credentials. The Organisation of the Islamic Conference left the Afghan seat vacant until the question of legitimacy could be resolved. Major world governments and international organisations instituted sanctions against the Taliban. The U.S. government imposed sanctions on Afghanistan in July 1999. The UN imposed sanctions on Afghanistan in November 1999.

During 1999 and 2000, the Taliban gradually extended its control northward, eventually ousting Masood's troops and capturing the city of Taloqan in September 2000.[22] After the defeat of the opposition and the fall of the northern Afghanistan provinces, the Taliban exercised authority virtually throughout the entire country. Taliban representatives immediately appealed for diplomatic recognition from the international community. The conflict has now moved into a new phase, as the Taliban seeks to establish diplomatic recognition as the legitimate government of Afghanistan.[23]

The 1206-km-long Afghanistan–Tajikistan border is defined for most of its length by the Pani (Pandzh) River. The Rahmonov government in Tajikistan views the threat to this border arising from instability in Afghanistan as the chief challenge facing the country's postconflict reconstruction. Without interruption since the disintegration of the USSR, Russian and Tajik military units have policed the Tajikistan border with Afghanistan.[24] The Russians see the border as a porous integument through which terrorism, weapons, and drugs penetrate on route to destinations in Eurasia. At the same time, the border is seen as a cultural divide between the values of Western civilisation and the lawlessness of Afghanistan.

Looking East to China

Modern Tajikistan has been physically and politically isolated from China. During the 1950s the USSR and China engaged in a considerable amount of "fraternal socialist cooperation." Military and commercial interactions were considerable. Cadres and technical information were exchanged. The USSR made significant investment in physical infrastructure to facilitate Sino–Soviet trade relations. But, when the ideologic differences regarding leadership in the world communist movement emerged in the 1960s, other policy differences surfaced as well. The Chinese government took issue in particular with the Sino–Soviet border, claiming that "unequal treaties" should not be considered legitimate.[25] Given that the population of Gorno-Badakhshan is not ethnographically Tajik, and given that much, perhaps most, of Gorno-Badakhshan lies on the eastern slope of Asia's continental divide, it should not be surprising that China questioned the legitimacy of the China–Tajikistan border.

Partly because of the remoteness and in part because of the lack of legitimacy, virtually no effort was made during the Soviet period to improve physical infrastructure relating to the border. By the end of the Soviet period, no road existed linking Tajikistan and China. No border post suitable for commercial purposes existed. No formal commerce of any kind was supported by the policy and physical infrastructures of the two countries.

The Sino–Soviet border relationship began to change after Mikhail Gorbachev introduced his ideas of "new thinking" in Soviet foreign policy. After Gorbachev's July 1986 speech in Vladivostok, the Chinese government sent a delegation to Moscow to start serious discussions regarding the Sino–

Soviet border.[26] Although, these discussions focused almost exclusively on the Far East, they nonetheless established a momentum that led to the conclusion of the May 1991 Agreement on National Boundaries.[27] After the USSR disintegrated, the individual border countries soon resumed the border talks, working on both multilateral and bilateral levels.

In April 1993, a five-country commission to draft border agreements met in Beijing.[28] In January 1996, the five border countries exchanged topographic maps, a first step in agreement on actual demarcation.[29] In April 1996, the Presidents of the five border countries met in Shanghai to sign a package of 14 cooperation agreements that became known as the Shanghai Accord. The "Shanghai Five" joined again in Moscow the following April to conclude an agreement on military confidence building.[30] The follow-up five-power summit of foreign ministers in July 1998 underscored the commitment to the continuation of earlier agreements on confidence building and to the goal of establishing a nuclear-free zone in Central Asia [31]. At the meeting in Dushanbe in July 2000, the countries adopted the term *Shanghai Forum* to describe their interactions.

At the same time, as the multilateral negotiations took place, China was conducting negotiationswith the Eurasian states on a bilateral basis. Kazakhstan was the first to make progress, opening its border to trade and traffic early on. In March 1999 the Kazakhstan and Chinese heads of state signed a comprehensive border agreement that was designed to resolve the border issue in perpetuity.[32] Kyrgyzstan too made good progress in normalisation. In August 1999, Kyrgyzstan President Askar Akaev and Chinese President Jiang Zemin signed an agreement that was described as "settling all disputes over the border between the two countries".[33]

In contrast, progress on Tajikistan's common border with China went slowly. Tajikistan, like the other Central Asian countries, is landlocked. But unlike the other Central Asian countries, Tajikistan's road and rail access has been exclusively westward-oriented. Tajikistan has a limited number of rail and road transit corridors. The two rail corridors are through Uzbekistan. Two remote and sparsely traveled roads connect Tajikistan with Kyrgyzstan, but road conditions do not permit regular freight. Road crossings with Afghanistan are under military control and are not used for routine commercial purposes.

The Tajikistan government has been particularly enthusiastic about a plan to develop a road that will link Tajikistan with Asian markets. Construction has begun on an "eastern access" road that will link the city of Murgab in Badakhshan with the city of Taxkorgan in the westernmost Xinjiang Uygur Autonomous Republic of the People's Republic.[34] In June 1999, the Tajikistan and China governments announced a decision to open a bordercrossing point on a temporary basis and complete the road through Eastern Tajikistan.[35] In August 1999, Tajikistan President Rahmonov and Chinese President Jiang Zemin signed an agreement on the demarcation of one section of their disputed common border. But, the leaders failed to reach a comprehensive agreement to resolve Chinese territorial claims on parts of Tajikistan's Gorno-Badashkhan Autonomous Oblast.[36]

Tactical Dimension

Russia's long-term, psychological commitment to an Asian sphere of influence and Russia's calculation of its strategic interests in the region explain the underlying commitment Russia has to Tajikistan. But, it is recent events in Russia and Central Asia that have mobilised the Putin government to adopt its current proactive posture toward security cooperation with the Central Asian countries. Russia and the states of Central Asia share a common fear of the spread of terrorism under the banner of radical Islam.[37] This fear has been mobilised by the campaign of terrorist bombings in Russia motivated by Russia's determination to retain control over Chechnya. In similar measure, in Central Asia this same fear was mobilised by Tajikistan's experience with the antigovernment uprising in Hujand in November 1998, by Uzbekistan's experience with terrorist bombings in Tashkent in February 1999, and by Kyrgyzstan's hostage crisis in the Fergana Valley in August 1999.

The Hujand uprising occurred in November 1998, when an irregular military formation led by Tajikistan civil war colonel Mahmud Khudoiberdiyev attempted to take over the government in the northern Tajikistan town of Hujand. Khudoiberdiyev's group of about 700 soldiers fought a government force of nearly 3000. After intense street fighting, the Tajikistan government troops repulsed Khudoiberdiyev's troops. According to a subsequent Tajikistan government report, 114 Tajikistan military members and 220 rebels were killed, 431 Tajikistan military members and 215 rebels wounded, 75 rebels taken prisoner, and 170 civilians injured during the operation.[38] Tajikistan President Rahmonov charged afterwards that the government of Uzbekistan rendered assistance to former Tajikistan Prime Minister Abdumalik Abdollojonov, whom Rahmonov claimed was the mastermind of the Hujand uprising. Uzbekistan President Islam Karimov on November 30, 1998, denied that Uzbekistan had any links to the rebels or provided any support for the uprising.[39]

Just a few months later, in February 1999, a series of explosions shook the nearby city of Tashkent, Uzbekistan. Uzbekistan President Islam Karimov attributed the explosions to an effort to assassinate him and to overthrow the government of Uzbekistan.[40] Two explosions took place in the Ministry of Interior building, one in the Ministry of Foreign Economic Relations, and one in Independence Square, not far from where President Karimov was riding in his car at the time. Uzbekistan officials later claimed that the bombings were the work of Hezbe Tahriri Islomiya, an Islamic political movement Uzbekistan officials said was established in Pakistan.[41]

Five months later, in August 1999, unrest broke out in the Fergana Valley in neighboring Kyrgyzstan. Like the Hujand uprising and the Tashkent bombings, the events in Kyrgyzstan's Fergana valley region also have their roots in the dislocations of the Tajikistan war. A large group of dissident ethnic Uzbeks from the Namangan area of Uzbekistan established themselves in the Garm region of Tajikistan as early as 1994, when the area was still outside the control of the Tajikistan government in Dushanbe. With the changes in Tajikistan that took place as a result of the reconciliation and peace process, the Garm area became less hospitable.

In Spring 1999, the group abandoned Tajikistan under pressure from the ongoing demilitarisation of the country. A group numbering between 700 and 1000 irregulars crossed into the Fergana Valley region of southern Kyrgyzstan near the town of Batken. Anticipating their arrival, Uzbekistan government troops already had taken up positions across the nearby Uzbekistan border. Tajikistan troops were at their rear. On the August 19, 1999, the guerillas, under the leadership of Juma Namangani, a field commander who had fought on the side of the opposition in the Tajikistan civil war, took a number of hostages, including four Japanese geologists. Namangani's troops took refuge in the rugged mountain passes of southern Kyrgyzstan.

Poorly equipped Kyrgyzstan troops were initially unsuccessful in dislodging the guerillas. The Kyrgyzstan government appealed for help from other countries in the Commonwealth of Independent States. Citing the Collective Security Agreement, Russia immediately provided technical support. Uzbekistan sent troops to fortify the border with Kyrgyzstan. Toward the end of August 1999, the Uzbekistan air force began air strikes against the guerrillas' suspected stronghold. There was considerable collateral damage. Negotiations mediated by the United Tajikistan Opposition resulted in the release of 13 hostages on October 25, 1999.[42] The four Japanese geologists were released. But 26 persons died as a result of the conflict. Later, Tajikistan deported Namangani's rebels by escorting them across Tajikistan to neighboring Afghanistan.

This series of conflicts dramatised to all the states of the region that they share the diplomatic goal of containing disorder and lawlessness. Over the past few years, a consensus has formed that a syndrome of lawlessness involving political opposition, radical religious doctrine, weapons, and illegal activities, principally gun running and narcotics trafficking, is drawing the countries of the region into common peril. As Kyrgyzstan's president Askar Akaev put it, the traffic in drugs and weapons has become "problem Number One" for Kyrgyzstan.[43] According to a recent report of the UN Offence for Drug Control and Crime Prevention, in 1998 the expansion of poppy cultivation in Afghanistan was particularly evident in the northern part of the country, "which may result in a further preferred use of Central Asia as a transit zone for opium and heroin trafficking".[44]

True to the pattern of development of many Latin American countries, in which high production and low indigenous use eventually gave way to high production and high indigenous use, the countries of West Asia also have witnessed a rise in local use despite the small profits that the depressed economies of the countries can support.[45] Although the evidence is not systematic, there are indications that drug use within Central Asia is on the rise too.

With the normalisation of the political situation in Tajikistan, there was some pressure for the Russians to reduce their presence in Tajikistan in line with the departure of UNMOT and the reduced profile of other international organisations. The Russian government announced that it was considering a reduction in the Russian infantry in favor of a new emphasis on long-term military aid, including advisors, technology, arms and ammunition.[46] At the same time, there have been discussions that suggest a wider, if different, military role for Russia in Tajikistan. There has been discussion of the establishment of a permanent Russian military presence in Hujand, for instance. In addition, Russia has made clear its willingness to assist its "strategic allies" in the event of any attack on their territory by international terrorists and has proposed joint measures to combat terrorism, banditry, religious extremism, and drug trafficking.[47]

Conclusion

This study presents arguments why, despite the realistic orientation of Russia's newly adopted foreign policy doctrine, Russia's commitment to Tajikistan should not be understood simply in terms of a calculation of narrow interests.[48] Rather, it should be viewed in terms of a much broader calculation that includes long-enduring features of Russian political psychology, long-term strategic considerations, and an array of shortterm tactical necessities.

Contemporary realist diplomatic calculations often follow the standard definition of strategy as simply the process of bringing ends into line with means in the pursuit of a country's national interest. In the view of some contemporary analysts, this simple formula would suggest that foreign policy analysis consists merely of making an objective assessment of a state's capacities with respect to its interests. But if the foregoing argumentation of this article is well founded, applying such realist formulas to the analysis of Russia's position in Central Asia can lead analysts to reductionism and over simplification. A more robust analysis must take into account the background of decision making and the fact that interstate commitments sometimes transcend what may appear, at least to the outsider, to be in the immediate, material interests of a state.

Tajikistan is a country whose geostrategic significance is out of proportion to its size, the size of its population, or the size of its economy. Tajikistan is a country whose future will define new diplomatic and strategic relationships that will reach well beyond the country's borders. This article describes the bases of the Russian government's commitment to Tajikistan. It is apparent from this description that the Russian government does not intend lightly to abandon the leverage it gains from its position in Tajikistan, the "pivot of Asia." Russian diplomats at the beginning of the 19th century sought to gain control of what was regarded as a crucial geostrategic redoubt in the center of Asia. The conquest of Asia's "high ground" gave the diplomats the capacity to lay claim to the territory reaching up to and beyond the Eurasian continental divide. For Russia to abandon its outpost in Asia would be equivalent to abandoning a claim to a sphere of influence in Asia. This is the reason that Russia is in Tajikistan.

NOTES AND REFERENCES

1. Boris Rumer, *Soviet Central Asia: "A Tragic Experiment,"* Boston: Unwin Hyman, 1989; William Fierman, *Soviet Central Asia: The Failed Transformation,*Boulder:Westview Press, 1991; Roald Sagdeev and Susan Eisenhower, eds, *Central Asia: Conflict,*

Resolution and Change, Chevy Chase, MD, CPSS Press, 1995); R.D. McChesney, *Central Asia: Foundations of Change,* Princeton: The Darwin Press, 1996; Martha Olcott, *The New States of Central Asia,* Washington: United States Institute of Peace, 1996; Gregory Gleason, *Central Asia: Discovering Independence,* Boulder: Westview Press, 1997; Lena Jonson, *Russia in Central Asia: A New Web of Relations,* London: The Royal Institute of International Affairs, 1998; Olivier Roy, *The New Central Asia: The Creation of Nations,* London: Tauris, 2000.

2. Tajikistan has witnessed a downward spiral of social and economic indicators in the post-independence period. Tajikistan's gross domestic product declined steadily from 1991 through 1996. This trend slowed and reversed in 1997 and 1998 when Tajikistan showed modest growth in gross domestic product. During this period, however, the incidence and severity of poverty continued to worsen. The World Bank World Development Indicators database rated Tajikistan's gross national product per capita in 1998 as 179th of 210 countries. See "Republic of Tajikistan: Recent Economic Developments," IMF Staff Country Report No. 00/27, March 2000, p. 50; *World Development Indicators Database,* Washington, DC: World Bank, 1999. Also see *Tajikistan Human Development Report 1999,* Dushanbe: United Nations Development Programme, 1999, p. 13.
3. Tajikistan's primary trading relations prior to independence were structured around the import of manufactured and consumer goods from the north and the export of primary commodities, particularly aluminum and cotton, to northern markets in the former Soviet Union. Trade was channeled through a small number of corridors, all of which passed through the former Soviet republic of Uzbekistan. Civil strife in Tajikistan interrupted shipping routes through Uzbekistan in 1992. Since 1992 these transit routes have remained subject to blockage, delay, and interruption. These routes have not been reestablished for normal commercial purposes.
4. Tajikistan is the world's third largest producer of hydroelectric power after the United States and Russia. At the same time, energy consumption per capita is among the lowest in the former Soviet states.

5. The largest enterprise in Tajikistan, the Tursunzade Aluminum Smelter, is in the centralwest part of the country, between Dushanbe and the Uzbekistan border. It has an overall capacity of over 520,000 tons per year, making it one of the largest aluminum plants in the world. In recent years, however, the plant has been functioning at a level beneath 50 per cent of capacity.
6. The 1989 Soviet census recorded a Russian population in Tajikistan of approximately 388,500. Five years later, that number had dropped to smaller than 140,000.
7. This is documented in Jeff Chinn and Robert Kaiser, *Russians as the New Minority*, Boulder CO: Westview Press, 1996.
8. "Republic of Tajikistan: Recent Economic Developments," IMF Staff Country Report no. 00/27, March 2000, table 46.
9. *RFE/RL Newsline*, 17 November 1999.
10. Owen Lattimore, *Pivot of Asia: Sinkiang and the Inner Asian Frontiers of China and Russia*, Boston: Little, Brown and Co., 1950, p. 32.
11. Lowell Tillett, "The National Minorities Factor in the Sino-Soviet Dispute," *Orbis*, vol. 21, 1971, pp. 241–260; Rasma Silde-Karklins, "The Uighurs Between China and the USSR," *Canadian Slavonic Papers*, vol. 17, 1975, pp. 341–364.
12. Ying Cheng Kiang, *China's Boundaries*, Chicago: Institute of Chinese Studies, 1984. Also see Lattimore, *Pivot of Asia*; Parshotam Mehra, *The Younghusband Expedition*, New York: Asia Publishing House, 1968.
13. Wars are not easily observed or described objectively. There are legitimate differences of perspective on these issues. Shahram Akbarzadeh offers another perspective on these events ("Why did Nationalism Fail in Tajikistan?" *Europe–Asia Studies*, vol. 48, no. 7, 1996, pp. 1105–1129.
14. "UNHCR report on Tajikistan, January 1993–March 1996," United Nations High Commissioner on Refugees, May 1996, p. 4; "Return to Tajikistan, Continued Regional and Ethnic Tensions," *Human Rights Watch/Helsinki* vol. 7, no. 9, May 1995, pp. 4, 7.
15. In a widely discussed newspaper article published just a short time before the Soviet breakup, Aleksandr Solzhenitsyn

proposed an expanded definition of the Russian border that, for instance, would have included area that is now located within the sovereign territory of Kazakhstan. *"Kak nam obustroit' Rossiiu? Posil'nye soobrazheniia"* ("How Shall We Reconstitute Russia? Feasible Observations"), *Komsomol'skaya Pravda*, 18 September 1990, p. 1.

16. Andrei Kozyrev, *Izvestiia*, 2 January 1992, p. 3.
17. *Egemendy Qazaqstan*, 10 April 1993, p. 1. Kyrgyzstan's Akaev sent a small detachment to the Tajik border in March 1993, but it was withdrawn in April 1993. See Christopher J. Panico, "Uzbekistan's Southern Diplomacy," *RFE/RL Research Report*, vol. 2, no. 13, 26 March 1993, pp. 39–45; Bess Brown, "Central Asian States Seek Russian Help," *RFE/RL Research Report*, vol. 2, no. 25, 18 June 1993, pp. 83–88; Casandra Cavanaugh, "Uzbekistan Looks South and East for Role Models," *RFE/RL Research Report*, vol. 1, no. 40, 9 October 1992, pp. 11–13; and Keith Martin, "Tajikistan: Civil War without End?" *RFE/RL Research Report*, vol. 2, no. 33, 20 August 1993, pp. 18–29.
18. FBIS SWB SU 1676 C1/1 RUSSIAN TV. 27 April 1993.
19. Andrei Kozyrev, *Izvestiia*, 4 August 1993, p. 4.
20. FBIS SWB SU/1753 C3/1 ITAR-TASS 26 July 1993.
21. Lena Jonson, *The Tajik War: A Challenge to Russian Policy*, London: The Royal Institute of International Affairs, 1998.
22. "Taliban Capture Key Northern City After Heavy Fighting," Associated Press, 7 September 2000.
23. Shortly after the fall of Taloqan, Turkmenistan president Niyazov dispatched Special Envoy Boris Shikhmuradov to Islamabad to initiate a dialogue with Pakistan of. cials on political recognition for the Taliban government. Raja Asghar, "Pakistan Backs Turkmenistan's Afghan Peace Move," Reuters, 31 August 2000.
24. Over the past several years, two border checkpointshave been maintained: one at Nizhniy Pyandzh near the western border with Uzbekistan and one at Ishkashim in western Badakhshan.
25. Alexei D. Voskressenski, *The Difficult Border: Current Russian and Chinese Concepts of Sino-Russian Relations and Frontier Problems*, Commack, NY: Nova Science Publishers, 1996.

26. Jing-dongYuan, "Sino-Russian Confdence-Building Measures: A Preliminary Analysis," Asian Perspective Vol. 22, No. 1 (1998), pp. 71–108 at p. 77.
27. Jing-dongYuan, *op. cit.*, p. 83. This treaty was ratified by the Russian Duma on February 13, 1992, and by the Chinese People's Congress Standing Committee on February 24, 1992.
28. Xinhua News Agency, 15 April 1993.
29. Xinhua News Agency, 12 January 1996.
30. ITAR-TASS News Agency, 21 April 1997, 23 April 1997, 23–24 April 1997, 26 April 1997.
31. RFE/RL Newsline, 7 July 1998; "Five Countries Sign Central Asian Security Agreement," BBC, 4 July 1998.
32. Interfax News Agency, 3 February 1999.
33. Shao Zongwei, "Border Accord Signed," *China Daily*, 27 August 1999.
34. The road leads east from Murgab over the Kulma Pass (4362 m) into the People's Republic of China to connect with the north-south running Karakoram Highway. From Taxkorgan, China, the road leads south for 120 km to the border with Pakistan. The road then turns west, climbing over the ridge above the Yorkant River, and leads through the Khunjerab Pass at the Pakistan frontier before turning downward 300 km through the mountains to Islamabad. From Islamabad a well-developed network of roads leads to the ocean port of Karachi.
35. Interfax, Moscow, 7 June 1999 (FBIS-Sov-1999-0607). RFE/RL Newsline, 8 June 1999.
36. *China Daily*, 14 August 1999.
37. Michael Rywkin, *Moscow's Muslim Challenge: Soviet Central Asia*, New York: M.E. Sharpe, 1990; Ahmed Rashid, *The Resurgence of Central Asia: Islam or Nationalism?* Karachi: Oxford University Press, 1994; Dilip Hiro, *Between Marx and Muhammad: The Changing Face of Central Asia*, London: Harper Collins Publishers, 1994; Mehrdad Haghayeghi, *Islam and Politics in Central Asia*, New York: St. Martin's Press, 1995.
38. "Tajikistan Authorities Prosecuting 197 for Rising against Government," Interfax 29 January 1999.
39. RFE/RL Newsline, 1 December 1998.

40. RFE/RL Newsline, 16 February 1999.
41. RFE/RL Newsline, 17 February 1999.
42. "Freed Japan hostages to Tokyo from Bishkek," Reuters, 26 October 1999.
43. RFE/RL Newsline, 15 December 1998.
44. United Nations, *Global Illicit Drug Trends,* New York, 1999: Drug Control and Prevention Program, p. 20.
45. Barry Bearak, "Adding to Pakistan's Misery, a Heroin Epidemic," *The New York Times,* 19 April 2000, p. A1.
46. Vladislav Komarov, "Is Russia Preparing For Tajik Pullout? Military Of. cials Say 'Scale Back' Will Not Hurt Operations There," *The Russia Journal,* April 13, 2000.
47. RFE/RL Newsline, 11 April 2000.
48. Russia's "New Foreign Policy Concept" was approved by the Russian Security Council on 24 March 2000 and approved by President Putin on 2 July 2000. The concept was printed in *Rossiskaya Gazeta,* 11 July 2000. The concept serves as a guidance document for the Ministry of Foreign Affairs, articulating the goals and objectives of Russian foreign policy. The last such doctrinal statement, often referred to as the "Kozyrev doctrine," was adopted in April 1993, during Andrei Kozyrev's tenure as Minister of Foreign Affairs.

7

INDIA'S POLICY TOWARDS POST-SOVIET CENTRAL ASIA

The strategic location, energy resources, competition for pipeline routes and the sheer number of regional and global players, were sufficient reasons for many analysts to create theories of the "New Great Game" in Central Asia. The race for military bases and the regime change experiments through "colour revolutions" have added a new dimension to this competition. Earlier, analysts felt the real competition was between Russia and the U.S.

However, as of late, China has created a huge profile for itself through trade, energy deals, military agreements and the Shanghai Cooperation Organisation (SCO). The growing Chinese influence in the region is an established fact. Both internationally[1] and in India[2], many scholars have commented on it and a lot of literature has been written on the subject. Yet, very few in India3 have directly looked at the implications of the growing Chinese influence on Indian security, energy deals and commerce. This article attempts to fill this gap.

Indian policy-makers and analysts believe that the region is important because of its strategic location, proximity—

Tajikistan is just 20 kilometers from Greater Kashmir—and of its energy resources.[4] Therefore, restoring traditional linkages with its extended neighborhood in Central Asia and beyond has been one of the primary strategic priorities of the government.[5] Despite the intentions and rhetoric, India was never really part of any competition there. With no direct road or transportation access plus difficult market conditions, the region never became attractive to Indian private companies. In the post-socialist period, economic relations with the region have declined considerably. In the last few years, the annual official trade between India and the whole of Central Asian region is about US$200 million. Kazakhstan itself accounts for half of this trade.

Still, opportunities are enormous as shown by London based Indian steel tycoon Laxmi Mittal who owns a 5.5 million ton capacity steel plant in Kazakhstan. His company employs 50,000 people in Kazakhstan alone from where it supplies the Chinese market. In May 2006, the Indian government also officially approved its participation in the US$5 billion Turkmenistan-Afghanistan-Pakistan- India (TAPI) gas pipeline project.[6] In another development, there are also reports that India has established an airbase in Tajikistan. The Indian Air Force is going to deploy a fleet of MiG-29 fighter-bombers at the Ayni airbase near Dushanbe. The airbase follows the establishment of India's first military "outpost" in Tajikistan at Farkhor, adjoining the Tajik-Afghan border.[7] The location is important as it is close to the bases of anti-Indian terrorist groups as well as near the territory where Pakistan and China are engaged in military cooperation.[8]

Indian policy makers have been more or less comfortable in dealing with Central Asian authoritarian leaders. They were part of the former Soviet elite, with whom India was dealing with for decades. They have provided stability and are committed to fight religious terrorism. Moreover, many analysts believed that Russia will continue to have a decisive role in Central Asia because of its advantage of history and geography. Although many Indian analysts still believe in the reemergence of Russia[9], a sober assessment is also made of a scenario in which over time China becomes a dominant player in Central Asia while maintaining very friendly relations with Russia.

As China increases its engagement in the region, India will be watching carefully. Despite many positive developments and fruitful diplomatic engagements, India is still very cautious in matters relating to China. Both India and China are still very much concerned with basic balance of power considerations, although officially, both deny this proposition. While delivering a speech at the Shanghai Institute of International Studies, the Indian Foreign Secretary recently declared that the theories of "balance of power" or "conflict of interest" are "outdated in today's fast-emerging dynamics of Asia's quest for peace and prosperity and its interconnectedness". He further asserted that "India and China, as two continental-sized economies and political entities, are too big to contain each other or be contained by any other country".[10]

Still, the Government of India's 2006 Ministry of Defense Annual Report notes that "China's military modernisation, with sustained double digit growth in its defense budget for over a decade, as also development of infrastructure in the India-China border areas, continues to be monitored". In addition, "close defense exchanges and nuclear and missile cooperation between China and Pakistan continue to elicit concern".[11] Yet, as both countries are concentrating more on domestic economic development, focusing on the positive and playing down the negative, this has been the defining characteristic of India-China relations in recent years.[12] One of the most encouraging recent developments in India-China ties is the rapid increase in bilateral trade. In 2005-06, it surpassed US$17.4 billion. In the last four years, it has grown at an average rate of more than 55 per cent per year. Encouraged by these trends, both have opened a historic trade route at Nathula in Sikkim that had been closed since 1962. This opening has more political significance than trade. Sikkim was incorporated with India in 1975. This move was opposed by China, which lay claim to Sikkim. With this opening, the question of Sikkim being recognised as a part of India is now permanently settled.

Emerging Scenarios Most analysts now believe that the Asian continent is going to become the new centre of gravity in global politics.[13] In an evolving Asian economic and security architecture, most Asian countries would be looking towards China or India for future economic and security alignments. As an economic and military superpower, the U.S. would also like to play an important role in this evolving situation. In Central Asia, India will be expected to play its role as a balancer in the backdrop of increasing Chinese dominance and declining Russian presence. In a rapidly evolving situation, "India would need to bring to bear its rapidly increasing political, economic and military capabilities to the table as a threshold great power with vital stakes in the region".[14] But how alignments will take place in Central Asia is still an open question.

A simple straightforward political logic of realism, with its power balances and security dilemmas would predict the emergence of a Washington-New Delhi-Jakarta-Hanoi-Tokyo axis in the context of a rising China and attempts by the U.S. to contain it.[15] This is a nightmare scenario for Chinese strategists. China would do every thing possible to avoid this situation, including accommodating some Indian security and economic concerns. With a rapidly growing trade and economic relationship with India, China may also try to build partnerships in other areas. Both have declared their intentions of cooperation in oil and gas biddings. India's earlier Petroleum Minister Mani Shankar Aiyer also embraced the idea of Asian regional cooperation in energy and initiated a dialogue between principal Asian suppliers (Saudi Arabia, UAE, Kuwait, Iran, Qatar, Oman) with principal Asian buyers (India, China, Japan, Korea).[16] These efforts showed some results when China National Petroleum Corporation (CNPC) and India's Oil and Natural Gas Corporation (ONGC) mounted a successful US$573 million joint bid to acquire Petro-Canada's 37 per cent stake in the al-Furat oil and gas fields in Syria.[17] Earlier they worked as joint operators in Sudan. India and China may be cooperating in other areas, but when it comes to Central Asian energy, competition is fierce. This was clearly illustrated in late 2005 when China outbid India to acquire PetroKazakhstan, Kazakhstan's third-largest oil producer with CNPC raising its bid to US$4.18-billion.[18]

It is also plausible to argue that an alternative axis running through Tehran-New Delhi-Kuala Lumpur-Beijing could be formed around Asian solidarity.[19] In the context of Central Asia, some scholars in India have forcefully argued that attempts by the U.S. to bypass Russia, Iran and China for transit of Caspian oil to international markets (like the Baku-Tbilisi-Ceyhan pipeline) could jeopardize the energy security of India and China. Therefore, they argue that India, China and Iran "need to evolve multiple strategies for security and economic cooperation in Central Asia, including trilateral framework involving the three".[20]

India-Russia-China cooperation in Central Asia is another pet theme of many anti-American enthusiasts both in India and Russia. Ever since visiting Russian Prime Minister Yevgeni Primakov suggested a Russia- China-India triangle in 1998, the idea has been discussed at various official as well as non official forums. Recently, Chinese President Hu Jintao put forward some proposals for trilateral political coordination on major international and regional issues as well as to uphold multilateralism.[21] The recent U.S. move to group countries of Central and South Asia under a new bureau in the State Department has added new dimension to India-Central Asia relations. At a very basic level, it is an attempt by the U.S. to shift the Central Asian region away from the Chinese and Russian orbit and bring them closer to South Asian countries. This also fits well with the emerging Indo-U.S. ties. According to U.S. policy circles, the emerging new partnership between Washington and New Delhi will be bound by many common interests, including "preventing Asia from being dominated by any single power that has the capacity to crowd out others and which may use aggressive assertion of national self interest to threaten American presence, American alliances, and American ties with the regional states".[22] So for them, the U.S. policy of developing a new global partnership with India "represents a considered effort at 'shaping' the emerging Asian environment to suit American interests in the twenty-first century".[23]

However, the proposition of linking Central and South Asian regions could only be attractive to Central Asians if they have direct access to the rapidly growing Indian market. This can happen only if Afghanistan stabilises and Pakistan provides direct access of Central Asian goods to India and vice versa. Afghanistan's on-going transformation from a failed into a viable democratic state with a market economy could facilitate this linkage.[24] From the commitments of the international community and multilateral institutions, it is clear that a massive effort to rebuild Afghanistan's transport network and economy is underway. Already, the Asian

Development Bank is working on many plans to improve institutional as well as infrastructural development in the region.[25]

Despite the recent Taliban resurgence in the South, Afghanistan will rebound much quickly because of the desire for peace and the entrepreneurial spirit of its population. Things are, however, very uncertain in India-Pakistan relations. Despite many positive developments (like the composite dialogue), India continues to have serious concerns about terrorist infrastructure in Pakistan targeting India. The recent July 11 bombings in Mumbai, which claimed nearly 200 lives and injured 770 people, have resulted in temporary suspension of peace talks. After the blasts, the Indian Foreign Secretary asserted that "as a result of these terrible terrorist incidents, it is becoming difficult to take this process forward".[26] Pakistan has also still not extended MFN status to India and has refused to implement the South Asian Free Trade Area (SAFTA) with India, which became operational on 1 July 2006.

Knowing these difficulties, India's major initiative in the region has been building the North-South trade corridor.[27] This is being built in cooperation with Russia and Iran.[28] Although this initiative will speed the flow of goods, especially energy, from Central Asia to India via Iran, the shortest route from India to the region is through Pakistan. This is the current major challenge for the U.S. administration, as promotion of regional cooperation between Central and South Asia is now their declared objective[29]. This is also crucial for the revival of Afghanistan's economy.

These developments indicate that India's growing future role and alignments in Central Asia will be determined by the actions of the U.S. and China and their military involvement with Pakistan. If the U.S. is unable to influence

Pakistan on dismantling terrorist infrastructure and facilitating transit facilities, and China continues to have close defense, nuclear and missile cooperation with Pakistan, India will have no option but to work closely with Russia and Iran instead to add value to its bilateral relations in Central Asia. There are no indications of China- Pakistan relations weakening in the near future. In fact, when the Indian parliament was debating the India-U.S. nuclear deal, China signed two defense agreements with Pakistan.[30]

The U.S.-Pakistan equation is uncertain. So far, Pakistan is a declared major non-NATO ally. The U.S. is counting on Pakistani security forces to neutralise the Taliban and Al Qaeda and their associates who are operating from the Afghanistan-Pakistan border. While President Musharraf has co-operated to some extent in the operations to capture some activists of Al Qaeda, he has taken no action against the neo- Taliban. Although the Pakistani administration admits that some of the Al Qaeda leaders may be operating from their territory, they have denied the presence of any Taliban leaders, camps or activities in Pakistan.[31]

Policy makers in Pakistan were hoping that U.S. forces would leave Afghanistan after initial operations so that after their withdrawal, they could have strengthened and use the Taliban card again to attain "strategic depth" in Afghanistan. Now, with the possibility of an enduring U.S. presence, the neo-Taliban are trying to replicate the anti- Soviet Jihad of the 1980's through conventional strikes and terrorist acts. The target is not the Soviets, but the "Western infidels led by the U.S. and the UK" and their Afghan supporters. The objective is to tire and weaken the western forces. They hope that as a result of continuous bleeding, western forces may finally decide to quit. Once that happens, the Karzai government is bound to fall.[32]

The Afghan government has repeatedly accusing Pakistan for harboring the insurgents. In these circumstances, it will become increasingly difficult for the U.S. to keep defending President Musharraf, who is making the West pay for his domestic democratic deficit. While some institutions in Pakistan promote the ideology of terrorism, others provide training to carry it out. There are reports that officials in the Pentagon are already rethinking the relationship with Pakistan.[33] The June visit of Condoleezza Rice to Afghanistan and Pakistan seems to get the message across that America is "not leaving" and going to stay in Afghanistan for a "very, very long time to come."[34]

NATO is also formalising its presence in Afghanistan to stay on a long term basis. Sensing these developments and in order to stay in power, President Musharaff may opt for cooperation in Afghanistan. For India, the enduring U.S. presence in Afghanistan can be leveraged to push Pakistan into a cooperative direction. To assert its economic and strategic power, India would be able to reach Afghanistan and central Asia over land.[35] This could also be a new beginning of India-Pakistan relations. While speaking at the launch of the Amritsar (India)–Nankana Sahib (Pakistan) bus service, the Indian Prime Minister said that "India and Pakistan must work together to open up new opportunities for economic cooperation, not only with South Asia, but also with West Asia and Central Asia. Cities like Lahore and Amritsar should once again become throbbing international commercial centers serving the entire region".[36]

On the other hand, China is also trying to improve its presence in Afghanistan through aid and other projects. If Pakistan is able to muster significant influence in Afghanistan, then triangular Pakistan-Afghanistan-China cooperation is also a possibility. Color Revolutions after witnessing the Rose revolution in Georgia, the Orange revolution in Ukraine, the Tulip revolution in Kyrgyzstan and the violent protests in Uzbekistan, Central Asian states have clearly moved towards Russia and China. This has happened because of the U.S. dilemma in trying to balance two of its major foreign policy goals—democratisation and counterterrorism—in Central Asia. Capitalising on this U.S. quandary and its overstretch in Iraq and Afghanistan, Russia and China in cooperation with each other have consolidated their position in the region. Most of the western governments and the western press consider these color revolutions as a move towards democracy. Among Indian academic circles, many scholars with mainly leftist leanings have raised a number of questions regarding the legitimacy and funding of these "revolutions". They have categorised these "revolutions" as "made-in-America coups" while emphasising the role of American embassies and western funded NGOs.[37]

At a higher level, these series of events have also been examined from the broader perspectives of security and stability in the region. It is argued that the evolution of these countries, which are situated at a sensitive geo-political location, to stable democratic systems and thriving market economies will remain extremely difficult and complicated.[38] Others, however, argue that these events have shown that that the Soviet-era leadership is not going to survive long in Central Asia. So rather than reacting to events, India should have a clear-cut futuristic policy which supports all domestic and outside actors pushing for democracy and market reforms in the region.[39]

The Indian government has been a more or less passive observer to these events. India was neither alarmed (like Russia and China), nor really excited (like many western governments) by these developments. The response to these developments is articulated by the Indian Defense Minister in his speech at Washington where he asserted that "by nature, India is not inclined to export ideologies, even ideologies it believes in and follows. India would rather promote democracy in the region by precept and example. Freer traffic between India and Central Asia would be a factor in favour of moderation and democracy there".[40]

In April 2006, Indian Prime Minister visited Tashkent and seven agreements including three agreements in energy and mineral sectors were signed between India and Uzbekistan.[41] The visit demonstrated that India is also willing to deal with authoritarian regimes in the region, if they are able to help India in the energy sector.

The SCO and India Since the formation of the Shanghai Cooperation Organisation (SCO), India is not quite sure what priority this organisation deserves. It provides China, Russia and the Central Asian states a delicate equilibrium in the new geopolitical situation. India was never featured in this equilibrium, though Central Asians perceived India's potential to be a countervailing factor.[42]

The major objectives of the SCO have been projected as promoting trans-border peace, security and counter-terrorism. With the increasing profile of the organisation, China's role is also becoming large within Central Asia. In the beginning, India showed interest in the SCO but the impression is that China never really wanted India in the grouping. India was welcomed as an observer in the SCO only when China was also admitted in SAARC as an observer.

In addition, China also brought Pakistan into the grouping. The way the SCO has conducted itself in the last two years has further aggravated India's dilemma.[43] India has a positive perception of the potential of the SCO as an instrument for promoting regional economic integration, trade and ensuring energy security. However, it has many reservations over the political direction of the SCO. Even with the main objective of fighting terrorism, it would be an uncomfortable position for India if the Dalai Lama and his followers, members of the Falungong and people asking for genuine democratic rights in Central Asian republics were clubbed together as terrorists/separatists/extremists. India will find it difficult to digest these interpretations when it is also an important contributor to the UN Democracy Fund, whose purpose is to support democratisation throughout the world.

Furthermore, the objective of multi-polarity, as often raised by China, is constantly being used to counter the U.S. influence in Asia-Pacific. At a time when its relations with the U.S. are steadily moving forward, India would be cautious in its participation in the grouping.

As a result of these dilemmas, India was the only country among members and observers, which was not represented at the latest SCO Summit by the Head of State but by Petroleum Minister Murli Deora. The official position was that there was no need for the prime minister to attend the meeting as India was only an observer.[44] The actual fact may be that India is giving serious thought to its involvement in the SCO. The way the organisation is developing, some Indian analysts have already warned that it would "be imprudent for India to join the SCO".[45]

India should work for a separate regional organisation. This new organisation should include all countries which have legitimate interest in the region cooperating on a la carte basis. These include the five Central Asian countries, Afghanistan, China, India, Iran, Japan, Russia, Pakistan, Turkey and the United States. The idea is somewhat similar to Frederick Starr's "Greater Central Asia Partnership for Cooperation and Development" concept.[46]

Although the region has a history of over-engagement with regional organisations, so far none of the organisations is able to accommodate all major players. Moreover, many of them are only on paper. Although SCO is already considered by some analysts as the *de facto* regional organisation, there are many uncertainties. These include possible Russian uneasiness over increasing Chinese dominance and complications arising with future enlargements etc. In the absence of any other dynamic organisation, India will continue to participate in the SCO to improve its standing in the region. In the long run, it will also further strengthen Russian position in the SCO. Despite very weak bilateral trade, which is about US$ 2 billion a year, India-Russia ties continue to be strong. Currently, about 75 per cent of its weapons imports come from Russia.[47]

Although, many Indian scholars have discussed the possibility of India-Russia cooperation in Central Asia in the past,[48] concrete examples are emerging now. These include military cooperation in Tajikistan, the North-South corridor, joint exploration of oil and gas in Central Asia[49] and Russian help with India's entry into the SCO. Therefore, "as an increasingly powerful China asserts itself in Eurasia and America scrambles to deal with the consequences, Delhi and Moscow still hold many cards."[50]

Conclusions

Chinese engagement in Central Asia is watched very carefully in India. It is becoming clear that China is going to provide tough competition to India in both energy and trade. If Chinese increasing engagement coincides with declining Russian influence, India will have no choice but to expand its political, economic and military capabilities in Central Asia. Simple realist logic would suggest close Indo-U.S. cooperation in Central Asia. These realities are fueling India's "forward" Central Asia policy. There is also a feeling of urgency in policy circles to discover a strategy, where India is able to reach the region over land. The new U.S. thinking of linking South and Central Asia with possibilities of a wider new grouping could fit into Indian thinking.

Improvements in India-Pakistan relations, however, would be a crucial input into this strategy. Sensing this alignment, China may try to accommodate some of India's security and economic concerns. If the U.S. is unable to influence Pakistan on dismantling terrorist infrastructure, India will continue to work with Moscow and Tehran to consolidate some control in Central Asia. Although, policy makers in India do not believe in the policy of exporting democracy, they would be very sympathetic to political changes as they know that Indian interests would be served better by opening the region to further democratic changes and more economic reforms.

NOTES AND REFERENCES

1. Niklas Swanstrom, "China and Central Asia: A New Great Game or traditional Vassal Relations", *Journal of Contemporary China* 14, 45 (2005): 569-584.
2. Sujit Dutta, "China's Emerging ties with Central Asia" in Nirmala Joshi, Ed., *Central Asia: The Great Game Replayed: An Indian Perspective* (New Delhi: New Century Publications, 2003); Nirmala Joshi, "An Appraisal of China's Policy Towards Central Asia" in K Santhanam and Bulat K Sultanov (eds.), *India-Kazakhstan Relations: Enhancing the Partnership* (New Delhi: Anamaya Publishers, 2006).
3. P. Stobdan, "Central Asia & China Relations: Implications for India" in K. Santhanam and Srikanth Kondapalli, Eds., *Asian Security and China 2000-2010* (New Delhi: Shipra Publications, 2004).
4. Kapil Kak, "India's Strategic and Security Interests in Central Asia" in V. Nagendra Rao and Mohammad Monir Alam, Eds.,

Central Asia: Present Challenges and Future Prospects (New Delhi: Knowledge World, 2005).

5. Speech by Indian Defense Minister, Mr Pranab Mukherjee at Carnegie Endowment of International Peace, Washington DC, June 27, 2005 <www.indianembassy.org/press_release/2005/June/11.htm> (July 10 2006).
6. Union Cabinet decision press release May 18, 2006, <http://pib.nic.in/release/release.asp?relid=17859&kwd= > (July 10 2006).
7. "IAF to Station MiG-29s in Tajikistan" *The Times of India,* April 20 2006 http://timesofindia.indiatimes.com/articleshow/msid-1498063,curpg-1.cms (August 14 2006).
8. Sudha Ramachandran , "India's Foray into Central Asia" *Asia Times,* August 12 2006, <www.atimes.com/atimes/South_Asia/HH12Df01.html> (August 17 2006).
9. M. K. Bhadrakumar, "The Rise and Rise of Russia" *Asia Times,* July 20 2006, <www.atimes.com/atimes/Central_Asia/HG20Ag01.html) (July 21 2006).
10. "Present Dimensions of the Indian Foreign Policy" An Address by Indian Foreign Secretary Mr. Shyam Saran at Shanghai Institute of International Studies, Shanghai, January 11 2006, <http://meaindia.nic.in/speech/2006/01/11ss01.htm< (July 15 2006).
11. Ministry of Defence, Government of India, *Annual Report 2005-06,* (New Delhi, 2006), p. 10.
12. B. Raman, "India and China: See No Evil, Hear No Evil, Speak No Evil, Paper No. 1857," *South Asia Analysis Group,* June 23 2006 < www.saag.org/papers19/paper1857.html> (July 10, 2006).
13. Ashley J. Tellis, " Military Modernisation in Asia" in Ashley J. Tellis and Michael Wills, Eds., *Strategic Asia 2005–06: Military Modernisation in an Era of Uncertainty* (Washington : The National Bureau of Asian Research, 2005).
14. Kapil Kak, "India's Strategic and Security Interests in Central Asia", p. 208.
15. Varun Sahni, "From Security in Asia to Asian Security," *International Studies,* 41, 3 (2004): 245-262.
16. Mani Shankar Aiyer, "What Lies Beneath: Getting to all that Oil and Gas," *The Indian Express,* February 25 2006.

17. Indrajit Basu " India, China Pin Down $573m Syria Deal," *Asia Times*, December 25 2005, <www.atimes.com/atimes/China_Business/GL22Cb06.html> (July 8 2006).
18. "India Loses Kazakh Oil firm to China," *The Tribune*, August 23 2005. <www.tribuneindia.com/2005/20050823/biz.htm#2> (July 5 2006).
19. Varun Sahni, "From Security in Asia to Asian Security", p. 257.
20. Ajay Patnaik, "Central Asia's Security: the Asian Dimension" in R. R. Sharma, Ed., *India and Emerging Asia* (New Delhi: Sage Publications, 2005), p. 228.
21. "China, India, Russia hold First Trilateral Summit" *People's Daily*, July 18 2006, <http://english.people.com.cn/200607/18/eng20060718_284028.html> (July 20 2006).
22. Ashley J Tellis, "The U.S.-India ''Global Partnership'': How Significant for American Interests?" Testimony before the House Committee on International Relations <www.carnegieendowment.org/publications/index.cfm?fa= view&id=17693&prog=zgp&pr oj=znpp,zsa,zusr> (August 10 2006).
23. *Ibid*.
24. S Frederick Starr, "A Partnership for Central Asia," *Foreign Affairs*, 84, 4 (July/August, 2005); Gulshan Sachdeva, "Rejuvenating Economic Relations between South Asia & Central Asia" *Shygys* (Almaty) 2 (2004).
25. ADB, *Central Asia: Increasing Gains from Trade through Regional Cooperation in Trade Policy, Transport, and Custom Transit* (2006); ADB, *Report on the Economic Impact of Central- South Asian Road Corridors* (2005).
26. Special Media Briefing by Foreign Secretary Mr. Shyam Saran on the eve of Prime Minister Dr. Manmohan Singh's Visit to St. Petersburg for G-8 Summit, July 15 2006 <http://meaindia.nic.in/pbhome.htm> (August 17 2006).
27. International North South Trade Corridor website: <www.instc.org> (August 14 2006).
28. Stephen Blank, "The Indian-Iranian Connection and its Importance for Central Asia," *Eurasianet*, <www.eurasianet.org/departments/business/articles/eav031203.shtml> (June 25 2006)

29. Richard A. Boucher, "Partnership, Trade, and Development in Greater Central Asia" Kabul, Afghanistan, April 1-2 2006.
30. "Pak, China Sign Defence Agreements," *The Nation*, August 17 2006. <www.nation.com.pk/daily/august-2006/17/index4.php> (August 19 2006).
31. S Raman, "South Asia & Al Qaeda—Emerging Trends," *South Asia Analysis Group*, Paper No. 1797 (May 12 2006) <www.saag.org/papers18/paper1797.html> (August 18 2006).
32. S Raman, "Afghanistan: Re-Run of the 1980's," South Asia Analysis Group Paper, No.1812, (May 26 2006) <www.saag.org/papers19/paper1812.html> (August 18 2006).
33. "Pakistan Leader Faces Increasing Political Challenges," *New York Times*, August 18 2006.
34. Secretary Condoleezza Rice, Remarks With Afghan President Hamid Karzai After Their Meeting, June 28 2006 <www.state.gov/secretary/rm/2006/68396.htm> (August 10 2006).
35. C Raja Mohan, "Recent Developments in Afghanistan," <www.ipcs.org/South_Asia_articles2.jsp?action=showView&kValue=2078&country=1016& status=article&mod=a> (August 15 2006).
36. http://pmindia.nic.in/speech/content.asp?id=302, (August 16 2006).
37. *The Hindu* carried specific articles on colour revolutions by Russian scholars. Some Indian scholars and journalists mentioned these events in broader foreign policy issues. For example, on writing President Bush's visit to India John Cherian wrote "The recent 'colour revolutions' that overthrew governments in the former socialist bloc were funded by U.S. agencies," <www. hinduonnet.com/fline/fl2304/stories/20060310004000400.htm> (August 12 2006).
38. M K Bhadrakumar, "Anatomy of a Revolution," *The Hindu*, May 29 2005; M K Bhadrakumar, "A Storm Sweeps the Post-Soviet Space," *Asia Times*, October 5 2005, <www.atimes.com/atimes/Central_Asia/GJ05Ag01.html > (April 15 2006).
39. Gulshan Sachdeva, "Do not Ignore Central Asia," *The Times of India*, June 15 2004, <http://timesofindia.indiatimes.com/articleshow/1142258.cms> (July 1 2006).

40. Speech by Indian Defence Minister, Washington DC, June 27 2005.
41. Ramakant Dwivedi, An Appraisal of the Indian Prime Minister's Visit to Uzbekistan <www.idsa.in/publications/stratcomments/RamakantDwivedi280406.htm> (July 15 2006).
42. P Stobdan, "Central Asia and China Relations: Implications for India", p. 355.
43. For an excellent summary of India's dilemmas with the SCO see B. Raman, *Shanghai Summit: Indian Misgivings* < www.saag.org/papers19/paper1847.html > (July 5, 2006).
44. Sudha Ramachandran, "India Gives Shanghai the Cold Shoulder," *Asia Times Online*, June 17 2005, <www.atimes.com/atimes/South_Asia/HF17Df01.html> (June 25 2006).
45. P. Stobdan, "Central Asia & China Relations: Implications for India", p.357.
46. S. Frederick Starr, *A Greater Central Asia Partnership for Afghanistan and Its Neighbours*, (Washington DC: Central Asia-Caucasus Institute & Silk Road Studies Program, 2005).
47. Gulshan Sachdeva, "Strengthening Indo-Russian Economic Relations," *Russia in Global Affairs*, August 2 2004 <http://eng.globalaffairs.ru/engsmi/0/563.html> (August 10, 2006).
48. Anuradha M. Chenoy, "A Defining Moment" *Frontline*, October 14-27 2000 <www.hinduonnet.com/fline/fl1721/17210150.htm> (July 14 2006); Nirmala Joshi, "Indian and Russian Security Perspectives on Central Asia" in Shamsudin, Ed., *India and Russia Towards Strategic Partnership* (New Delhi: Lancer Books, 2001).
49. "India, Russia to Explore Oil and Gas in Central Asia,," <www.rediff.com/news/2005/dec/05pmrus2.htm> (August 15 2006).
50. C. Raja Mohan, "Why Delhi Must Rediscover Moscow," *The Indian Express*, December 3 2005 <http://iecolumnists.expressindia.com/full_column.php?content_id=83161> (August 20 2006).

8

ROLE OF THE SHANGHAI COOPERATION ORGANISATION IN CENTRAL ASIAN SECURITY

On June 15th and 16th 2009, the Shanghai Cooperation Organisation (SCO) will hold its ninth annual heads of state summit in the Russian city of Yekaterinburg. It will be attended by the presidents of its six full members—China, Russia, Kazakhstan, Kyrgyzstan, Tajikistan and Uzbekistan—and by representatives of various ranks from its four observer states—India, Iran, Mongolia and Pakistan—and from several aspiring partner nations yet to be announced.

The SCO as an institution and as a concept represents the world's greatest potential and in ways is its major paradox as its capacities and their realisation to date are so far apart. Its six full members account for 60 per cent of the land mass of Eurasia and its population is a third of the world's. With observer states included, its affiliates account for half of the human race.

At its fifth and watershed summit in the capital of Kazakhstan, Astana, in June of 2005, when representatives of India, Iran, Mongolia and Pakistan attended an SCO summit for the first time, the president of the country hosting the summit, Nursultan Nazarbayev, greeted the guests in words that had never before been used in any context: "The leaders of the states sitting at this negotiation table are representatives of half of humanity."[1]

Former Joint Chief of Staff of the Russian Armed Forces and political analyst Leonid Ivashov later described the significance and unique nature of the SCO in asserting that, "Contrary to Samuel Huntington's concept of the allegedly inevitable clash of civilisations, the conclusion drawn in the SCO framework was that harmonised interactions between civilisations and their mutual assistance were possible.

"The contours of an alliance of five non-Western civilisations—Russian, Chinese, Muslim, Hindu, and Buddhist—began to materialize."[2] To emphasise the world-historical prospects of the organisation, he added: "The SCO is supposed to be a special world without a clearly defined boundary, a world spanning the entire global space.

"The quadrangle of the new global entity – Brazil, Russia, China, and India – is already taking shape....The above and certain other formations are related to the SCO."[3]

The quartet, Ivashov mentions above—Brazil, Russia, China, and India—has since 2001 been known by the acronym formed by the first letters of the nations' names, BRIC, the world's fastest and most consistently growing economies with the largest foreign currency and gold reserves.

BRIC held its first summit last May in the same city as this year's SCO summit will occur, Yekaterinburg, and will be holding the next in June.

Three of the four members of BRIC are also members or observers of the SCO, as are four of the world's seven official nuclear states.

As a Russian daily said in 2006, "The SCO is a momentous organisation which occupies territory from the Arctic to the Indian Ocean and from Kaliningrad to Shanghai. "It may become the second political pole of the world."[4]

SCO members and observers also take in a stretch of Eurasia from the South China Sea to the Baltic Sea and from the Persian Gulf to the Bay of Bengal.

At the 2006 heads of states summit in Shanghai the presidents of Afghanistan, Iran and Pakistan—Hamid Karzai, Mahmoud Ahmadinejad and Pervez Musharraf—attended as observers. Photographs of the three standing side by side appeared on numerous websites at the time and abounded in importance, both symbolic and substantive. The Afghan and Pakistani presidents had been hurling mutual accusations for years over the other's nation being the base of destabilisation of his own and there even had been loss of life in military exchanges between the two states' armed forces.

Iran was the intended victim of thinly veiled threats of US military strikes. In fact the granting of observer status to the nation in 2005 and Ahmadinejad's attendance at three successive heads of state summits—China in 2006, Kyrgyzstan in 2007 and Tajikistan in 2008—played no small role in thwarting whatever plans the United States and Israel have nurtured for attacking Iran.

To see the three above-mentioned leaders in the founding city of the SCO under the auspices of a multinational security alliance headed by Russia and China, as all three of their nations were at war or could soon be, revealed the regional and global prospects for the SCO as a new model for conflict resolution and cooperation.

During the 2007 summit, the SCO discussed establishing a "unified energy market" and then Russian president

Vladimir Putin stated, "I am convinced that energy dialogue, integration of our national energy concepts, and the creation of an energy club will set out the priorities for further cooperation."[5]

The following year Kazakh Prime Minister Karim Massimov speaking in reference to an impending meeting of SCO energy ministers and in affirming that "the existing system of pipelines on the SCO space connecting Russia, Central Asian states and China is a serious basis for the establishment of an SCO unified energy space," said:

"The projects on the establishment of a unified energy market and the SCO common transport corridor could become bright examples of the global approach to defining the forms and mechanisms of cooperation."[6]

By 2007, the SCO had initiated over twenty large-scale projects related to transportation, energy and telecommunications and held regular meetings of security, military, defense, foreign affairs, economic, cultural, banking and other officials from its member states. No multinational organisation with such far-ranging and comprehensive mutual interests and activities has ever existed on this scale before.

America's First Afghan War and its Aftermath in Central Asia

Leaders of SCO member states routinely deny that the organisation is a military alliance or one in the process of formation or that it entertains plans to model itself after or to directly challenge NATO. The first half of the claim is perfectly true, the second may be an obligation forced on it.

A penetrating Iranian analysis of late last year, "Iraq Smoke Screen" by Hamid Golpira, had this to say on the topic:

"According to Brzezinski's theory, control of the Eurasian landmass is the key to global domination and control of Central Asia is the key to control of the Eurasian landmass....Russia and China have been paying attention to Brzezinski's theory, since they formed the Shanghai Cooperation Organisation in 2001, ostensibly to curb extremism in the region and enhance border security, but most probably with the real objective of counterbalancing the activities of the United States and NATO in Central Asia."[7]

The SCO grew out of the Shanghai Five alliance of Russia, China, Kazakhstan, Kyrgyzstan and Tajikistan formed in 1996 on the basis of the Treaty on Deepening Military Trust in Border Regions to insure border demarcation and security in an area of the world thrown into turmoil by the precipitate break-up of the Soviet Union five years earlier.

Mutual concerns of the five nations also included cross-border armed extremism based in the Ferghana Valley that takes in parts of Uzbekistan, Kyrgyzstan and Tajikistan and the threat of violent secessionist movements often connected to it.

What Russia, China, Kazakhstan, Kyrgyzstan and Tajikistan were in fact contending with was the aftermath of the American Afghan proxy war of 1978-1992 which had spread, as its architect Zbigniew Brzezinski intended it to, into the Central Asian republics of the Soviet Union during that period and continued to expand in the region after 1991.

When Uzbekistan joined the Shanghai Five in June of 2001 the group was formalised as the Shanghai Cooperation Organisation and commenced annual heads of state and heads of government (prime ministers) summits.

Less than three months later the attacks on New York and Washington, D.C. occurred and in October the US and its NATO allies invaded Afghanistan and began establishing military bases in that nation and in Pakistan, Kyrgyzstan, Tajikistan and Uzbekistan.

It was at that point which, whatever the SCO's original purpose and goals envisioned, it was brought face-to-face with the US and NATO deploying troops, warplanes and military installations on SCO territory and in adjoining nations.

After the September 11, 2001 attacks on the Twin Towers of the World Trade Center and the Pentagon, SCO members like the rest of the world seemed inclined to give the US the benefit of the doubt and take it at its word: That it would launch a—limited—military operation in Afghanistan to avenge the attacks and perhaps along the way address the situation in the country and its environs that its own actions had in large part brought about.

These included the destruction of Afghanistan as a nation state after Washington's mujahedin clients took the capital of Kabul in 1992 and soon reduced much of it to rubble with mortar attacks and other acts of factional fighting.

Collapse of the National Economy and Infrastructure

The second-generation invasion of the shattered country by Taliban and their capture of Kabul in 1996 with the support of American favorite Benazir Bhutto and the active connivance of the US. Earlier this month current Pakistani President Asif Ali Zardari told NBC News, concerning Taliban, that it is a "part of our past and your past, and the ISI [Inter-Services Intelligence] and CIA created them together."[8]

By the time of the fifth SCO heads of state summit in Kazakhstan in 2005, with few of the claimed objectives of the US - and NATO which joined the fray by invoking its Article 5 mutual military assistance clause - accomplished and no sign of the Pentagon and NATO ever preparing to remove their military forces from Afghanistan and four neighboring nations, patience had worn thin among SCO member states.

The United States and its NATO allies had launched three unprovoked wars in four years - Yugoslavia in 1999, Afghanistan in 2001 and Iraq in 2003 - as well as waging counterinsurgency and proxy conflicts and subversion campaigns in Colombia, Macedonia, Ivory Coast, Yemen, the Philippines, Liberia and elsewhere.

What alarmed SCO members as much as the preceding was the so-called Tulip Revolution in Kyrgyzstan in March of 2005 and what government authorities in Tashkent saw as a variation on the theme of regime change in Uzbekistan in May of that year, a month before the SCO summit.

The uprising in Kyrgyzstan and the overthrow of its president Askar Akayev was the fourth in a series of Western-backed "color revolutions" in the Balkans and the former Soviet Union following those in Yugoslavia in 2000, Georgia in 2003 and Ukraine in December of 2004, only three months before that in Kyrgyzstan. The dominoes were falling with an increasing rapidity and now were occurring on the Chinese as well as Russian borders. And in the very heart of the SCO community.

The newspaper of the Chinese ruling party, People's Daily, wrote a month after the summit:

> "The recent SCO Summit was held against a background featuring major changes taken place in the regional political situation. After the wars in Afghanistan and Iraq and other direct military actions, the United States and other Western powers have basically completed integration of the world

security pattern, launched offensives of 'democratic reform' and 'elimination of tyrannical outposts' in former Soviet states and the Greater Middle East region and started 'color revolutions' one after another."[9]

At the summit in Kazakhstan the SCI issued a Declaration of Heads of Member States of the Shanghai Cooperation Organisation which addressed a broad panoply of concerns and which contained a general statement on the situation obtaining in the world at the time and an elaboration of the organisation's principles. It included:

"The heads of the member states point out that, against the backdrop of a contradictory process of globalisation, multilateral cooperation, which is based on the principles of equal right and mutual respect, non-intervention in internal affairs of sovereign states, non-confrontational way of thinking and consecutive movement towards democratisation of international relations, contributes to overall peace and security, and call upon the international community, irrespective of its differences in ideology and social structure, to form a new concept of security based on mutual trust, mutual benefit, equality and interaction.

"Diversity of cultures and civilisations in the world is a common human value. At a time of fast developing information technologies and communications it must stimulate mutual interest, tolerance, abandonment of extreme approaches and assessments, development of dialogue. Every people must be properly guaranteed to have the right to choose its own way of development.

"The heads of the member states are convinced that a rational and just world order must be based upon consolidation of mutual trust and good-neighborly relations, upon the establishment of true partnership with no pretence to monopoly and domination in international affairs. Such order will become more stable and secure, if it comes to consider the supremacy of principles and standards of international law, before all, the UN Charter. In the area of human rights it is necessary to respect strictly and consecutively historical traditions and national features of every people, the sovereign equality of all states."[10]

The SCO is composed of six member states and four observers representing a true diversity of cultures, civilisations, histories and political systems, from many of the world's oldest and most venerable traditions to some of its newest nations, from the world's two most populous states to Kyrgyzstan with slightly over five million citizens, and political structures ranging from secular to religious and multi-party to single-party. The internal demographic composition of the ten members and observers, excluding Mongolia, is also a rich tapestry of ethnic, national, linguistic and confessional pluralism and variety.

In additional to calling for a just, rational and peaceful world in a global situation that was little enough of any of the three, the Declaration contained both an appeal and blueprint for the sort of international order required as an antidote to the current one of unipolarity, unilateralism, cutthroat competition, cynical complacency, brute force and war.

The summit declaration was the opening salvo in a long-overdue campaign for a multipolar international system, one not dominated by a self-appointed sole superpower or by several powers with presumptions to global domination or respective spheres of influence, but a democracy between nations that would augment the development of democracy within nations.

In November of 2005, Russian Foreign Minister Sergey Lavrov reiterated that the "Shanghai Cooperation

Organisation (SCO) is working to establish a rational and just world order" and that "The Shanghai Cooperation Organisation provides us with a unique opportunity to take part in the process of forming a fundamentally new model of geopolitical integration."[11]

It also recognised that no single, standardised model of political, economic, social, cultural and ethical development and practices could be forced on the 88 per cent of humanity that lives outside the Euro-Atlantic world, not a parliamentary system devised in the British Isles centuries ago nor a consumerist culture and pseudo-civilisation designed on Madison Avenue and in Hollywood.

That genuine structural problems exist in the political systems of SCO member states is indisputable. Five of the six were thrust into sudden independence in 1991 with the near instantaneous break-up of the Soviet Union in 1991 and the USSR's former Central Asian republics were among the most adversely affected by that catastrophic occurrence. Social dislocation, economic destitution, cross-border armed incursions and general destabilisation are not conducive to the optimal development of electoral and other political institutions.

The SCO Declaration evinced a recognition that even if trends in all nations and societies should evolve in the direction of government that is equitable, accountable, accessible and humane, each nation and culture will arrive at that destination by its own path as well as that of universal principles.

The West that presumes to dictate, often to the point of blackmail and bombs, that its increasingly constricted and impracticable model of governance must be enforced always and everywhere, even where the native soil rejects such transplantation, would be better advised to examine its own deficiencies.

The standard bearer of Western values, the United States, held federal elections last year in which two billion dollars of private funds were expended in an effort to buy influence. And that in a system, where only two established political parties are given automatic ballot status and thus have a monopoly on fielding candidates broadly and surely in winning posts.

Challenges for the USA and NATO

The Declaration adopted at the 2005 SCO summit also contained this provision:

> "Considering the completion of the active military stage of antiterrorist operation in Afghanistan, the member states of the Shanghai Cooperation Organisation consider it necessary that respective members of the antiterrorist coalition set a final timeline for their temporary use of the above-mentioned objects of infrastructure and stay of their military contingent on the territories of the SCO member states."[12]

Which is to say that the US and NATO had outlived whatever usefulness their presence in South and Central Asia had served and it was now time for them to leave.

A Chinese daily expressed the matter in these terms:

> "The Declaration points out that the SCO member countries have the ability and responsibility to safeguard the security of the Central Asian region, and calls on Western countries to leave Central Asia. That is the most noticeable signal given by the Summit to the world."[13]

On July 7 of 2006, Uzbekistan issued an eviction notice to the 800 US military personnel housed in its base at Karshi-Khanabad, stating that the use of the base had been allowed "for the sole purpose of ousting Taliban rulers from Afghanistan" which had been achieved almost four years earlier.

The government demarche said "Any other prospects for a U.S. military presence in Uzbekistan were not considered by the Uzbek side."[14]

On the 17th, Kyrgyzstan's newly elected President Kurmanbek Bakiyev "stressed ...that with the appeasement of the situation in Afghanistan, it is the time for the United States to schedule its pullout of forces from the base in his country," where an estimated 1,500 US and NATO military personnel were stationed.

On July 20, Tajik Foreign Minister Talbak Nazarov said "it is time for the United States and its allies to set a date to pull their conventional troops out of Central Asia as the situation in Afghanistan has stabilised," with local reference to the use of the former Soviet Kulyab airbase and the use of Tajikistan's airspace.[15]

"Nazarov reiterated the call made jointly by the six member states of the Shanghai Cooperation Organisation (SCO) earlier this month that the US-led anti-terror coalition should set a deadline for the withdrawal of their troops and the temporary use of infrastructure in Central Asian countries."[16] Later in the month, Russia signed an agreement with the government of Tajikistan for the use of a military base in the country.

The US Secretary of State at the time, Condoleezza Rice, denounced the SCO Declaration's call for the removal of US and NATO bases in Central Asia with the pat response that "there is still a lot of terrorist activity in Afghanistan and US troops were needed to train the Afghan army to counter it,"[17], a state of affairs that from the Western perspective persists to this day, four years later, and into the indefinite future with the war now fully extended into Pakistan.

So concerned was Washington that its plans for permanent military deployments in Central and South Asia under the guise of the so-called Global War on Terror were in jeopardy that it deployed Defense Secretary Donald Rumsfeld on a hastily scheduled tour to the region, visiting Kyrgyzstan and Tajikistan.

At the time the US had "1,000 planes in the Ganci military base" in Kyrgyzstan and "about 1,500 military staff and planes in the Khanabad base in Uzbekistan."[18]

"Rumsfeld planned his trip after the Shanghai Cooperation Organisation called for a timetable for US withdrawal in an early June summit in Astana.

"During his talks in Bishkek, Rumsfeld will demand the lease of Ganci military base, in the vicinity of Bishkek's Manas Airport, to be extended."[19]

Washington had leverage with the governments of Kyrgyzstan and Tajikistan in two respects: The ever-looming threat of another "color revolution" could be activated against any government that defied US diktat and America could offer economic incentives to the two Central Asian nations that had no substantial oil and natural gas resources, unlike Kazakhstan, Turkmenistan and Uzbekistan.

In August what were described as anti-terrorist exercises were conducted in the Caspian Sea with the participation of the Shanghai Cooperation Organisation, the post-Soviet Collective Security Treaty Organisation (comprised of Russia, Armenia, Belarus and the four Central Asian nations in the SCO) and the Commonwealth of Independent States anti-aircraft defense allied command.

Participants included the chiefs of anti-terrorist units and secret services from Azerbaijan, Armenia, Belarus, Kazakhstan, Kyrgyzstan, Russia, Ukraine, Moldova, Tajikistan and Uzbekistan and officials from the Iranian Security Ministry attended the exercise in the capacity of observers for the first time.[20]

This was while US Defense Secretary Rumsfeld was conniving to establish a Western-dominated Caspian Guard in the region.

Days later, Russia and China launched their first-ever joint military exercises, the eight-day Peace Mission 2005, in Eastern Russia and in China's Shandong Province, consisting of land, sea and air components and 10,000 troops.

In December, the Chief of the Russian General Staff at the time, Yuri Baluyevsky, announced "Our goal is to organise such multi-country military exercises with both India and China within the framework of the Shanghai Cooperation Organisation."[21]

A Pakistani commentary in the same period drew attention to the purpose of such exercises:

"NATO was often regarded as the hidden fist behind a peaceful US-led drive for equal access to the vast energy resources of the successor states of the Soviet Union."[22]

SCO Appeal Resonated Throughout Eurasia

But, the most significant aspect of the period following the SCO June summit was the eagerness with which nations outside the organisation welcomed its new enhanced role and the underlying call for global multipolarity. Indian External Affairs Minister K. Natwar Singh, who had represented his nation at the summit, announced a month afterward "To deepen engagement with the region, India plans to apply for full membership of the SCO,"[23], a position he repeated in November when stating that India planned to expand its engagement with the SCO and "declared India's intention for a greater role in the organisation."[24]

At the same time, the Pakistani Prime Minister Shaukat Aziz "stressed that the SCO...represents 3 billion population of the world"[25] and said his country "wanted to become a full member of the Shanghai Cooperation Organisation," adding, "This organisation is of immense strategic importance" and "that if the SCO conducted military exercises like those performed by Russia, China, and India recently, Pakistan would consider participating."[26]

New observer state Iran also expressed its desire to become a full member and stated that it would offer the SCO access to the Middle East and, according to Iran's First Vice-President Mohammad-Reza Aref, "Iran would play a key role in linking the Shanghai Cooperation Organisation to Persian Gulf states and even Europe."[27]

Malaysian Ambassador to Russia Mohamad Khalis, who had attended the Astana summit, said "Malaysia completely supports the goals set by the SCO and is ready to cooperate with the organisation and its members for common interests."[28]

In the ensuing months similar interest was expressed by nations as diverse as Bangladesh, Belarus, Nepal, Turkey and Azerbaijan.

On November 4, 2005 a ceremony was held at the SCO Secretariat to sign a protocol on the establishment of a Contact Group between the Shanghai Cooperation Organisation and Afghanistan.[29]

The SCO has also established relations with the United Nations, where it is an observer in the General Assembly, the European Union, ASEAN (Association of Southeast Asian Nations), the Commonwealth of Independent States and the Organisation of the Islamic Conference.

The response to the prospects of an expanded SCO was such that a Pakistani commentator considered "The new contenders for admission are Afghanistan, North Korea and

South Korea. If the SCO continues its southward expansion, Vietnam, Thailand, the Philippines, Malaysia and Indonesia may join in the future."[30]

US Strikes Back: India

The US counteroffensive was not long in coming nor was it limited to attempts at maintaining airbases in Central Asia. It targeted the most populous new SCO observer state and that nation which can tilt not only the region but the world either toward Western dominance or a new multipolar international order: India. July 18, 2005 American President George W. Bush and Indian Prime Minister Manmohan Singh issued a joint statement on the Indo-U.S. civilian nuclear agreement that came into effect three years later and that permitted a waiver to be granted to India to commence civilian nuclear trade.

This was the economic enticement to lure India away from the SCO and closer security arrangements with Russia and China and begin the process of its orientation toward strategic military ties with Washington and its serving as the fourth pillar of an emerging Asian NATO along with Japan, Australia and South Korea. India as a full member of the SCO would insure the demise of global unipolarity, of bloc and power politics on the world stage and of Western domination on not only the military but the diplomatic and economic fronts. India as a US military ally will perpetuate divisions in the world and hostilities in Eurasia.

An Indian analyst warned two years ago that "Washington is not interested in New Delhi's official admission to the nuclear power club because that would enhance the latter's influence in international affairs. An important objective of the Americans in the region is to turn India into a major factor capable of counterbalancing a rapidly growing China.

"In order to reduce the SCO's role and influence in the region and to promote realisation of the American concept of a 'Greater Central Asia,' Tokyo and Washington are trying to drag New Delhi into a so-called Quadrilateral of Democracies aimed at building an alliance-like relationship between the US, Japan, Australia and India."[31]

Another Indian writer at the time echoed the same concern in stating, "It is indeed sad that New Delhi should continue to underestimate the importance of the Shanghai Cooperation Organisation.

"So enamoured are our foreign policy mandarins of the new found friendship with Washington that they have found no time to evaluate the SCO's great potential strategic importance to India.

"The US has sought to undermine the SCO and given an opportunity, it would have loved to throttle it in its infancy.

"India is the most important 'swing state' in the international system. It has the potential to emerge as a strong, independent centre of power. Must India allow the US to play midwife to the birth of a new great power?"[32]

India is, as a member of the BRIC (Brazil, Russia, China, India) and RIC (Russia, India, China; the Strategic Triangle that former Russian foreign minister and prime minister Yevgeny Primakov spoke of in 1998) group of nations, as a major economic power in its own right and as a nation of over one billion citizens, that country in the world which can decide whether efforts by the SCO and complementary ones in Latin America, Africa and the Middle East toward securing a democratic, peaceful, prosperous and safe world system are successfully expedited or are made more laborious, painful and costly by artificially prolonging the disproportionate and by now manifestly unjust and disastrous power of the major Western states in and over the world.

Sino-Russian Strategy of Containment of the West

Yet, the 2005 SCO summit has not been without effects. Since that time, the cycle of wars waged by the US and its NATO allies from 1999-2003 has been halted. There have been no more successful "color" coups in the former Soviet Union, notwithstanding apparent attempts in that direction in Belarus, Armenia and most recently Moldova.

The current president of Turkmenistan, Gurbanguly Berdymukhammedov, attended the 2007 heads of state summit as did Afghan President Hamid Karzai, the second for two years in a row.

In early October of 2007, the SCO and the Collective Security Treaty Organisation signed a memorandum of mutual understanding to integrate regional and international security cooperation and the following month agreed on a collaborative approach to Afghanistan.

This May 15th Russian Foreign Minister Sergey Lavrov informed the news media that the SCO had recommended what is described as dialogue partner status to Belarus and Sri Lanka, which would extend the geographical range of the SCO to a nation entirely in Europe and to another not part of the Eurasian landmass.

And not only has the post-World War II global domination of the West, given an extended and virtually unbridled license after the end of the Cold War, been curtailed by the new assertiveness of a revived Russia, a democratised and progressively more integrated Latin America and new formations like the SCO, but its power to dictate economic, financial, trade, copyright, political and energy terms to the rest of the world—and its ability to reserve the exclusive prerogative of using military force outside its own borders—has begun to collapse under its own weight.

Not that the military, including strategic, threats have abated. A Turkish analyst reminded readers last September that "the SCO has seen the unipolar mentality of the US as a source of conflict rather than a cure for the world's common challenges.

"Stressing the necessity of a multipolar world for the sake of international security, the SCO has supported the maintenance of a strategic balance of power.

"The SCO has thus warned that the US endeavor to create a global missile defense system, as in Poland and the Czech Republic, is a futile attempt, as such efforts will neither help uphold the strategic balance nor prevent the spread of weapons of every kind, including nuclear."[33]

In the same month, the head of Russia's Center for Contemporary Studies on Iran, Rajab Safarev, indicated the outlines of an alternative: "If Iran would become a SCO member, the SCO would become the third most influential, most powerful international body after the United Nations and the European Union."

"I even believe the SCO would rank second, next to the UN, from the competence point of the view, after Iran's membership."

"The SCO would also get stronger following Iran's membership, because its member states would be the owners of two thirds of the world's energy sources which gives them a great financial power."[34]

Caucasus War as Turning Point

On August 1st of last year, Georgian armed forces launched artillery barrages against the capital of South Ossetia, Tskhinvali, killing several people including a Russian peacekeeper. Only the preceding day a US-led NATO military exercise had been completed in Georgia and American troops and hardware remained in the country. Six days later Georgia, hours after its US-educated leader Mikheil Saakashvili announced a unilateral ceasefire, unleashed a full scale invasion of South Ossetia.

Russian forces beat back the Georgian offensive and decisively defeated an army that for years had been armed and trained by the Pentagon and NATO.

The Caucasus war was a double precedent. It marked the first time that a US and NATO proxy army had come into direct armed conflict with Russia and its defeat put the first dent in the West's post-Cold War image of invincibility.

After the war last August and in response to it Iranian President Ahmadinejad affirmed his country's intention of joining the SCO and added, "The thing is that every organisation has its own functions. We have our own expectations related to the SCO. The world does not consist only of NATO and the United States."[35]

Addressing the Georgia-Russia war also, the head of Russian Center of Political Information Alexei Mukhin took the above point to the next level: "If we are talking about SCO's move from an economic organisation to a military one, then this has already happened....All the member states were willing to respond to the strengthening of NATO."[36]

The director of the Russian Academy of Sciences' center for SCO and regional problems, Anatoly Bolyatko, added:

"The recent conflict in the Caucasus underscored the need for a multipolar world order. If NATO and even the UN are unable to settle this conflict, the SCO could well become a viable platform for resolving such problems....

"The SCO should eventually start playing a new role both in and outside the Caucasus. What we see now is a real crisis of the idea of a unipolar world now that the US and its NATO allies pretend they are unable to get to the core of what's been happening in the Caucasus.

"I believe that organisations like the SCO and BRIC, that brings Russia together with Brazil, India and China, should play an important role here."[37]

Russian political analyst Andrei Areshev also noted on this score that "Following the August crisis in the Caucasus, political consultations within the SCO have intensified....The SCO's transformation into an organisation capable of effective resolution, inter alia, of joint defense issues will become ever more relevant as the tension on the Eurasian continent, which is provoked from without, increases further."[38]

An even more forceful assessment is that which follows:

> "Changes in world politics that 'took place after 'the awakening of the Russian bear' could open the SCO's doors for Tehran, which remains one of the key oil suppliers for China.
>
> "If this should be the case, it may be possible to speak of an unprecedented consolidation of the countries of the Eurasian continent around Beijing and Moscow.
>
> "This will render the US's attack on Iran impossible and put an end to America's plans of redrawing the lines in the Middle East and Central Asia. "Such developments...change the entire world order formed after the collapse of the USSR."[39]

Prospects

In late October of 2008, the prime ministers of the SCO member states met in Kazakhstan against the backdrop of the worst world financial and economic crisis since the Great Depression of the 1930s.

At the summit Russian Prime Minister Vladimir Putin said that "Amid the global financial turmoil the SCO function acquires new meaning."[40]

He specified that each member of the organisation "offers its competitive advantages to be added to the common asset of interaction on international markets."

"In this sense, the organisation's role doubles today, since we are going through a complicated process in the international financial system and in the world economy. God has blessed the countries of our region to make use of their competitive geographical and historical advantages."[41]

What Putin was alluding to was a central hallmark, indeed the very foundation, of the SCO and its model of horizontal rather than vertical integration. What provides the organisation the vast potential it has both as the major multifaceted alliance and structure in Eurasia and also as microcosm and prototype alike for an international transformation in all realms is not only the individual or even collective resources of its members, but its principle and practice of complementarity, of avoiding inefficient and costly repetition and redundancy and what in the West is uncritically celebrated as "competition."

It is that precise variant of myopic and avaricious, ruthless and asocial policy practiced over the past twenty years - when the US and its allies held practically uncontested sway over the world and were free to fashion it just as they chose to - that has led to the people of the West and the world staring into an economic and social abyss. The last mechanisms left available to power-obsessed Western political elites is to rob their own citizens and those of the world to subsidize the institutions and individuals that created the crisis and to maintain war as their ultimate trump card.

At last October's SCO summit Iranian Vice President Parviz Davudi addressed an initiative that has been garnering greater interest and assuming a heightened sense of urgency when he said, "The Shanghai Cooperation Organisation is a good venue for designing a new banking system which is independent from international banking systems."[42]

The address by Russia's Putin also included these comments: "We now clearly see the defectiveness of the monopoly in world finance and the policy of economic selfishness. To solve the current problem Russia will to take part in changing the global financial structure so that it will be able to guarantee stability and prosperity in the world and to ensure progress."

"The world is seeing the emergence of a qualitatively different geo-political situation, with the emergence of new centers of economic growth and political influence.

"We will witness and take part in the transformation of the global and regional security and development architectures adapted to new realities of the 21st century, when stability and prosperity are becoming inseparable notions."[43]

The world is at a historical crossroad with the security and even survival of humanity at stake. One path continues along the way that has been pursued to date, of the right of might and every person for himself regardless of the consequences. The other is one of a more rational, just, peaceful and multipolar alternative.

NOTES AND REFERENCES

1. Kazinform, July 5, 2005
2. Strategic Culture Foundation, January 8, 2008
3. *Ibid.*

4. From Pravda as quoted in Daily Jang (Pakistan), June 14, 2006
5. Eurasia.net, August 16, 2007
6. New Europe (Belgium), November 4, 2008
7. Tehran Times, November 20, 2008
8. Press Trust of India, May 11, 2009
9. People's Daily, July 6, 2005
10. The Shanghai Cooperation Organisation, July 13, 2005 http://www.sectsco.org/news_detail.asp?id=407&LanguageID=2
11. UzReport, November 28, 2005
12. *Ibid.*
13. People's Daily, July 8, 2005
14. New York Times, July 8, 2005
15. Xinhua News Agency, July 21, 2005
16. *Ibid.*
17. Xinhua News Agency, July 21, 2005
18. Cihan News Agency (Turkey), July 26, 2005
19. *Ibid.*
20. Itar-Tass, August 17, 2005
21. The Hindu, December 4, 2005
22. Daily Times, December 2, 2005
23. Indo-Asian News Service, July 6, 2005
24. Indo-Asian News Service, October 27, 2005
25. Pakistan Tribune, October 27, 2005
26. Russian Information Agency Novosti, October 27, 2005
27. Islamic Republic News Agency, July 5, 2005
28. Vietnam News Agency, December 9, 2005
29. Shanghai Cooperation Organisation, November 4, 2005
30. Daily Jang, June 14, 2006
31. Mansoor Ali, Choice between Quadrilateral of Democracies and SCO Mainstream, October 9, 2007
32. Ash Narain Roy, Shanghai Cooperation Organisation - Towards New Dynamism Mainstream, September 18, 2007
33. Guner Ozkan, Russia and the remaking of the 'near abroad' part 2 Zaman, September 23, 2008

34. Islamic Republic News Agency, September 15, 2008
35. Interfax, August 29, 2008
36. Deutsche Presse-Agentur, August 27, 2008
37. Voice of Russia, September 7, 2008
38. Strategic Culture Foundation, December 24, 2008
39. RosBusiness Consulting, August 30, 2008
40. Voice of Russia, October 31, 2008
41. Interfax, October 30, 2008
42. Mehr News Agency, October 31, 2008
43. Russia Today, October 30, 2008.

9

CHINA-CENTRAL ASIA ECONOMIC RELATIONS IN THE ERA OF GLOBALISATION

Trade between China and Central Asia

In the rapid growth of Sino-Central Asian exchanges, several strategies are at play. First, the PRC, using a voluntary implantation policy in vital economic sectors, is seeking to consolidate its political influence in Central Asia. Secondly, it wishes to contribute to regional development and opening in order to avoid political and social destabilisation, which could have domestic consequences in Xinjiang and slow Chinese economic growth. Lastly, the Central Asian states also provide new markets for Chinese products, markets that could open up to the whole of Russia: the Chinese authorities have even mentioned several projects for merging the SCO and the Eurasian Economic Community.

To manage these strategies well, China utilises several different approaches in developing both bilateral relations and collective structures like the SCO. Many Western companies consider the states of Central Asia, with the notable exception of Kazakhstan, as risky countries where investment conditions are unfavorable or unpredictable. The local authorities therefore seek pragmatic, foreign partners who are undeterred by the political environment and are capable of investing in large projects, as well in small- and medium-sized ones. Though they may not be profitable, these projects can profoundly change the lives of local populations who benefit from them.

The Chinese authorities have understood the extent to which poverty and the decay of basic state infrastructure constitute the key elements of the potential destabilisation of the Central Asian states. Beijing has thus played the investment card by opening-up highways and railroads, improving electrical grids and hydroelectric resources, exploiting precious mineral resources, and of course developing trade relations.

Chinese Investment in China

China is also one of the only investors present in Central Asia that attaches importance to the frequently-neglected banking sector, which permits the Central Asian republics to pursue large-scale projects with Beijing. With the exception of Kazakhstan, however, the countries of the region have a particularly weak banking system. Kazakh banks have increasingly established themselves in Kyrgyzstan, as well as invested in the rest of Central Asia. The Bank of China and the Chinese Industrial and Commercial Bank opened branches in Kazakhstan. In 2006, the Kazyna Development Fund and the Development Bank of China decided to create a Sino-Kazakh development fund to invest in infrastructure collective projects worth up to five billion dollars. Kazyna also hopes to send representatives to Beijing, Hong Kong, and Urumqi and to gain privileged access to the Hong Kong Stock Exchange.[1]

It is also necessary to mention the conjoint desire of the Chinese and Central Asian authorities to participate together in large projects to develop trans-Eurasian continental relations. Thus, when at the start of the 1990s the USSR imploded and China opened-up, the European Union, in the TRACECA (Transport Corridor Europe Caucasus Asia) framework, decided to give more than 100 million euros to rail and road infrastructure projects with the intention of opening-up Central Asia and the Caucasus and restoring them to their former roles as trade crossroads. International organisations such as the World Bank, EBRD, and the Asian Development Bank have, for their part, invested more than a billion dollars in the development of port, road, and railway infrastructure. Further, the Transit Asia Europe (TAE) Fiber Cable System has assisted the states of Central Asia and China in strengthening their cooperation in the telecommunications sector. Very much a part of the current logic of globalisation, the development of Sino-Central Asian economic relations is bound to profoundly transform the societies of the five new states.

China-Central Asia Trade Relations Since 1991

Trade relations between China and Central Asia have had to overcome many obstacles. The first of these problems is geographical: the Tian-Shan mountains, the Pamir mountains, and the Taklamaklan desert hardly facilitate the development of relations and the rapid opening-up of the region. On both sides of the border, the regions in question are relatively sparsely populated (less than 60 million inhabitants in the five post-Soviet states and 20 million inhabitants in Xinjiang) and the distances to reach major urban centers, whether situated in Oriental China or in Siberia, are particularly long. The second factor curbing development has its roots in the history of the 20th century: the Sino-Soviet border has always been one of the most secure borders in the world. Not even a single regular trading route was ever opened between the federal republics of Central Asia and the autonomous region of Xinjiang, despite some tentative agreements in the beginning of the 1960s and the 1980s. The border towns were considered strategic zones: special permits were required for them; they contained several military installations; the inhabitants were subject to rigorous controls; and both central powers, Moscow and Beijing, regarded these populations as likely to be disloyal. After the demise of the USSR in 1991, the new states, thus, had to set up the necessary infrastructure to enable the development of trade: border posts, roads, railways, electrical grids, pipelines, etc.

Since the fall of the USSR, Chinese and Central Asian trade has gone through three principal phases. The first period covers the years 1992-1996 and is marked by the opening of the first Sino-Kazakh border post at Dostyk-Alatau and the signing of multiple Friendship Treaties and accords for Cooperation between the new states and China. The Uighurs largely managed initial shuttle trade on the Chinese side. On the Central Asian side, meanwhile, the Dungans played an important role, since their knowledge of Chinese facilitated relations. The volume of trade exchanges at the time was between 350 and 700 million dollars per year.[2]

Although, the magnitude of these exchanges was unprecedented, they do bear a certain historical continuity: despite the fact that the borders were officially closed during the second half of the 20th century, limited relations between the local populations were maintained due to familial, clan, and regional networks.[3]

The second period concerns the years 1997-2001, during which exchanges between China and Central Asia underwent a slow but appreciable increase of approximately 25 per cent. After a first phase of promises and hopes, the setting up of Chinese firms was somewhat hindered by the economic crises of the Central Asian states, which were further exacerbated by the Russian crash in the summer of 1998. Diplomatic relations had become complicated, furthermore, due to border disputes and renewed separatist claims in Xinjiang. The political pressure that Beijing was putting on Central Asian governments spread a negative image of China in the region.

Beijing, indeed, compelled Kazakhstan, and to a lesser degree Kyrgyzstan, to dissolve the associations the Uighur Diaspora set up on their territories and forced the Institute of Uighur Studies, which had been created within the Institute of Oriental Studies in Almaty, to close down.[4] During this second phase, the Uighurs were stripped of their major role in the development of border trade and were replaced by the Han, the reason being that Beijing did not want to see these exchanges reinforce the political and cultural links between the newly independent states and its own Muslim minority.

The third phase in the history of relations between China and Central Asia began in 2002: with the difficult political problems either resolved (border issues) or obviated (Uighur separatism), dealings henceforth became much more pragmatic, i.e., based on mutually advantageous economic cooperation.

This third phase is marked by several factors: the trade boom; the consolidation of Chinese economic ventures in Central Asia in key sectors such as hydrocarbons and infrastructure; the economic development of Xinjiang; and the strengthening of the role of the SCO. Between 2002 and 2003, trade increased by more than 200 per cent, going from about one billion dollars per year to more than three billion. An exponential increase of 150 per cent followed between 2004 and 2006, with trade reaching a value of more than ten billion dollars.[5] This dynamic, which till then had mainly been limited to Kazakhstan and Kyrgyzstan, now spread to all the states: it happened in 2004 for Tajikistan with the opening of a border post; in 2005 for Uzbekistan following its geopolitical turnaround after the events in Andijan in the same year; and is now likely to be occurring in Turkmenistan following the death of President Saparmurad Niyazov in December 2006, which has so far had the effect of re-opening up Turkmenistan to regional developments and to Chinese economic influence.

Structure of Sino-Central Asian Trade

Despite the good will of the authorities, there is still a lot of wariness on both sides resulting from political fears (Uighur separatism for the Chinese) and social fears (the "unleashing" of Chinese migrants for the authorities of Central Asia who are largely supported in this by their populations). The Central Asian states and China have maintained a visa system in place which does not make business travel easy, even if strategies of facilitation have been put in place.

In addition, at present only China and Kyrgyzstan are members of the WTO and so only they benefit from trade agreements facilitating issues like customs duties and tariff obligations. With the exception of Uzbekistan, which has a high level of protectionism, the level of customs duties the Central Asian states impose on goods is relatively low, which in itself is favorable to developing trade, but they often subject the most widespread Chinese products to special regulations (textiles, toys, shoes, small electrical and electronic goods).[6] Furthermore, Chinese traders complain that the legislative environments of these states are not conducive to investment and denounce in particular the level of corruption and the recurrent absence of contracts.

In order to facilitate trade, Beijing has vigorously supported the applications of Kazakhstan, Uzbekistan, and Tajikistan to join the WTO (only Turkmenistan has yet to make an application). Kyrgyzstan has done likewise; its wish is that all the members of the Eurasian Economic Community are admitted to the WTO so that the ballooning trade with China will be subject to consistent regulations. It is in the interests of the Central Asian states, as much as it is in China's, to develop their mutual relations because their economies are more complementary to, rather than in direct competition with, one another. China, for example, has the capacity to export consumer products to Central Asia at low prices, i.e., at prices suited to the low standard of living of the Central Asian populations, whereas Russian, Turkish, and Iranian, not to mention Western, products are too expensive.

The result is that more than 85 per cent of Chinese exports to Central Asia consist of finished goods. The reverse is true for the Central Asian states: more than 85 per cent of their exports consist of raw materials, petrol, and ferrous and nonferrous metals.[7] As Hsiu-Ling Wu and Chien-Hsun Chen have shown, there is a particular lack of diversification in Central Asian exports: a quarter of Kazakhstan's exports to China consist of petrol, a quarter of nonferrous metals, and a quarter of iron, steel, and other metals. Metals constitute one third of Kyrgyzstan's exports to China, whereas chemical products and nonferrous metals comprise 20 per cent and 25 per cent, respectively.[8]

By contrast, Chinese exports are much more diversified consisting of consumer products, machinery, processed foodstuffs, textiles, shoes, electronic goods, pharmaceutical products, automobile spare parts, etc.[9]

According to Gaël Raballand and Agnès Andrésy, trade between China and Central Asia can be divided into three categories: First, border trade which is dominated by shuttle trade. Bartering, for example the trading of skins for foodstuffs, appears to have retained its importance in China's trade with the border populations of Kyrgyzstan and Tajikistan, who live in partially demonetarised economies. The second category consists of trade organised by the Xinjiang Production and Constructions Corps or the XPCC (Xinjiang shengchan jianshe bingtuan), one of Beijing's political instruments. This trade is thought to account for more than a third of total trade between China and Central Asia. The third category, private entrepreneurs, is no longer made up of the Uighurs, who were ousted in the second half of the 1990s, but are rather ethnic Han from the maritime provinces. The majority of them originate from Zhejiang province, especially from the city of Wenzhou, considered to be one of the biggest centers of Chinese entrepreneurs. In fact, more than 80,000 traders from Wenzhou have established themselves in Xinjiang, principally at Kashgar, and half of these engage in trade with Central Asia.[10]

It is, however, difficult to assess the trade figures between China and Central Asia, since these are official statistics that take little account of the realities of border trade, and even less of the contraband networks. In addition, the information provided by China, on the one hand, and the Central Asian states, on the other, are not often in agreement. It seems preferable, however, to go with the Chinese statistics, since Chinese exporters have very little incentive to undervalue their sales to Central Asia because the customs duties are practically non-existent. Thus, Chinese statistics include petty trade, which the Central Asian authorities do not count. Thus, for 2006, China announced trade figures of 13 billion dollars, that is, 23 per cent more than the official figures given by the Central Asian republics. For the two countries with which China's border trade is the greatest, Kazakhstan and Kyrgyzstan, the figures are especially divergent. Thus, in 2005, Kazakhstan is, according to Astana, supposed to have imported goods worth 1.2 billion dollars from China, but Beijing puts the figure at close to 4 billion; Astana estimated exports to be worth 2,423 million dollars, while Chinese figures include an additional 500 million.[12] With Kyrgyzstan, the divergences are even greater: for 2005, Chinese figures are ten times higher than Kyrgyz figures (30 million in exports and 100 million in imports according to Bishkek; 300 million and 1 billion respectively according to Beijing).[13] The divergences are smaller (around 10 per cent) with the three other states, Tajikistan, Uzbekistan, and Turkmenistan. China and Tajikistan's figures are in relative agreement: 350 million dollars according to Beijing; 37 million less, i.e., 11 per cent less, according to Dushanbe. For the two others, the relatively small divergences in calculations can be explained by the fact that most trade is organised at the level of the state and that there is a low level of small business, a result of them not sharing a border with China.

Beijing has declared trade figures of 900 million dollars with Tashkent and 133 million with Ashgabat. According to Vladimir Paramonov and Aleksei Strokov, trade not taken into account by official statistics would have reached somewhere between 4.5 and 6.5 billion dollars in 2006 for the five states, of which nearly two-thirds was with Kazakhstan, between 500 and 800 million dollars with Kyrgyzstan, approximately half a million with Uzbekistan, between 100 and 200 million for Tajikistan, and less for Turkmenistan.[13]

Thus, the total value of trade between China and Central Asia for 2006 would have amounted to approximately 18 billion dollars and not 13 billion.

China–Central Asia, Unequal Trade Relations

Trade between China and Central Asia mostly concerns trade between China and Kazakhstan (70 per cent of the total), or more precisely, trade between Kazakhstan and the Xinjiang region, which amounted to 3 billion dollars in 2004. Astana quickly rose to become the second largest of China's trading partners in the CIS after Moscow and has for quite some time already held the mantle of being Xinjiang's largest foreign trading partner.[14]

Between 1992 and 2002, the total of Chinese investments in Kazakhstan reached 800 million dollars. This amount is continuing to grow rapidly, placing China among the five largest foreign investors in the country.[15] In 2005, trade between the two countries reached close to 7 billion dollars, an increase of 50 per cent over the previous year.[16] The volume of trade between China and Kazakhstan is much higher than for the rest of Central Asia. Of the total trade, Uzbekistan and Tajikistan each have 9 per cent, Kyrgyzstan 7 per cent, and Turkmenistan only 2 per cent. However, trade with Turkmenistan is likely to become much greater in volume if the gas contracts signed between Ashgabat and Beijing are confirmed.

The astonishingly low levels of trade between China and Kyrgyzstan, as a percentage of the total trade between China and Central Asia, can be explained by weaknesses intrinsic to the Kyrgyz economy. However, this situation is likely to be offset by the development of transit: Kyrgyzstan is earmarked to become one of the main transit centers for the re-exportation of Chinese products throughout the rest of Central Asia. The Dordoi Bazar in Bishkek, for example, is already a kind of crossroads for Chinese products that are being expedited to Kazakhstan and Uzbekistan. Similarly, the Karasuu Bazar in the Ferghana Valley directly feeds into the Uzbek market.

Indeed, it is likely that in reality Sino-Uzbek trade is far greater than the official figures suggest, but this trade is difficult to measure precisely because it is transited through Kyrgyzstan. According to some economists, one can now estimate that 75 per cent of Chinese imports to Kyrgyzstan are reexported to other Central Asian countries. The extent of this commercial growth is such that the re-exportation of Chinese goods has become one of the two largest economic activities of Kyrgyzstan.[17]

Xinjiang is set to become the main economic power of wider Central Asia (the five post-Soviet States, Afghanistan, and Xinjiang). Its GDP (220 million dollars in 2004) is already four times that of the combined total of the five Central Asian States.[18] Though Xinjiang is the least developed of the 13 provinces of the Great West, it nevertheless benefits from some special economic conditions (abolition of taxes and duties for Chinese and foreign companies setting up there) that are designed to enable it to become a regional economic power, specialising mostly in hydrocarbons, metals, electricity, and textiles. This dynamism is in large part the fruit of a project launched in 2000 to develop the Far West (*xibu dakaifa*): Beijing has injected more than 8 billion dollars into the road, railway, gas, petrol, and hydroelectric sectors of this autonomous region. In the coming years, a great deal of this financial "manna" will flow into the Central Asian states, such that Xinjiang will be the door not only to the rest of China but also to Pakistan, South Asia, and the Pacific edge. Since September 1995, Beijing has allowed Kazakhstan the use of the Lianyungang port so it can transit commodities arriving from the Pacific.

Inequalities in political and geopolitical relations between China and Central Asia are thus also present in the economic sphere: while the Chinese state is investing in the strategic sectors of the five Central Asian states, and small and very dynamic Chinese enterprises are setting themselves up in the Central Asian market, the Central Asians themselves have very little presence in China.[20] In 2005, a census taken revealed that 744 Chinese enterprises have been established in Kazakhstan (40 large companies and close to 700 small ones), one hundred in Uzbekistan, a dozen in Kyrgyzstan, and a similar number in Tajikistan.[21] The role of the various Chambers of Commerce of each of the countries in facilitating meetings between traders has proven to be crucial. But even in the cases of states with significant economic development such as Kazakhstan, the inequality in Sino-Central Asian relations is not going to be easy to reduce.

In 2006, Central Asia only represented 0.6 per cent of the foreign trade of the People's Republic of China, far behind the United States and Russia. *A contrario*, the position of China in Central Asia is already major, as it accounts on average for 12 per cent of Central Asian foreign trade. Differences between Central Asian countries are, however, still particularly glaring: China accounts for 34 per cent of Kyrgyzstan's foreign trade, 15 per cent of Kazakhstan's, 10 per cent of Tajikistan's, 5 per cent of Uzbekistan's, and only 1 per cent of Turkmenistan's.[22]

Role of Border Posts

One of the main thoroughfares between Central Asia and China is the Urumqi airport, which offers a large number of flights to the capitals of Central Asia—Almaty, Astana, Bishkek, Tashkent, and Dushanbe are served, the first three by China Southern Airlines and Hainan Airlines, the latter two by Uzbekistan Airways and Tajikistan Airlines. Ashgabat does not currently enjoy any direct flights with Urumqi, but this may quickly change in the course of 2007. Despite Urumqi's superior position, Kashgar is also fast staking out a place as one of the main crossroads for trade between

China and Central Asia. The capital of Uighur culture, the city has for this reason aroused the concern of the Chinese authorities who prefer the largely Hanized Urumqi. Yet Kashgar's proximity to the Torugart Pass and the Karakorum Highway may prove to be one of the driving forces of Sino-Central Asian trade, particularly after the revitalisation of the Karakorum Highway in Sino-Pakistani relations. For Central Asian countries this remains the one and only point of access to Pakistan so long as the situation in Afghanistan prevents the establishment of more direct connections.

The Sino-Central Asian border posts that were opened during the 1990s are all situated in isolated and mountainous regions, and so are not as such conducive to the development of large-scale trade. Of the eight posts currently in operation, only four—Dostyk, Khorgos, Irkeshtam, and Torugart—have actually succeeded in making an impression on regional trade, while the others have mainly served only as points of passage for the local populations. River trade is still quite marginal, and the Premier Secretary of the CP of Xinjiang, Van Lentsiuan, has made no attempt to hide his skepticism concerning the possibility of establishing river trade in the cross-border rivers.[23]

In a bid to counter the geographical situation of the border posts and their distance to large urban centers, China has opened many free trade zones. Xinjiang includes 17 special economic zones with a Republican statute. The regional government has also opened its own free trade zones, the main function of which is to be home to large industrial exhibition parks, such as is the case with, for example, the capital Urumqi (3,000 m2 of exhibition space), the town of Yining, and the small railway town of Kuytun. The Chinese authorities have also granted the town of Shihezi a special status. Situated 150 km from Urumqi, Shihezi serves as a *carrefour* both on the road between Xinjiang and Central Asia and on the Urumqi-Almaty railway.

The development of cross border trade also depends in part on the existing visa system between China and the Central Asian states, which is slowly becoming more simplified. Kazakhstan and Kyrgyzstan, for example, have opened consulates in Urumqi to accelerate the visa process for Chinese businessmen who were otherwise obliged to get one in Beijing. Lastly, several measures have been implemented to make it easier for the border populations to obtain visas, and persons who travel to the free trade zones of the border posts on a day-trip can now do so without a visa. The simplification of these procedures would truly facilitate the flow of persons between the two borders and make China a destination as accessible as Russia is now. Yet, for the present time, security issues are paramount for the Central Asian states and China, which hope above all to avoid destabilisation caused by border traffic they cannot control, like drugs, arms, and terrorism.

Sino-Kazakh Border Posts

The first border post, at Dostyk-Alatau (Alashankou), was opened in 1992. Located in the Almaty region close to the town of Zharkent and the regional capital of Taldy-Kurgan, it quickly became the main transit point between the two countries: in 2003, it was responsible for 50 per cent of the total trade between Kazakhstan and Xinjiang and 90 per cent of the border and petty trade. The commodities that pass through there are not only bound for the Kazakhstan market but also for the Russian, Azerbaijan, Uzbek, Kyrgyz, and even Afghan markets.[24]

The exponential rise in economic growth Dostyk-Alatau has enjoyed in only fifteen years was made possible by the willingness of the Kazakh and Chinese authorities to increase the means of trade: the post in effect manages highway trade, rail trade, and, as of 2006, the Atasu-Alashankou pipeline, which has freed up railway freight to make room for other types of commodities. The small city of Dostyk is home to more and more small companies. The Kazakh Deputy Minister for the Economy,

Berdibek Saparbaev, stated in 2006 that the authorities would like to create an economic free trade zone in order to accelerate development in the region.[25] In 1993, the first free trade zone was scheduled with the support of companies based in Hong Kong, but the city's retrocession to China in 1997 and fears of a "flood" of Chinese products onto the Kazakhstan market, which was very weak at the time, put an end to the project.[26]

China, as much as Kazakhstan, would like to transform the Dostyk-Alatau post into a veritable transit point of international proportions. In terms of road systems, several major works are in need of being undertaken because of the bad condition of the road leading from Dostyk to Zharkent. In the railway sector, the railway track linking Almaty to Urumqi also passes through Dostyk.

The first railway line going to the border was constructed in the 1930s. The idea of linking up the Soviet and Chinese lines was toyed with in 1969 but quickly abandoned due to the deterioration in relations between the two communist countries. Opened in 1990, this link is at present the only railway line connecting Kazakhstan to China, and in fact the only one linking Central Asia and China. This railway carries 75 per cent of all Sino-Central Asian trade. The journey between Almaty and Urumqi lasts forty hours, eight of which are spent at the border crossing, during which time customs formalities are undertaken and the train's wheels are changed because of the differences in Chinese and Soviet gauge-widths. For the merchandise, the wait at customs and manual off-loading takes several days.[27]

The rail trade going through Dostyk is increasing exponentially: it reached 7 million tonnes in 2004, around 13 in 2005 (about 10 million tonnes going from China to Kazakhstan and 3 million in the opposite direction) and will reach an estimated 16 million in 2007. The authorities hope to be able to handle as much as 25 million tonnes by 2010.[28] To achieve this, the Kazakh Prime Minister, Danial Akhmetov, announced in April 2006 that the line linking Dostyk to Aktogai—a major rail point for redistribution to the South, the North and the East of the country—would be reinforced by 2011.

The aim is to increase the passenger and freight traffic and to implement simplified customs procedures to reduce transit time.[29] This rail development is part of Kazakhstan's strategy to become one of the transport links of the old continent, a wish that will be realised by the existence of a transcontinental line joining the Lianyungang port on the Pacific side to Lanzhou, Urumqi, Dostyk, Russia, and then Western Europe. This line would have a total transport capacity of 40 million tonnes per year and would cost Astana approximately 3 billion dollars, a sum that would in large part be financed by Hong Kong firms interested in having land and not only maritime links with Europe.[30]

The second Sino-Kazakh border post was opened at Khorgos in 2004. It is located further south on the Khorgos River (a tributary of the Ili), not far from the Chinese town of Yinin and around 90 km from Kuldja. By contrast to Dostyk, the road joining Khorgos to Zharkent (33 km) and then to Almaty (370 km) is in good condition. For this reason Khorgos has quickly become the foremost Sino-Kazakh road transit point, and far outstrips Dostyk. In 2006, freight passing through Khorgos was worth an estimated billion dollars, an increase of 35 per cent over the previous year.[31] Once the Shihezi-Yining-Khorgos route is rehabilitated, the distance between Urumqi and Almaty will be reduced by 200 km, which accentuates the profitability of the route.

In 2003, the Kazakh and Chinese authorities announced the creation of a free trade zone in order to boost trade. Khorgos thus became the first free trade zone in Xinjiang and China's foremost cross-border free trade zone.[32] It includes a tax-free trading zone and an industrial zone whose area straddles both states—on the Kazakh side, it includes the Panfilov district, and on the Chinese side, the autonomous Kazakh region of Ili. An ethnographical park presenting the various cultures of Central Asia and of Russia is to be created on the Chinese side. And a system of one-day travel without visas has been set up. Again on the Chinese side, more than 200 companies, including China's largest leather company, are to be set up, and a number of them are specialised in new technologies and manufactured products.

In order to keep the momentum going, both countries raised the possibility, in 2004, of linking up their railway lines using Dostyk-Alatau as a model. An office representing the Chinese national company of railways opened in Almaty, and a branch of the Kazakhstan Temir Zholy is now in operation in Beijing.[33]

In 2005, Chinese railways proposed extending the already existing Lyanyungan-Lanzhou-Urumqi line by adding a section between Urumqi-Kuldja-Khorgos-Sary-Ozek, this last town being situated half way between Almaty and Taldy-Kurgan.[34] Despite opposition from the executive director of Kazakh Railways, Erlan Atamkulov, who thinks the project too difficult to implement given the mountainous nature of the zones to be traversed,[35] both countries signed an agreement in February 2006 making provision for the linking up of their respective railways at the Khorgos Pass by 2009. When finished, this electrified line of nearly 300 km in length on Kazakh territory will run parallel to the existing highway and will have a capacity of 25 million tonnes per year. It will permit the opening of a connection to the main network that passes through Almaty and will enable a second Sino-Central Asian railway line to be opened so that capacity can be freed up in Dostyk.[36]

As in Dostyk, this connecting section will be accompanied by the construction of a dry port which will be home to a logistical center for redistribution, significant storage facilities, communications services, enterprises for product certification, and insurance companies.[37] Before 2010, Kazakhstan thus wishes to provide itself with a capacity of 50 million tonnes for rail freight to be set aside for Chinese products, half of which will pass through Dostyk and half through Khorgos. This strategy is part of the CATIC project (Development of Uniform Transport and Logistical System of Central Asian Transport and Industrial Corridor), which the political authorities in Kazakhstan are backing so that three large border logistics centers can be developed, with one in Khorgos, one in Taskal (on the border with Russia), and one in the Aktau port on the Caspian sea.[38] Astana's desire to become an essential thoroughfare for trans-Eurasian highway trade was given confirmation in 2006, when China and Kazakhstan reached agreement on six new roads joining Urumqi to Ust-Kamenogorsk, Semipalatinsk, and Almaty to run variously through Dostyk and Khorgos. China has officially opened 22 roads linking it to Kazakhstan.[39]

In addition to the two main posts at Dostyk and Khorgos, which are open all year round, Kazakhstan and China have three other border posts, which are presently limited to border trade and which are not always open to foreigners. The Kolzhat-Dulart border post, located further to the south between Narynkol and Khorgos, however, seems to have a bright future ahead of it: The section of road running through Aksai-Chundzha-Kolzhat presently being reconstructed passes through several small towns in the autonomous Uighur region that are all well-placed to benefit from this trade, and once completed the old capital of Almaty, 340 kilometers away, will be reachable in less than 5 hours.[40] On the Chinese side, Durlat has been regarded as an international port since 1994 and in 1999 a free trade zone was opened there. The passage of freight and people through it is nonetheless minimal: in 2002, a total of 6,000 persons, 3,000 vehicles, and 24,000 tonnes of freight transited through it.[41]

Further to the north, above Dostyk in the region of Eastern Kazakhstan, two other posts were opened, those of Bakhty-Tacheng and Maikapchagai-Jeminay, both close to Lake Zaisan. These two border posts have the capacity to service the whole of North-East Kazakhstan, and also Altai on the Russian side of the border. The Kazakh authorities are financing the reconstruction of the Taskensken-Bakhty highway (35 km) so its freight transport capacity can be augmented, while on the Chinese side, at the Tasheng post, a small airport was opened to enable it to handle commercial flights. The Maikapchagai-Jeminay post is likewise in full development. In March 2006, the Chinese authorities made it into a free trade zone. It is the second largest after Khorgos, and is capable of handling a maximum of 10,000 stands and 3,000 tonnes of freight.[42] A sixth post at Narynkol-Muzart, situated in the area surrounding the Kyrgyz border 320 km away from Almaty, was made official in 1992.

Prior to 1953, it had only ever been partially opened for temporary trade between the two countries. It has a potential capacity of up to 50,000 tonnes of freight and 30,000 passengers annually but has been closed due to a lack of traffic, the existing traffic being redirected to other more efficient posts. A seventh point of passage might be opened at Alekseevka-Aheytubiek, which is located more than 800 km away from Urumqi. Both countries officially agreed to open it in 1992, but it is still not yet operational. It has a potential capacity for 20,000 tonnes of products and 10,000 passengers annually.

Sino-Kyrgyz Border Posts

The main Sino-Kyrgyz border post is that at the Torugart Pass, situated on the Bishkek-Naryn-Kashgar stretch of highway. At an altitude of 3,900 meters, the post is not easy to access and is often closed during the floods in spring. Indeed, between Torugart and Naryn the highway is not even asphalted: it takes trucks around 16 hours to complete a journey of only 190 km. And the pass is always only ever open in one direction at a time: during the morning, the traffic is authorised to flow from Kyrgyzstan to China, and in the afternoon from China to Kyrgyzstan. It is closed on weekends and on public holidays, and private automobiles are rarely given authorisation to use it. Authorised companies on the Chinese side of the border must meet foreign tourists. Nor are Kyrgyz trucks allowed into China, which means that all commodities must be unloaded and then reloaded onto Chinese trucks. Neither the geographical nor the technical conditions at the Torugart Pass, then, are particularly optimal for the development of Sino-Kyrgyz trade.

A second post at Irkeshtam in the south of the country was opened only in 1997. China and Kyrgyzstan had wanted it to be operational much earlier but the Sino-Kyrgyz border was at the time run by Russian troops as part of CIS agreements and they were not favorable to the idea. From 1997 to 2002, Irkeshtam was opened uniquely to commodity transit and not to passengers, and even then only for a few months a year. In the summer of 2002, authorisation was given to allow individuals to cross. Situated 240 km from Osh and 250 km from Kashgar, the Irkeshtam post is the most direct road between the Ferghana Valley and Xinjiang. It is not, however, the quickest, since the road is not always asphalted and it winds through a particularly mountainous region. So, it takes on average four hours to get to the town of Sary-Tash only 45 km away and a whole day to get to Osh. Irkeshtam's strategic position, however, has aroused the interest of the international community. Hence, the Chinese Development Bank has decided to provide 7 million dollars to finance the reconstruction of the first 18 km of the highway. The Asian Development Bank for its part has approved a loan of 32 million dollars for the reconstruction of the 80 km section from Osh to Irkeshtam, and the China Road & Bridge Corporation won a tender for it in March 2007. [43] The Islamic Development Bank is also contributing with financing for a 44 km stretch.[44]

Once the works are finished, sometime around 2010, travel time between the border post and the markets of Osh and Karasuu will be cut in half. Irkeshtam, in fact, seems destined to enjoy a really substantial economic boom: whereas the Torugart Pass supplies Bishkek and the northern regions of Kyrgyzstan, Irkeshtam provides Chinese products with access to the rich Ferghana Valley, to the Tajik provinces, and to a substantial Uzbek market (more than 25 million people). Indeed, more than 2,000 small Chinese companies are reported to be already registered in Osh.[45] The Uzbek authorities have had their sights on the Irkeshtam Pass since the end of the 1990s, since it is Uzbekistan's quickest route to China. The idea of a road linking Ferghana and Andijan to this border post has been backed by Tashkent because it would lower the costs of Chinese products entering its markets. The Uzbek authorities are also favorable to the construction of a section of railway connecting Andijan to Irkeshtam and Torugart, a particularly expensive project (three billion dollars).[46]

A feasibility study, undertaken at China's expense in 2001, has not as yet led to anything concrete, since deteriorating political relations have put a halt to the plans. In addition, Kazakhstan has made an effort to hold up the project because once it is finished Astana will lose part of its transit traffic, i.e., traffic bound for Uzbekistan. However, the 2006 rapprochement between the Uzbek and Kyrgyz Presidents, respectively Islam Karimov and Kurmanbek Bakiev, has made the project more likely. In addition, Beijing has given financial backing to the project, allocating to it part of the 900 million dollars of credit offered to the Central Asian states under the auspices of the SCO. The rapid construction of a road from Irkeshtam to Osh is likewise vital for Tajikistan and will be a key element in a much larger project, namely the reconstruction of the Kyrgyzstan-Tajikistan corridor connecting Irkeshtam to Dushanbe (550 km). Financed to the tune of 25 million dollars by the Asian Development Bank,[47] this project would allow Tajikistan to "disenclave" itself and to strengthen its ties with Kyrgyzstan so it can bypass its Uzbek neighbor.

Sino-Tajik Border Posts

At present there is a single Sino-Tajik border post, which was opened at Kulma-Kalasu in May 2004. Located in Far East Pamir on the Kulma Pass at an altitude of 4,300 meters, access to it is difficult and due to climatic conditions it is only open from May through November. In 2006, close to 10,000 tonnes of freight were transited through it: Tajikistan's exports totaled more than 200,000 dollars and its imports valued over 800,000.[48] The volume was thus modest.

In order to increase its trade potential, China would like to create a free trade zone based on those already in operation close to the Kazakh and Kyrgyz borders, one for which Tajikistanis would not need a visa. While the Tajik government is researching strategies that would allow it to disenclave the autonomous Republic of Gorno-Badakhshan, this border post will be called upon to play a major role if commerce with China along the border grows.

The main town of the region, Murghab, mainly populated by Kyrgyz, is 140 km from the border and more than 85 per cent of the products sustaining the population are from other regions.[49] The road is bad between Kulma and Toktamysh but the stretch to Murghab has already been reconstructed. In addition, Murghad itself is the main thoroughfare on the Pamir Highway on the way to Khorog, the capital of Gorno-Badakhshan: the potential market for Chinese products could in this way extend as far as the Tajik-Afghan border.[50] Despite geographical conditions that are on the face of it quite unfavorable, the development of Sino-Tajik trade relations along the Pamir Highway would enable the country to be at least partially disenclaved and allow it to access consumer products that are otherwise unobtainable via its neighbors, Uzbekistan and Afghanistan.

Chinese Investments in Central Asian Infrastructure

China's economic presence does not only bear on the trade sector: beyond the consumer products that are now supplying Central Asian markets, China is likewise setting itself up in the domain of infrastructure. Infrastructure has often been neglected by the Central Asian states, because since independence they have not had the means to invest the large sums of money required, and so have ended up relying on infrastructure inherited from Soviet times. It is precisely in this area that Beijing has many trump cards up its sleeve. Its companies, whether public or private, have cutting-edge expertise in numerous technology sectors and at the same time offer much more attractive prices than other international companies.

Backed by political power, Chinese firms can also offer the Central Asian states particularly advantageous financial conditions: the Development Bank, the State Bank, and the Import-Export Bank of China manage these investments through low-interest loans, essential for Central Asian states which often have only little by way of banking resources. These foreign ventures may be undertaken by Chinese firms either as part of bilateral agreements or within the framework of the SCO.

The proposal made by Beijing in June 2004 to grant 900 million dollars of credit to the five states in order to finance projects that involve Chinese companies, has already enabled several large projects to get up and running. China is in this way staking out an increasingly stronger position for itself within strategic sectors like ferrous and nonferrous minerals, hydroelectricity, railways and roads, and telecommunications. The geopolitical impact of this Chinese strategy should not be overlooked. These sectors are vital for the economies of Central Asia states and make up key elements for a commercial opening-up—again still in its infancy—toward southern countries.

Exports of Ferrous and Nonferrous Metals

Central Asia possesses considerable reserves of minerals: not only does it possess gold, uranium, and silver, but also aluminum, copper, zinc, and lead as well as rare minerals like tungsten and molybdenum—minerals necessary for the blossoming development of China's industries. China is especially interested in Kyrgyzstan's gold reserves. In January 2005, the Chinese government offered Bishkek an investment of several hundreds of millions of dollars as part of the "investments for natural resources" scheme. The terms of the offer were that Beijing would buy gold, tungsten, and tin in exchange for the construction of a section of railway linking Uzbekistan to Kyrgyzstan and China, investments in the hydroelectric stations of Eastern Tian-Shan, and the construction of two metallurgic complexes.[51] In June 2006, China made a new offer: to form a joint Sino-Kyrgyz venture that would be responsible for extracting Kyrgyz gold deposits, between 10 and 20 tonnes of which would be held at the Chinese Development Bank as a guarantee. Many Kyrgyz politicians and economists, including for example the director of the Entrepreneurs Union, Omurbek Abdrakhmanov, protested at the proposal citing the security risk that the country might run: according to them, in getting rid of its gold reserves too quickly and allowing other countries control over its strategic minerals, Kyrgyzstan would risk losing its political autonomy.[52]

Tajikistan is in a similar situation to Kyrgyzstan: it cannot do without foreign investment to exploit its reserves. In 2005, this led to an 11 per cent drop in the exportation of precious minerals from 2004 levels, yielding the authorities the meager sum of 18 million dollars. To develop the sector, a meeting with businessmen from Xinjiang was organised in Dushanbe in November 2005, and several projects were raised, although for the moment none have been finalised.[53] In Kazakhstan, cooperation in this sector has turned out to be easier because the country has enough financial capacity to participate in the exploitation of its own reserves. Thus, in 2005, the China National Gold Group Association and the metallurgic complex Kazakhaltyn Mining signed a contract for a joint-venture to exploit Kazakhstan's gold deposits.[54]

China requires uranium to complete the construction of the many tens of nuclear power plants designed to respond to its growing energy needs. In 2020, it is projected that

Chinese nuclear electrical stations will produce approximately 40 million kw/h, or four per cent of global electrical production. Beijing therefore seeks to diversify its partners. It already buys uranium from the world's foremost producers, Australia and Canada, and is becoming increasingly interested in Kazakhstan's reserves. As of 2001, negotiations have been underway between Kazatomprom and the China National Nuclear Corp. (CNNC) concerning a joint-venture to extract and export uranium from the deposits in the south of Kazakhstan. [55] In the summer of 2004, the Ulbinsk metallurgy plant owned by Kazatomprom and based in Ust-Kamenogorsk opened a branch in Shanghai so it could sell its beryllium on the Chinese market.[56]

The first contract—valid until 2020—for uranium extraction was signed between Kazatomprom and CNNC in November 2004, and was accompanied with a strategic cooperation treaty designed to strengthen Sino-Kazakh ties in matters of atomic energy.[57] The two countries signed a new strategic cooperative agreement in December 2006. Within this framework, in June 2007, the China Guangdong Nuclear Power Holding (CGNPC) and Kazatomprom signed an agreement to supply nuclear fuel to Chinese stations. According to the terms of the contract, Kazakhstan will send natural uranium to China, which will enrich it, and then send it to Ulbinsk, where it will be converted into fuel. By this contract, Ulbinsk will become the first foreign firm to obtain rights to supply nuclear fuel to China National Nuclear Corp.[58]

Kazatomprom will, therefore, be the sole foreign supplier to the Chinese nuclear market, a strategic recognition of which the authorities in Astana are especially proud. China is also looking to shore up its supply of rare metals, particularly from Kyrgyzstan. Bishkek presently exports mercury to the PRC produced by the Khaidarkan factory, which resumed its activities in 2004 after a failed attempt at privatising it. China is likewise seeking to import tungsten: its own reserves, as well as its molybdenum mines, were destroyed by the floods in Yangtze and Huang He.

Nevertheless, a tender put out in October 2006 for the exploitation of the tungsten mine in Kensu was not won by a Chinese company. On the other hand, the Western Mining Co., China's second largest lead production company, made a proposal in June 2006 for the exploitation of the Kyrgyz tin mines for a cost of 24 million dollars and a predicted annual extraction of 330,000 tonnes.[59] Beijing would also like to get involved in extracting the silver deposits in Zhetymskoe, which are situated in the Naryn region: presently underexploited, it has the advantage of being situated along the Sino-Kyrgyz-Uzbek railway line that Beijing would like to construct, thus facilitating the export of silver to China. Moreover, China is interested in the deposits of tin, tungsten, molybdenum, and gold to be found along the Enylchek and Sarydzhaz Rivers in Eastern Tian-Shan, which is precisely where some Beijing-financed hydroelectric plants are due to be constructed.[60]

After Kyrgyzstan, Tajikistan has turned out to be the second most promising country for China in terms of precious minerals. Beijing's interest has been piqued by the country's deposits of tantalum and niobium in the Kuristik mine. Of the overall total of Chinese investments in Tajikistan, investments in the mineral sector already stand at 29 per cent.[61] China has also been asked, notably by the economist Hajimahmat Umarov, to participate in the construction of the Dushanbe cement factory. In the case of Turkmenistan, Chinese cooperation has so far not focused on the extraction of metals but on industrial cooperation in the chemical industry. In January 2007, for example, the companies Capital-Lonqji Sci-Tech Co. Ltd and SINOMASCH won a tender launched by the government for the turnkey construction of a glass factory which will be the largest in Central Asia; it is to be operational by 2009. The 67 million dollar cost of the project is to be financed by a lowinterest loan from the Import-Export Bank of China to the Turkmen authorities. Indeed, the total loan is close to 300 million dollars over a period of 20 years, and should also enable the modernisation of the Maryazot chemical complex and the construction of a carbamide factory in the Mary region.[62]

Hydroelectric System

Hydroelectric issues between Central Asia and China have not been extensively discussed.[63] However, the possibilities for cooperation between these two regions in this sphere are numerous. The Central Asian hydroelectricity sector, still relatively underdeveloped, appears promising. With demand for electricity expected to remain weak due to a industrial crisis coupled with high production potential, exports of electricity are destined to experience considerable growth. Beijing effectively views Central Asia as an area capable of supplying it with cheap electricity.[64]

Contrary to its hydrocarbon policy, the aim of the Chinese here is not, at least not primarily, to have this hydroelectricity delivered to its large cities in the east (the electrical lines required would need to stretch over at least 6,000 km) but rather to make up for the energy shortfall in Xinjiang. China would also like to be able to sell Central Asian hydroelectricity to countries of the meridional corridor (Afghanistan, Pakistan, Iran, and India) because of the significant transit fees it would accrue. The establishment of Chinese companies in the region, like those it has set up in Russia and Mongolia, has thus been centered on two axes: First, the construction of new hydroelectric stations and second, the installation of new electricity lines, in particular high-voltage ones.

The majority of Kazakhstan's hydroelectric stations date back to the Soviet era and require costly repairs. Astana and Beijing are currently discussing the construction of an electrical power station (between 5,500 and 7,000 MW capacity) on the Irtysh near the city of Ekibastuz in the Pavlodar region. Its cost (estimated between four and seven billion dollars) will be totally covered by Beijing.[65] The production will be exclusively destined for China via a high-voltage line of 1500 kV, which will export the electricity produced as far as Xinjiang, 4,000 km away. The second project involves the Khorgos River at the Sino-Kazakh border. The construction of a Sino-Kazakh hydroelectric station called Dostyk ("friendship") was negotiated in 2005. The station will consist of a cascade of small stations with a combined capacity of 21 MW and will be situated near the village of Baskunchi 20 km from Khorgos.[66] An 11 km long canal will also provide irrigation for more than 40,000 hectares of land on both sides of the border.[67] The third common project concerns the hydroelectric station in Moinak, situated on the Charyn River approximately 200 km from the former capital, Almaty.

During a summit of the Shanghai Cooperation Organisation in June 2006, the Kazakh President N. Nazarbayev signed the final contract to finance the Moinak station with the National Development Bank of China. The total cost of constructing this station is an estimated 310 million dollars.[68] The project is scheduled for completion in 2009 and the station will have a capacity of 300 MW, meaning it will partly be able to make up for the electricity deficit in the south of the country.[69] The Moinak hydroelectric station represents the first Chinese turnkey construction project for a new station since Kazakhstan's independence.

In Tajikistan, China has decided to invest mainly in the Zarafshan River, which is located in the Penjikent region in the north, while Russia is dominant in the meridional projects. In December 2005, Tajik Prime Minister Oqil Oqilov received a loan from the Chinese Development Bank for three investment projects involving hydroelectric stations on the Zarafshan.[70] Out of three proposals, only one has been signed.[71] The state-run Sinohydro Corporation will take on the construction of the Yavan power station, which is supposed to supply close to 600 million kWh per year.[72] Once operational, the Penjikent region, which currently imports its electricity from Kyrgyzstan and Uzbekistan, will be energy-independent.

The project includes the construction of a 60 km long electric line of 220 kV from the station to the town of Penjikent. In September 2006, the Tajik Minister for Energy, Abdullo Yorov, and the Chinese Prime Minister, Wen Jiabao, formalised the signing of two contracts between Tajikistan's state-run company Barki Tojik and the Chinese Theban Electric Apparatus Stock Company (CTEAS) to construct electric lines.[73] The first contract is for the construction of an electrical line (Lolazor-Obi Mazor) in the Khatlon region in the country's south. With a length of 93 km and a capacity of 220 kV, it will be capable of transporting four billion kWh per year for a cost estimated at 59 million dollars. The second contract is for a 350 km long, 500 kV high-voltage line that will connect the north and the south of the country. Estimated to cost 281 million dollars, it will have the capacity to transfer eight billion kWh to Afghanistan, Iran, and Pakistan. Out of a total cost of 340 million dollars, the Exim Bank of China has put forward 300 million. The Tajikistan state budget will pay for the remaining 40 million.[74] A primary agreement to supply electricity in exchange for oil was signed between Beijing and Bishkek in 1995.[75]

In June 2006, the two countries reached a new principle agreement for the export of 50 MW to Xinjiang, but so far they have been unable to agree on the price per kWh. The Kyrgyz authorities would like a consortium to be created that would include Kazakhstan, Russia, and China for the joint financing and exploitation of the new stations Kambarata I and II. It is therefore possible that Chinese companies will become involved in one way or another in the Kambarata I and II projects, but that this will happen without undermining the supremacy of Russian companies. The second zone after the Naryn for the Chinese-Kyrgyz hydroelectric cooperation is in Oriental Tian-Shan, in the region of Lake Issyk-Kul on the border with China.[76] The privately owned company Sarydzhaz-Energo plans to begin the construction of a cascade of five stations with a capacity of 750 MW (thirteen million kWh).

Negotiations are currently underway for the Chinese financing of the construction of three stations for three cross-border rivers—the Sarydzhaz, the Enilchek, and the Akshiirak—which run down from Kyrgyz glaciers toward China.[77] The Chinese would like also to construct high-voltage lines, starting at these stations and heading toward Xinjiang. In July 2006, Chinese experts visited the Kyrgyz sites, and at present the most promising seems to be that of Sarydzhaz.[78]

As is the case in the hydrocarbon sector, China has arrived somewhat late on the Central Asian hydroelectricity market. The largest projects for hydroelectric stations were already launched during Soviet times and are today in the hands of Russian companies, in particular RAO-UES. Beijing is thus mostly concentrating on projects of small to medium size. Though they may not meet expectations for large-scale export, these projects nevertheless play a very important role in local economic development. China does not pretend, in any case, to be able to take possession of the Central Asian market in exclusivity. The financial weakness of Kyrgyzstan and Tajikistan quite often requires the alliance of several foreign investors to guarantee the feasibility of these costly projects.

Transportation: Roads, Tunnels, and Railways

Chinese presence in the railway sector is particularly important, so much so that China appears to be on the verge of dethroning the traditional predominance of Russia in the sector. Turkmenistan is turning out to be China's main client: in 2005, the first contract was signed between Ashgabat and a Chinese company, Capital-Lonqji Sci-Tech Co, Ltd., for the purchase of 48 diesel locomotives diesel and 50 carriages adapted to local climatic conditions (air conditioned). They are intended mainly for the new Ashgabat-Dashoguz line, and on some other sections. So, that they could afford the purchase, the Chinese firm granted the Turkmen authorities an eight-year loan. The first carriages and locomotives were delivered in 2006. In the same year, another contract was signed with the CITIC Company. The terms of the contract will see Turkmenistan purchase more than 200 carriages, 160 of which are passenger carriages, for a total of around 80 million dollars.[79]

Uzbekistan also seems interested in Chinese expertise in the rail sector and has ordered a dozen locomotives. Kazakhstan for its part began by buying only three electric locomotives, saying that it wanted to wait to test their compatibility with its network.[80] The authorities in Astana had in fact yielded to pressure from Moscow, which until then had enjoyed a quasi-monopoly over Central Asian railway infrastructure.

Indeed, Russia today refuses to allow Kazakhstan trains that include Chinese carriages into its territory, arguing that they are incompatible with the security standards in place in the post-Soviet space.[81] All the same, in 2006, the national company Kazakhstan Temir Zholy, concerned by the increasing shortage of carriages in operation in the country, decided the step needed to be taken. Astana had not bought any new foreign carriages for more than 10 years, and if this had continued by 2010, it would have had a shortage of more than 1,200 units.[82] The Kazakh State company has therefore ordered 152 passenger carriages from the Chinese factory Tian- Shan for a total cost of 60 million dollars, financed thanks to a loan from the Kazakhstan Development Bank and the Import-Export Bank of China.[83] Astana is also studying a proposal to buy carriages from China Railway New Express Transportation Equipment Co., as well as some carriages intended for agricultural products.[84]

China has also invested in the Central Asian road system. It has a twofold strategy: it is seeking to improve the roads heading toward border posts in order to increase the rhythm of trade and to disenclave the most isolated regions so as to facilitate internal communications. In Kyrgyzstan, as previously stated, Beijing has partly financed the reconstruction of the Irkeshtam-Osh highway, and the company China-Road & Bridge Corp. won the tender to construct a section of nearly 80 km on the Osh-Dushanbe highway for a cost of 15 million dollars.[85] Beijing has also financed two strategic tunnels for Tajikistan.

In March 2006, the Chinese railway company, in collaboration with some Tajik firms, began construction on the Shar-Shar tunnel located 80 km from Dushanbe. With a length of 2 km, it will allow half an hour to be saved on the road connecting the capital to Kuliab. Its cost is estimated at 40 million dollars and is to be completely financed with a loan to the Tajik government from China. The China Road Company is, for its part, involved in a different tunnel construction project at Shakhristan, situated 180 km from the capital on the road leading to Khujand. The reconstruction of the Duschanbe-Khujand-Chanak highway on the Uzbekistan border has also been financed with a Chinese loan of 280 million dollars, 70 million of which is for the tunnel.[86] These two projects are being carried out as part of the 900 million dollars in credit that China has offered to the countries of Central Asia.[87]

In both cases, Chinese aid will help communication between the capital and the remote regions of Tajikistan—Khujand in the north and Kuliab in the south—which will reinforce the country's stability. Finally, the Chinese company ECI has declared its interest in reconstructing a section of the 56 km-long railway linking Dushanbe, Kurgan-Tiube, and Nizhnii Piandzh, a project that has yet to be realised.[88]

Telecommunications

The telecommunications market is experiencing rapid expansion in Central Asia. The Central Asian states have not only to modernise their inherited Soviet-era telephone systems but also to respond to growing demands for the internet as well as to the explosion in the market for mobile telephones. In October 1998, China Telecom, a participating member of the Transit Asia Europe (TAE) Fiber Cable System, a link connecting Shanghai to Frankfurtam-Main, is developing a telephone network for four of the Central Asian states (Turkmenistan only came on board the project in 2004). The negotiations are today being undertaken principally within the SCO, which has decided to implement an Information Highway enabling better connections between the networks of member states so that they can buy and sell telephone services from each other. Thus, in 2005, all the national telecommunications operators, Rostelecom, Kazaktelecom, Tojiktelecom, Kyrgyztelecom, Uzbektelecom, and China Telecom held the first work meeting about coordinating their activities.[89]

The Sino-Central Asian rapprochement in this sector can be partly explained by Chinese expertise but also by the political situations in the two zones. That is, the Central Asian authorities are keen to buy technology limiting access to the Internet; so more and more Central Asian internet providers are functioning with Chinese software capable of blocking dissident sites. That is why, in February 2007, when the new Turkmen President Gurbanguly Berdymukhammedov reopened internet cafes, this act was accompanied by the signing of contracts with Chinese companies for software designed to control access to sites.

The principal Chinese firms in the market are, for the service sector, China Telecom and Shanghai Bell-Alcatel, and, in the technology domain, ZTE (Shenzhen Zhongxing Telecom Equipment Corporation) and Huawei Technologies. Thanks to its strong economic development, the Kazakhstan market has turned out to be the most substantial. In 2001, Kazaktelecom decided it should take advantage of the Transit Asia Europe Fiber Cable System to access the Internet via Chinese channels and not via European ones, which it considered too costly.[90]

In 2002, ZTE signed a contract with Kazaktelecom for the development of wireless telephone networks in the republic and for the installation of a more effective system of message switching (commutation system). In 2004, it invested more than 200 million dollars in setting up the CDMA-450 (Code Division Multiple Access) network in Kazakhstan as part of a joint Sino-Kazakh venture, Kazakhstan Engineering, 51 per cent of which is owned by Astana.[91] In June 2006, as part of the "Go beyond China" strategy, the national company China Telecom opened an office in Almaty.

Its aim here is not simply to establish itself in the Central Asian market but, above all, to be able to provide the necessary services to Chinese companies setting up in

Kazakhstan.[92] The second largest market is the Uzbek one: even if the standard of living in Uzbekistan is well below that of Kazakhstan, the population is larger and the demand for mobile communications is considerable. In June 2005, the Chinese Information Industry Minister, Si Gohua, went on an official visit to Tashkent accompanied by representatives from several large Chinese firms to discuss a range of agreements. During the visit, Shanghai Bell- Alcatel signed a contract with Uzbektelecom to modernise the Uzbek capital's telecommunications system. The Information Technologies University of Tashkent also plans the creation of a training center for 600 specialists from CIS countries to be partly financed by China.[93]

China Mobile Communications Corp. has expressed its desire to become a shareholder in Uzbekistan Telecom, which the authorities are in the process of privatising.[94] Several meetings between representatives from both companies took place in the summer of 2005, but appear not to have resulted in anything concrete. At the end of the same year, the Uzbek company Perfectum Mobile, one of the principal operators of the CDMA link in Uzbekistan, signed a contract with Huawei Technologies, the terms of which engage the latter to supply the necessary material to permit the whole of the country's CDMA network to be modernised.[95]

In Kyrgyzstan, the privatisation of the state-run Kyrgyztelecom, a process begun in 2001, has experienced many twists and turns, with many potential buyers later retracting offers or demanding conditions unacceptable to the authorities. In June 2006, the Kyrgyz Parliament authorised the sale of part of Kyrgyztelecom's state-held shares in order to modernise the company without privatising it *in toto*. According to its director K. Zhumaliev, since the Russian firm Rostelecom is no longer interested, the principal bidders for this new tender ought to be Chinese companies.[96]

Indeed, during a visit by the Kyrgyz President Kurmanbek Bakiev to China in June 2006, ZTE Corp. expressed its wish to buy parts of Kyrgyztelecom. The government intends to make a final decision on the matter in the second half of 2007. In addition, Huawei Technologies has been working in the country since 1998 in partnership with Kyrgyztelecom and supplies materials to all of the republic's mobile communications companies.[97] In Tajikistan, ZTE's installation attracted major attention.

In 2002, it received an order from Tojiktelecom for a commutation station between Dushanbe and Kurgan-Tiube. Then, in 2003, it won the bid for codification of the Tajik national network (CDMA), a project made possible by a loan from the EBRD and special financing from the Chinese government. And, in 2004, it became the sole shareholder of TK Mobile, which is the fifth largest mobile communications company in Tajikistan, while the third largest in terms of the number of subscribers, Babilon-Mobile, made a decision to buy its supplies exclusively from Huawei Technologies.[98] In May 2006, Huawei Technologies and the Vympelkom firm, which is active in many countries within the CIS, came to an agreement about installing GSM BTS networks in Tajikistan.[99] In June of the same year, during a visit by Tajik President Emomali Rakhmonov to Shanghai, ZTE announced its intention to invest 70 million dollars in three large telecommunications projects, the details of which have not yet been released.[100]

The situation is very similar in Turkmenistan. Mobile communications in the country still being very limited, Chinese companies have been able to invest primarily in the domain of modernising standard telephone networks. At the beginning of 2000, for example, ZTE won the tender for the codification of Turkmenistan's national network.[101] In 2004, Huawei Technologies supplied Ashgabat with modern equipment for a total of nearly 5 million dollars. This Chinese company has committed itself to establishing new telephone cable networks for the capital and the main cities in the country.

It has also agreed to modernise the commutation systems and to link Turkmenistan to the Transit Asia Europe Fiber Cable System. These projects are being carried out as part of an agreement signed between both countries in December 2002, which makes provision for interest-free loans from China to Turkmenistan in order to facilitate cooperation in the telecommunications sector.[102] In April 2006, both countries signed a new cooperation agreement which provides Ashgabat with a credit of 200 million yuans from the State Bank of Foreign Trade and Import-Export Bank of China so that it can buy Chinese supplies for fixed telephony, mobile communications, and radio networks.[103]

Hydrocarbon Question

The Chinese appetite for energy contributes to the strengthening of relations with the Central Asian regimes, which are all in search of new export markets for their hydrocarbons in order to loosen their reliance on Russia.[104] Even if production costs for Central Asian hydrocarbons prove higher than those in the Middle East, they hold two advantages: Beijing considers them reliable long-term investments and insists on political alliances and solid coordination of interests between the involved states.[105]

However, the construction of gas and oil pipelines connecting Central Asian fields to Chinese markets is a technically and financially complex affair. The distances involved range from 3,000 to 10,000 km, and the costs run up to several billion dollars. In addition, China arrived several years after the main international companies, which established themselves on the most promising sites. Beijing failed to take part in the exploitation of the Kashagan field, one of the five largest in the world with an estimated production of 1.5 Mbbls/d in 2015, and of Tengiz, the production of which should reach 700 kbbls/d in 2015.[106] China can certainly continue to be an actor in the Central Asian and Caspian petroleum sectors without these fields, but one with only secondary importance. Chinese firms tend to acquire second-rate fields and seek to establish themselves in countries like Uzbekistan, which are somewhat overlooked in petroleum and gas matters. However, China's breakthrough, accomplished in just a few short years, is still very visible. With various pipeline start-up projects, it is also considered quite significant.

This Chinese presence, increasingly visible on those markets more marginal than Kazakhstan, like Uzbekistan, could profoundly modify the geopolitics of the entire region, reorienting it, and its hydrocarbons, to the south and to the east.

Expansion of Chinese Demand

Until 1993, the People's Republic of China was petroleum self-sufficient, even becoming a net exporter of oil in the 1980s. But, its exponential economic development, with growth rates nearing ten per cent per year, suddenly highlighted China's dependence on foreign suppliers. Today the country imports more than 40 per cent of its energy consumption, a figure that could rise to 85 per cent by 2030. In a few years, China became the second-largest consumer of energy in the world after the United States. It also passed Japan as the world's No. 2 importer of energy, after the United States, buying more than 140 Mt of oil in 2004. According to the U.S. Department of State, Chinese demand for petroleum will more than double by 2020, reaching 11 million b/d, while that of natural gas will triple to 3.6 bcm per year.[107]

Though the country still consumes massive amounts of coal, petroleum represents a quarter of current energy consumption.[108] Natural gas remains scarcely utilised, around three per cent, but the Chinese authorities hope to expand its use to ten per cent of national energy consumption.[109]

To address this increasing demand for energy, in 1997, Chinese authorities decided to put offensive strategies into place, of which their principle, unifying element is the purchase of oil fields abroad. The main state actors included the China National Petroleum Corporation (CNPC) and its affiliates, such as the China National Offshore Oil Corporation (CNOOC) specialising in foreign investment, the National Oil and Gas Exploration and Development Corporation (CNODC), and the firm Sinopec (China National Petrochemical Corporation), which invests in refineries. They benefited from the new resources allotted to them and the support from authorities to secure provisions for the country. Reinforcing Beijing's energy choices was the war in Iraq, which was perceived as a threat to energy security. The priorities of China are thus clearly defined:

1. The authorities want to continue to develop the domestic production of oil and gas, a policy pursued since the 1980s. Indeed, China has its own crude oil reserves, estimated in 2005 by BP at 2.3 billion tonnes, or 1.4 per cent of world reserves. They are located mainly in the north and west of the country, far from the centers of consumption in the east and south. The fields exploited since the 1960s and 1970s, mainly Daqing and Shengli, started to become exhausted or increasingly expensive to operate. Beijing thus decided to develop new fields in Tibet and especially in Xinjiang, which could contain up to one-third of the country's oil and gas reserves. The Tarim Basin, considered the most promising, opened for investment in 1993. Numerous

multinational companies speculated, but the actual reserves there proved somewhat disappointing.[110]

However, Xinjiang quickly became the third-largest oil-producing province, at 35 million tonnes per year, and Beijing hopes to make it the energy center of the country by 2010. The authorities also expanded offshore oil exploration, in particular in the South China Sea, but these sites are both difficult to exploit and the object of territorial disputes with Vietnam, the Philippines, and Japan.

2. China wants not only to diversify its imports, but also to secure them by directly acquiring foreign oil fields. In less than one year, between 1997 and 1998, China spent more than eight billion dollars in purchasing oil fields in the Sudan, Venezuela, and Kazakhstan.[111] This strategy aims to decrease dependence on the states of the Persian Gulf (Saudi Arabia, Iran, Oman, Yemen, Kuwait, and Iraq), which currently supply more than half of China's petroleum imports. The authorities worry about the volatility of the Middle Eastern market and the risks of political destabilisation. For this reason, Chinese firms seek to establish themselves in areas such as the former Soviet Union, sub-Saharan Africa (especially the Sudan), and Latin America. However, these new markets cannot replace the dominance of the Middle East.[112]

3. China also seeks to reduce its dependence on energy importation by tankers, which are much too subject to the geopolitical risks of the market. The country worries about the risks of "energy containment" by the United States, in particular the control of the Strait of Malacca, through which 60 per cent of Chinese oil exports pass.[113]

Therefore the Chinese strategy is to avoid tanker transportation as much as possible and give priority to continental oil and gas pipelines. This includes the expansion of gas consumption, as Chinese authorities see gas as less dependent on geopolitical issues and more in line with the continental logics that Beijing endorses. At the same time, this policy must remain marginalised because China does not have the ability to build the dozens of pipelines that would be necessary to satisfy the demands of consumption.

The Chinese "energy thirst" obliges the country to develop paradoxical commercial logics. As large Western companies already control the majority of exploitable oil fields, Chinese companies must specialise in old or difficult-to-exploit fields, or settle in countries seen as unstable or have sanctions imposed on them by the international community. In addition, they do not benefit from the same technical skills as the large Western firms, and prefer to minimise the risks of exploration by utilising already-known extraction sites. On their side, however, Chinese firms have the diplomatic and financial support of Beijing, which enables them to outbid competitors during negotiations and put forward complementary "good neighbor" measures. These strategies elicit angry reactions from competitors, who often perceive Chinese energy policy as overly aggressive.

Chinese Desire for Kazakh Oil

Sino-Kazakh negotiations over petroleum began in 1994, during the visit of Chinese Prime Minister Li Peng to Kazakhstan. Some preliminary discussions with China National Offshore Oil Corporation took place over the common exploitation of offshore fields in the Caspian Sea. The real beginning of cooperation on petroleum dates to 1997, when two important contracts were signed within the framework of a general agreement between the two countries that invited the CNPC and its subsidiaries to invest in Kazakh fields. A second turning point in Sino-Kazakh energy relations occurred in 2003 with the start up of the Atasu-

Alashankou pipeline project and the purchase of new fields. In less than one decade, Chinese companies thus succeeded with their grand entrance into the Kazakh market, mainly by accepting the authorities' requirement that all oil companies include the state firm KazMunaiGaz in their activities.

Purchase of Fields

The Chinese strategy for the purchase of oil and gas fields is influenced by the fact that Beijing was late in its arrival in the Kazakh market, and can thus acquire sites only of relative marginal importance. In spite of this negative initial condition, China sought to follow logic in its acquisitions. It invests in fields located in the Aktobe region and near the Caspian Sea, so as not to be absent from the energy center of Central Asia, and is also involved in more isolated fields that have the advantage of being located along the path of the Sino-Kazakh pipeline.

Aktobemunaigaz, the Success of the CNPC

In 1997, the CNPC created surprise when it gained a tender from the Kazakh government. It thus acquired 60 per cent of the shares of the oil company Aktobemunaigaz, based in the Aktobe region. It has a twenty-year user license for the Zhanazhol gas site and the Kenkiyak oil site. To gain this tender, the CNPC knew it had to win the favor of the Kazakh authorities for itself. It was committed to investing four billion dollars by 2010, of which 540 million came in the first five years, returning 71 million of company debt, guaranteeing pensions for 5,000 employees, and giving a 325 million dollar allowance to the Kazakh government.[114] In 2003, the CNPC reinforced its presence in Aktobemunaigaz when it acquired an additional 25 per cent of shares in the company, formerly held by the Kazakh government, for 150 million dollars.[115] The Aktobemunaigaz Company currently controls oneseventh of oil production in Kazakhstan, and is essentially Chinese property, as CNPC owns more than 85 per cent of it.

Since 2001, the company has increased its production by more than one million tonnes per year. In 2006, it produced nearly 10 million tonnes of oil and 1.5 bcm of gas. The CNPC functions in an autonomous way, because all of its extractive equipment comes from China. It manages the entire cycle (extraction, production, and infrastructure) and has built or renovated several gas processing plants (GPP) since 2002. In 2003, it opened the Zhanazhol GPP, with an annual capacity of 1.4 bcm. The following year it finished a 160 km pipeline connecting Zhanazhol to the compression station KS-13, a junction on the Bukhara-Ural gas pipeline.[116] In 2003, the CNPC purchased a network of retail petroleum products at a cost of 25 million dollars. It planned to build factories producing asphalt and refined oil for Kazakhstan. In 2007, it announced an investment of more than a half-million dollars in production, that is to say one-third more than investments in 2006. The estimated total reserves of Zhanazhol and Kenkiyak are 570 million tonnes, less than five per cent of the reserves in Kazakhstan.

Chinese Disengagement from Uzen

Also in 1997, the CNPC beat Amoco, Texaco, and Unocal-Petronas for a second tender to develop the Uzen oil structure, a field located on the Mangistau Peninsula (formerly Mangychlak). The CNPC accepted the terms, according to which the Kazakh state retained ownership of the field, and proposed to invest nine billion dollars in the development of the field and pipeline construction, a financial promise that has proved impossible to keep.[117] These two acquisitions in 1997—Uzen and Aktobemunaigaz—were indeed accompanied by two pipeline construction projects, one of 3,200 km toward Xinjiang, the other toward Iran via Turkmenistan. However, the second project immediately ran afoul of US embargoes against Iran (the 1996 Iran and Libya Sanctions Act, renewed in 2001). The first project was sidelined when the low price of hydrocarbons in the second half of the 1990s made its construction unprofitable. In 1999, Chinese authorities officially abandoned the idea because the reserves of the Uzen field were not sufficient to ensure the profitability of the pipeline. [118] The CNPC ended up withdrawing from the project and yielded 100 per cent of its shares to Uzenmunaigaz, a subsidiary of KazMunaiGaz. Since then, only the Kazakh authorities, with international financing, have exploited Uzen.[119]

Collapse of Chinese Participation in Kashagan

In 2003, the CPNC launched a new wave of acquisitions in Kazakhstan. In May, the CNPC and Sinopec attempted to acquire 16.67 per cent of the shares of the Agip KCO international consortium, or the North Caspian Sea Project (NCSP), which exploits several Caspian sites, including Kashagan. Indeed, the firm British Gas wished to sell its shares for 1.23 billion dollars, and had accepted China's offer, which also enjoyed the support of the Kazakh government. The other members of the consortium (Shell, Exxon-Mobil, TotalFinaElf, Conoco Phillips, and Agip) refused such Chinese participation, and requested to exert their right of pre-emption over British Gas' shares.[120] After repurchasing British Gas' shares, China sold half of them to KazMunaiGaz under pressure from the Kazakh authorities. This rejection of Chinese participation created a conflict between Shell and Beijing that threatened to block the investments of that company in China.[121] China then failed to directly establish itself within the Kashagan structure, the most dynamic of the Caspian area, in spite of support from Astana.

Purchase of North Buzachi

Not able to take part in Kashagan, the company decided to invest massively in onshore fields in order to prepare for the filling of the Sino-Kazakh pipeline. In August of that year, it repurchased 35 per cent of its shares in the North Buzachi field, which is located in the Mangistau region north of Aktau, from the Saudi company Nimir Petroleum. Two months later, it repurchased the remaining 65 per cent from Texaco North Buzachi Inc.[122] For a total of 210 million dollars, the CNPC became the sole holder of this field, with reserves estimated between 40 and 70 Mt (approximately 10,000 b/d). It also acquired the Bars exploration site at 5,600 km2 located around the Buzachi field.

However, in December 2003, the CNPC suddenly decided to transfer half of its shares to a Kazakh-Canadian company, Nelson Resources Ltd.[123] The two companies planned to invest nearly 100 million dollars in the field and reach a maximum extractive capacity of 40,000 b/d in 2017. The site's reserves are estimated at 205 million tonnes of oil, that is to say oneeightieth of the total reserves in Kazakhstan. Nearly all, 85 per cent, of the oil extracted there is sold to the West through the Atyrau-Samara pipeline. It is also suspected that some of the oil from Buzachi is exported to the Iranian port of Neka on the Caspian Sea, where it is then sold according to a barter agreement. The common management of the field was complicated when Lukoil (cf. infra) purchased Nelson Resources Ltd. The CNPC then announced its intention of acquiring the 50 per cent stake belonging to Nelson Resources. According to them, Lukoil's repurchase broke a contract giving the CNPC a right to acquire Nelson's shares in a pre-emptive way.[124] The legal status of the field remains complex today.

Contested Purchase of Petrokazakhstan

In 2005, the CNPC pulled off the most important foreign acquisition ever undertaken by a Chinese company, that of Petrokazakhstan (formerly Hurricane Hydrocarbons). The CNPC outbid its Indian competitor ONGC (Oil and Natural Gas Corp.) by offering to pay 4.2 billion dollars, regarded by some as an overvaluation. Kazakhstan thus became the second-largest foreign base of production, after the Sudan, for the CNPC. Petrokazakhstan, based in Canada, possesses twelve per cent of Kazakhstan's oil production at 150,000 b/d, or nearly 10 Mt. It manages twelve oil-bearing fields, including North Kumkol (entirely under its control) and Southern Kumkol (shared control with Lukoil).[125] Faced with this Chinese offensive, the Kazakh Parliament passed a law guaranteeing itself a right of pre-emption on energy issues, and, thus, preventing Petrokazakhstan from selling its shares without the agreement of the political authorities. Kazakh President Nursultan Nazarbayev finally agreed to this repurchase, but forced the CNPC to yield a third of its shares to KazMunaiGaz. The Chinese firm also sold half of the shares of the Chymkent refinery, the most modern in the country, which Petrokazakhstan had held up to that point.

However, the legal saga became particularly complex and quickly became internationalised. The transaction elicited the reaction of Lukoil, which shares a subsidiary with Petrokazakhstan—Turgai Petroleum. The two companies had already been in litigation since 2004 over questions of financial compensation. Since the announcement of the repurchase by the CNPC, Lukoil appeared before an Alberta court in order to block this transfer based on its 50 per cent ownership of Turgai Petroleum. The court refused this request, but Lukoil appealed before the Court of Arbitration of Stockholm, which confirmed in 2006 that the Russian company had a right of pre-emption over half of Turgai Petroleum. The CNPC counter-attacked by invoking its right of pre-emption over half of the Buzachi field.[126]

At the end of 2006, Lukoil acquired Nelson Resources Ltd. for two billion dollars. The firm controls one per cent of Kazakh oil, and manages several fields, two of which, Alibekmola and Kozhasay, are located near Aktobe.[127] It includes several companies that are influential in Kazakhstan, such as Central Asia Industrial Holdings, Energy Investments International, and Cott Holdings.

Competition between Chinese firms and Russian firms in Kazakhstan is likely to experience more fluctuation, as Lukoil announced its desire to continue its presence in Kazakhstan, where it has already invested 4.5 billion dollars.

Sinopec's Purchases

In 2003, Shengli Oilfield, a subsidiary company of Sinopec, purchased 50 per cent of the shares of Big Sky Energy Kazakhstan, a company based in Canada that belongs to China Energy Ventures Corp. Big Sky has licenses to develop three small onshore sites: Morskoe, located near Tengiz, Karatal, and Dauletaty, close to Atyrau. In addition, China Energy Ventures Corp. owned two other blocks: Liman-2 and Atyrau. In 2004, Sinopec withdrew from Big Sky and announced its intention to invest itself in larger and more expensive projects. It did so by acquiring American First International Oil Company (FIOC), in Houston, for more than 160 million dollars. FIOC first established itself in Kazakhstan in 1997, buying the user licenses of small fields (like Fedorov, Mezhdurechensk, Sagiz, Begaidar, and Sazankurak) spread out over more than 17,000 km2 in the west of the country, and often exploiting them with Russian partners. FIOC also manages, with Rosneft, the promising site of Adai. Its reserves are estimated at 100 million tonnes of oil and nearly 400 bcm of gas. This repurchase will thus make it possible for Sinopec to invest in several Kazakh fields and to eventually supplement acquisitions of the CNPC.[128]

Offshore Darkhan Site

In August 2005, CNOOC and KazMunaiGaz signed an agreement to jointly explore the Darkhan field in the Kazakh area of the Caspian Sea. Located east of the Kurmangazy site and 60 km south of Bautino, its reserves are estimated at 480 million tonnes of oil with approximately nine exploitable areas.[129] The Kazakh government long sought a partner for this venture, and only the Indian ONGC displayed interest. China hopes to attain a production of 60 million tonnes in 2015, a figure that seems particularly optimistic. Even if the Darkhan site is not Kashagan, its acquisition makes it possible for Beijing to finally be a player in the vast, offshore Caspian reserves after its failure to take part in the exploitation of Kashagan in 2003.

Purchase of Energy Nations and the Karazhanbas Site

In December 2006, the Chinese state firm CITIC Group (China International Trust and Investment Company, based in Hong Kong) announced that it had just concluded the purchase of Nations Energy (Indonesia) for nearly two billion dollars. In 1997, Nations Energy acquired the KarazhanbasMunai firm, which holds twenty-year exploitation rights for the Karazhanbas field, located 230 km north of Aktau.[130] Nations Energy invested more than one billion dollars in this site, whose proven reserves are more than 340 million barrels of oil and whose production is more than 50,000 b/d. CITIC Group proposed that KazMunaiGaz buy half of the field at a discount, and promised the Kazakh government to build a refinery near Mangistau to make Kazakhstan independent in the production of asphalt.

Construction of Pipelines

The two Chinese establishment strategies in Kazakhstan—the purchase of fields and the construction of pipelines—are intrinsically linked, as China seeks to insure its investments. The two objectives are, however, not entirely unified. For instance, Russian pipelines and the CPC (Caspian Pipeline Consortium) export westward the production of some Caspian sites acquired by Beijing, while the pipeline bound for China will not only be filled with the oil of Chinese companies, but also with oil coming from Russia or international firms in Kazakhstan. Overall, the Chinese strategy remains the connection of all of the acquired fields with the gigantic Sino-Kazakh pipeline under-construction.

Competition over Siberian Projects

The Sino-Kazakh pipeline project quickly took form at the beginning of the 2000s, indirectly due to the difficulties China encountered in its negotiations with Russia. It seems that when the first pipeline project was abandoned in 1999, Beijing was clearly under the influence of Yukos, which wanted to be perceived as a priority, to the detriment of Kazakhstan. Boris Yeltsin launched the project of a Sino-Russian pipeline connecting Angarsk, in Yakutia, to Daqing, in the Heilongjiang province, at the beginning of the

1990s.[131] A feasibility study was carried out in 2000. Moscow and Beijing had agreed to a 2,400 km pipeline at an estimated cost of nearly three billion dollars. However, since 2002, the project underwent several important changes. Japan pressured the Russian authorities to give priority to a competitor project that would join the port of Nakhodka, giving a glimmer of hope in Russia to the possibility of reaching several prospective customers:

Japan, China, South Korea, and Taiwan. Finally, as Yukos supported the Chinese project, the arrest of Mikhail Khodorkovsky in 2003 seems to have slowed the Angarsk-Daqing plans for the long term. This situation led the Chinese authorities to favor Kazakhstan and to restart their interest in the Caspian Sea. In the mid-term, imports from Russia remain the least expensive option, but complex Sino-Russian relations serve to weaken Moscow vis-à-vis Central Asian regimes, which are willing to grant more concessions in order to attract Chinese investment.

Three Sections of the Atyrau-Alashankou Pipeline

In 1999, the first pipeline project proposed by China during its acquisition of the Aktobe and Uzen fields was shelved. After the discovery of the gigantic offshore Kashagan site, Kazakhstan returned this project to the negotiation table. The idea of a pipeline connecting the Caspian Sea to Xinjiang was revived in 2002. This pipeline, known as Atyrau-Alashankou, is divided into three sections.

The first, located in the west of the country, connects the Kenkiyak field to Atyrau over a length of 448 km. For its construction, the CNPC and KazMunaiGaz founded the company MunaiTas, held in equal portions by the two companies. Operational since 2003, the Kenkiyak-Atyrau section had the capacity to transport six million tonnes each year, but a new phase completed in 2006 has increased this to fourteen million.[132] It allows the oil extracted from the Chinese fields in Kenkiyak and Zhanazhol to join the Atyrau-

Samara pipeline and the CPC for export to European markets. The second section, located in the east of the country, connects the pumping station and railway terminal in Atasu, in the Karaganda region, to the Dostyk-Alashankou station on the Sino-Kazakh frontier. Atasu has the advantage of being en route to the Omsk-Pavlodar-Chymkent pipeline, making possible a connection to Russian oil.

The joint construction venture between CNODC and KazMunaiGaz was negotiated in 2003 and began in 2004.[133] The Atasu-Alashankou section, 988 km in length, cost 700 million dollars. It was inaugurated in December 2005, and has been operational since May 2006. The third section (KAK) will connect Kenkiyak to the Kumkol fields via the town of Aralsk over a length of 750 km and at an estimated cost of 511 million dollars. It will be complete in 2011. The last part of the pipeline, between Kumkol and Atasu, has existed since the Soviet period. Thus, once Kenkiyak-Kumkol is in operation in 2011, China will have a direct link with the Caspian Sea at its disposal.

During his December 2006 visit to China, President Nazarbayev, accompanied by his energy and mineral resources minister, Baktykozha Izmukhambetov, continued to promote energy cooperation between the two countries. Astana and Beijing signed two letters of intent. The first concerns the construction of the missing section of Kenkiyak-Kumkol. The second seeks to double the capacity of the Atasu-Alashankou pipeline to 400,000 b/d.[134] With the operational median section, the Sino-Kazakh pipeline will have a total length of more than 3,000 km, or 2,818 km in Kazakh territory and 270 km in Chinese territory.

During this first phase, the export capacity of the pipeline will be approximately ten million tonnes, but this will increase to twenty million after 2011. On the Chinese side, it is supplemented by an intra-Chinese pipeline, the Alashankou-Dushanzi Crude Oil Pipeline, which connects the border-post refinery at Dushanzi to Xinjiang. In 2010, the refinery will become a petrochemical complex capable of treating over one million tonnes of oil per year.[135] Indeed, the strategy of the CNPC in Kazakhstan makes sense only when placed in its intra-Chinese context. The objective of these acquisitions is not only to provide energy to Xinjiang, but also to the densely populated, maritime East China. Thanks to the new east-west, intra-Chinese pipeline, Kazakh oil can henceforth be expedited over 2,000 km to Lanzhou and its refinery.

Issue of Filling the Pipeline

Once complete in 2011, the Sino-Kazakh pipeline will have the capacity to transport twenty million tonnes of oil each year—the amount necessary for it to be profitable. From that point, it could later be increased up to 50 million tonnes. Thus, the question of filling the pipeline is strategic as it ensures the profitability of the operation, justifies China's policies of purchasing fields, and requires negotiations with other operators.

The Chinese import of Kazakh oil seems exponential in its growth. In 2005, China exported 1.3 million tonnes of oil by rail via Alashankou, while in 2007, the country hoped to transport up to eight million tonnes of oil through Atasu-Alashankou. Since China will use only 80 per cent of the pipeline capacity, it must be supplemented by Russian oil. In 2005, Chinese production in Kazakhstan reached six million tonnes, with 5.5 million tonnes coming from Aktobe and 500,000 tonnes from Buzachi. Such production in the west of the country will be difficult to export to China as long as the third missing section of the pipeline remains unfinished. A small part of the Chinese oil produced in

Zhanazhol, Kenkiyak, and Buzachi is sold in Western Europe via the CPC; the majority is refined on the spot, however, and sold locally, and what remains joins Atasu by railroad. However, the CNPC hopes to direct most of this oil toward China after the completion of the pipeline in 2011.

For the moment, the Atasu-Alashankou section accommodates mainly oil from the Kumkol fields. They particularly interest Beijing because they are closest to the Chinese border and are located on the halfway point of the pipeline. Since 2001, Petrokazakhstan has delivered, by rail, nearly 500,000 tonnes of oil (128,000 b/d), extracted in Kumkol, to China. Since 2006, this flow passes by the pipeline, to which China hopes to add either the reserves managed by Petrokazakhstan, approximately five million tonnes, and those of Turgai Petroleum, at three million. Lukoil also wishes to use the Atasu- Alashankou section by re-orientating the production of its parts of Turgai Petroleum in the direction of China. Up to then, the CPC exported them westward. In addition, while purchasing FIOC, Sinopec awarded a contract of one million tonnes of oil (and several bcm of gas) that will eventually be added to the fields the CNPC manages.[136] In 2010, Chinese production in Kazakhstan should reach 14 million tonnes, and therefore occupy approximately two-thirds of the pipeline's 20 million tonne capacity. For its part, KazMunaiGaz plans to transport nearly five million tonnes of oil from Kashagan to China.

But, to be profitable, the Sino-Kazakh pipeline must find additional provisions from Russia. China hopes to convince Russian companies to launch barter operations, exchanging Chinese oil produced in Zhanazhol and Kenkiyak, exported via the Atyrau-Samara pipeline, for Russian oil exported to China via the Atasu-Alashankou pipeline. Several Russian companies have demonstrated interest. Because of this pipeline, they could enter the Chinese market well before the Siberian and Far East pipelines are complete.[137] Transneft, for example, indicated its desire to send a part of its production to China, via the Sino-Kazakh pipeline. Rosneft stated its interest in exporting its oil from Western Siberia to China by connecting Atasu at a junction with the Omsk-Pavlodar-Chymkent pipeline. The Russian company was also committed to building with the CNPC, and its PetroChina subsidiary, a refinery to treat Russian oil near to Beijing in 2010. The fields of Khvalynsk and Tsentralnoye, which Lukoil exploits with KazMunaiGaz, could also see part of their production shift toward China.[138]

Thus, the issue of production volume is crucial for Kazakhstan. A few years ago, Kazakh production seemed insufficient to supply just one pipeline, which became profitable only with the participation of Russia. Since the discovery of Kashagan, as well as the exploitation of the onshore fields of Tengiz and Karachaganak, Kazakhstan has become an autonomous partner. Astana estimates that the country will produce 120 million tonnes of oil in 2007 and 180 million in 2015. Kashagan will be operational around the year 2010. By this time, the Atyrau-Samara pipeline and Caspian Pipeline Consortium, which connects Caspian fields to Russian ports on the Black Sea, will no longer be sufficient to export all of Kazakhstan's production. However, the Atyrau-Alashankou pipeline could be partially in competition with the Baku-Tbilisi-Ceyhan pipeline (Kazakh oil has arrived by tanker at Baku from the port of Aktau.)[139]

Future of Sino-Kazakh Oil Relations

China's rise to power on the Kazakh energy market seems to elicit increasingly sharp reactions from official circles. By fall 2006, several members of the Kazakh parliament were worried about China's many purchases of Caspian fields. Deputy of the Parliament Valery Kotovich, member of the presidential party Otan, declared that the country was losing its energy independence. He presented distorted figures, according to which China will soon control 40 per cent of Kazakh oil production.[140] Faced with the reactions that the announcement of the purchase of Energy Nations caused, Energy Minister Bakhytkozha Izmukhambetov declared that he would do everything possible to block the project; which proved not be the case. The deputies also worried about the announcement made by Central Asia Petroleum (Jakarta), which seeks to sell its shares in the company MangistauMunaiGaz (115,000 b/d) to China.

In spite of these reactions, the authorities in Astana have done little to diminish their favor for Chinese investment in the country. At all costs, Kazakhstan wants to distance itself from Russia, which dominates the two principal export routes, Atyrau- Samara and the CPC. In addition, Astana did not appreciate the Kremlin's recent rejection of support for its project to buy a refinery in Lithuania. Russia also refused to increase the transport capacity of the CPC, which is likely to force Chevron Texaco to transport surplus production by rail instead of pipeline in the coming years.

The clearly Sinophile choice of the Kazakh authorities thus confirms that China will become a privileged partner of Kazakhstan; however, in its current state, Beijing cannot compete with the large Western companies that dominate the Caspian basin. Indeed, the consortiums Agip KCO and Tengizchevroil possess 67 per cent of the total hydrocarbon reserves in the country. In 2006, China managed approximately 24 per cent of Kazakh production: Aktobemunaigaz (5.8 million tonnes, or ten per cent), Turgai-Petroleum (three million tonnes, or five per cent), Kumkol Resources (3.1 million tonnes, or five per cent), and KarazhanbasMunai (2.2 million tonnes, or four per cent.)[141] Even if the production figures of Chinese companies in Kazakhstan increases quickly, however, due to technical improvements, the exploration of still-undiscovered sites, and the strategic purchase of new fields, China's proportional share of total Kazakh oil production will decrease as the exploitation of Tengiz and Kashagan increases the size of the pie. For its part, Kazakhstan will play an increasingly important part in the supply of oil to China. In 2004, Astana represented less than one per cent of Chinese supply, but it will reach five per cent with the completion of the pipeline in 2011 (20 Mt out of the 400 that China will need to import). Still, in spite of this successful Sino-Kazakh cooperation, Central Asia will not be able to replace China's dependence on Middle Eastern oil.

Other Chinese Projects in the Central Asian Oil and Gas Sector

Kazakhstan largely dominates Sino-Central Asian oil sector cooperation; however, some new and more modest partners, such as Uzbekistan, are starting to make their appearance known. With large Western companies being absent from the Uzbek oil market, China can more easily establish itself there, and hopes that the under-developed Aral Sea and Ustiurt Plateau areas will fulfill their potential. From the beginning of the 2000s, Kyrgyzstan tried to interest China in its few oil and gas fields, too. In 2002, Beijing announced its desire to invest 300 million dollars in fields located in the south of the republic in order to help enhance its own energy independence. CNNC and Kyrgyzneftgaz signed a cooperative agreement.[142]

In 2004, Sinopec subsidiary, China's Shengli Oil Company, confirmed that it would participate in the reconstruction of Kyrgyzstan's outdated, eroding oil wells.[143] Nevertheless, the majority of these projects remain on paper, and Sino-Kyrgyz cooperation has moved to other sectors. In the oil sector,

Kazakhstan is therefore destined to remain Bejing's premier partner, with Uzbekistan following as a distant second. The gas issue is more complex because its transportation is much more expensive than that of oil. It also necessitates a favorable regional context, since many countries must agree to allow the gas pipeline to cross their respective territories. In spite of a challenging regional situation, Sino-Central Asian gas projects continue to grow, and could be finalised in the years to come if Kazakhstan, Turkmenistan, and Uzbekistan are able to agree among themselves to jointly sell their gas resources to China.

Kazakh Gas

Sino-Kazakh gas negotiations began in 2002 between Kazakh Deputy Prime Minister Karim Masimov and Chinese National Oil and Gas Corporation President Mi Fucai. The first feasibility studies examined the possibility of a connection with Turkmen gas via the Central Asia-Center gas pipeline, although the latter could then enter into competition with Kazakh gas.[144] In 2006, the Kazakh authorities signed an initial construction agreement with the CNPC and its PetroChina subsidiary. A new feasibility study will take place during 2007 and construction will begin in 2008. The gas pipeline will have a capacity of 10 bcm in 2009, and then expand to 30 bcm in 2012. Two routes are currently being studied, one southern (Chelkar, Kzyl-Orda, Chymkent, Almaty) and one through the center (Astana-Karaganda). The southernmost route appears to be the most profitable because it would also fulfill the need for gas delivery to energy-poor southern Kazakhstan.

The new layout could join with the already-existing Bukhara-Tashkent-Bishkek- Almaty gas pipeline.[145] The gas would come from the Kazakh Karachaganak, Tengiz, and Kashagan fields, and maybe from Turkmenistan. In 2010,

Kazakhstan hopes to produce nearly 50 bcm annually, of which half would be intended for the domestic market and approximately 20 bcm for export.

These Central Asian gas pipeline projects have only made sense since China decided to build an intra-Chinese pipeline, the West-East Gas Pipeline. It goes from the Tarim Basin in Xinjiang (Lunnan gas field) to join Shanghai through Gansu, Ningxia, Shaanxi, Shanxi, Henan, Anhui, and Jiangsu over a distance of more than 4,200 km. The first section was started in 2003, and it was put in operation at the end of 2004. Plans exist to upgrade its capacity from 12 bcm to 17 bcm by 2007. The West-East Gas Pipeline will thus have sufficient capacity to accommodate a portion of Central Asian gas and to transfer it to Shanghai.

Turkmen Gas

Since 1992, the Japanese firm Mitsubishi has proposed a Sino-Turkmen gas pipeline project in the hope that it would then join Japan from the Chinese coast. The subject was broached in 1994 during meetings between former Turkmen President Sapamurat Niyazov and Chinese Prime Minister Li Peng.[146] The CNPC prepared a preliminary feasibility study in collaboration with Mitsubishi and Exxon-Mobil, which envisaged a gas pipeline of almost 6,000 km able to transport up to 30 bcm each year from the Turkmen Dauletabad field to Shanshan in Xinjiang.[147] The excessive cost of this project—more than ten billion dollars—and the need for negotiations with several transit states contributed to its eventual shelving, although, since 1999, Kazakhstan has declared itself ready to become a transit country.

At the beginning of the 2000s, the rising price of oil and gas, the growth of the exploitation of the Tarim Basin fields, and the construction of the West-East Gas Pipeline renewed interest in the project. Indeed, the CNPC argued that additional provisioning from Central Asia would make it possible to guarantee the profitability of the West-East Gas Pipeline in the event of failure of the Tarim fields.

In 2004, Turkmengaz and the China Petroleum Technology and Development Corporation signed a 14.5 million dollar contract to supply equipment for repairs of gas wells in Turkmenistan.[148] Debate over the East Asia Gas Pipeline started again in 2005, when Niyazov announced that he had negotiated the price of Turkmen gas with Beijing at approximately 80 dollars per 1,000 m3, and discussed the construction of a pipeline to China through Kazakhstan and Uzbekistan.

In 2006, Beijing demonstrated its goodwill to the authorities in Ashgabat by financing the restoration of the Seidi oil refinery. In April of the same year, during Niyazov's visit to Beijing, the two countries signed an energy agreement according to which Turkmenistan will deliver 30 bcm of gas to China in 2009, hoping to reach 50 bcm in 2010.[149] During his trip to China in December 2006, Nazarbayev made it clear that the Sino-Turkmen gas pipeline could pass through Kazakhstan to avoid Uzbekistan, which is considered too unstable.[150]

In addition, China calmed Russian fears by reaffirming that it did not plan to take over areas intended *a priori* for Gazprom, but rather new fields in the Amu-Darya region. Negotiations must be held during 2007 to determine the methods of implementation of the agreement with regard to the construction of the gas pipeline, but also the exploitation of four oil and gas blocks on the right bank of the Amu-Darya River. In March 2007, the Import-Export Bank of China and the Turkmen State Bank for Foreign Economic Affairs signed two loan agreements totaling 26 million dollars for the purchase of drill material.[151]

Chinese Investments in Uzbekistan

Energy relations between the PRC and Uzbekistan became extensive only after Chinese President Hu Jintao's visit to Tashkent in June 2004. On this occasion, the CNPC and the state firm Uzbekneftegaz signed several projects confirming that the CNPC, which had already exported 80 million dollars of equipment necessary for the exploitation of ten wells, hoped to establish itself in Uzbekistan in a more significant way. For instance, the Harbin Xiandai Group set up liquefied petroleum gas and water meter factories in Tashkent. Sino-Uzbek cooperation in energy matters became more extensive in 2005, after the geo-strategic rapprochement that followed the events in Andijan. During Islam Karimov's visit to Beijing on May 25, 2005, the two leaders introduced several new projects.[152] The CNPC and Uzbekneftegaz signed an agreement instituting UzCNPC Petroleum, a joint venture responsible for exploration and the exploitation of oil-bearing fields in Bukhara and Khiva areas. It proposes up to 600 million dollars of investment in a score of small fields located in eastern Uzbekistan. Beijing also granted a 35 million dollar loan to Tashkent for the improvement of its oil and gas transport system.

Another joint venture was created in July 2005 between Uzbekneftegaz and Sinopec to develop still non-operational wells and to explore fields near Andijan. An overall investment of more than 100 million dollars over five years was agreed upon, half of which was intended for exploration, with the other half slated for the redevelopment of old sites.[153]

However, the project was suddenly abandoned in April 2007, without explanation from Uzbek or Sinopec authorities.[154] This cooperation between the CNPC and Uzbekneftegaz continued in 2006 with two projects. The first was signed in June. One of the subsidiaries of the CNPC—CNODC—announced that it planned to invest 210 million dollars in Uzbekistan over the next five years for the exploitation of five gas and oil blocks located on the Ustiurt Plateau, the Bukhara-Khiva region, and in the Ferghana Valley. The drilling of about fifteen new wells and evaluations on a dozen others are also envisaged in several areas of the country. If prospects appear profitable, a joint venture will be established and a new contract of exploitation signed.[155] CNODC also committed itself to training the Uzbek personnel of Uzbekneftegaz for half a million dollars.

The second agreement was signed on August 30, 2006, between the CNPC, Uzbekneftegaz, Lukoil, Petronas (Malaysia), and the National Company of South Korea. This production-sharing agreement stipulates that the international consortium in which these five companies take part will carry out the exploration of gas and oil fields located in the Aral Sea for the next 35 years. Uzbekistan places many of its energy aspirations in these three under-explored areas—the Aral Sea, the Ustiurt Plateau, and the right bank of the Amu-Darya River.

China-Central Asia Gas Pipeline Imbroglio

China hopes to finalise its Central Asian pipeline project by the end of 2007. It is holding direct bilateral negotiations with Kazakhstan, but is struggling to find a viable solution for a Sino-Turkmen or Sino-Uzbek pipeline. In 2006, the Chinese authorities seemed to give preference to its Kazakh neighbor over Tashkent. Uzbekistan would then have lost an important market of transit duties and been at least partially marginalised from new export routes. However, the situation has dramatically changed since the April 30, 2007, meeting between Uzbek president Islam Karimov and Ma Kai, the Chinese minister of development and reforms. Tashkent and Beijing decided to sign an accord pertaining to the construction of a 30 bcm capacity, 530 km long pipeline.

Details remain unclear with regards to its path and construction. Two routes were proposed. The first, according to the experts at the Economist Intelligence Unit, would pass through the Ferghana Valley, then Kyrgyzstan, before entering China.[156] The advantage of this route includes the contract the CNPC signed with Uzbekneftegaz to exploit the Mingbulak field, located in the Namangan region, which would allow for the rapid export of this new production.

The disadvantages include its passage through the mountainous regions of Kyrgyzstan, the fact that the main field of departure is not mentioned, and that it cannot depart from the Ferghana fields, which are too insignificant to warrant their own pipeline. Rather than pass through Kyrgyzstan, the second proposed route would pass through Kazakhstan. The pipeline would begin in the small town of Alata, 20 km from the Turkmen border in the Bukhara region, to join the already-existing Bukhara-Ural pipeline. Once in Kazakh territory, it will join the Sino-Kazakh pipeline east of Kumkol, that is to say the already-operational section that links to the Dostyk-Alashankou border post.[157] This second option seems more realistic.

From the technical point of view, it is restricted to a non-mountainous steppe region, which reduces its cost. From the logistical point of view, it uses already-functional structures to its advantage. In addition, the Turkmen- Kazakh growing alliance facilitates *a priori* this second solution. On May 7, 2007, the Kazakh energy and natural resources minister, Baktykozha Izmukhambetov, confirmed Astana's interest but acknowledged that the route was still under consideration. The negotiations between the different countries concerned will therefore be arduous. The Sino-Uzbek working group, established in April, will present its opinion on a final route by the end of 2007. In addition, the signed contract was never precise on the subject of Turkmen or Uzbek gas in the pipeline. In 2006, Uzbekistan produced 62 bcm of gas, of which 50 bcm went on domestic consumption. Only 12 bcm were exported, 9 of these by Gazprom to Russia, the rest to Kyrgyzstan and Kazakhstan. A pipeline limited to Uzbek production therefore seems overly ambitious. Tashkent is not able to dedicate 30 bcm, or half of its total production, to China, especially as Gazprom expects 13 bcm in 2007.

It is thus, likely that this pipeline will be a collaboration between Uzbekistan and Turkmenistan. In 2006, the latter produced approximately 65 bcm, of which 40 bcm were exported by Gazprom and 10 bcm by Iran. Again, no evidence exists that 30 bcm is free to redirect. Uzbekistan and Turkmenistan risk becoming modus vivendi by sharing this future Chinese pipeline, which supposes rapid political rapprochement between Tashkent and Ashgabat, estranged for many years.

Moreover, Gazprom continues to establish itself in the Central Asian market, such as the three-state agreement signed on May 12, 2007 between the Russian, Kazakh, and Turkmen presidents, which announced the construction of a Caspian gas pipeline (prikaspii). Although its capacity will be initially limited to 10 bcm, the agreement confirms Russian supremacy in matters of Central Asian gas export and puts concurrent Chinese and Transcaspian pipeline projects at a disadvantage. If the Caspian project is confirmed, China, like the West, will have to content itself in the hope that the new gas fields in South Yolotan and Osman live up to their potential claimed by Ashgabat.

However, on August 18, 2007, Chinese president Hu Jintao and his Kazakh counterpart signed two important agreements in Astana. The first one concerned the extension of the Atasu-Alashankou oil pipeline: its final section which is to be completed by 2011, will link the Kenyiak fields to those in Kumkol, and thus directly connect Xinjiang to the Caspian Sea. The second deal related to the construction of the Sino-Kazakh-Turkmen gas pipeline, which will be managed in equal parts by KazMunaiGas and the Chinese company CNPC. Its cost is estimated at four billion dollars for a total capacity of 40 billion m3. According to the map presented at the press conference, it will run from the Sino-Kazakh border post of Khorgos to the city of Chymkent, and then split into two branches.

One will head towards Uzbekistan and Turkmenistan in order to transport up to 30 billion m3 of Turkmen gas, as stipulated in the Chinese-Turkmen contract signed in April 2006; the other will link up to the Beineu field in Kazakhstan, and transport 10 billion m3.

These debates on Central Asian gas pipelines take place within a more global energy context. The vice director of Uzbekneftegaz, Shavkat Majitov, has recognised that China presents more attractive offers in terms of price than Gazprom, which refuses to this day to pay more than 100 dollars per 1,000 m3 for Uzbek or Turkmen gas. Thus, both Tashkent and Ashgabat have an interest in finding new buyers willing to pay the market price (like Iran in its purchases of Turkmen gas) or, more mundanely, convince Gazprom to accept higher tariffs. China will therefore be able to serve as an alibi to Central Asian states seeking to put pressure on Moscow.

Moreover, the Sino- Turkmen gas pipeline project is in direct competition with the objectives of Russia, which continually reaffirms its sole control over Turkmen exports, by the terms of their April 2003 agreement. In addition, Moscow wishes to sell its own gas to China, and to build a new pipeline increasing Russian gas flowing to China to 80 bcm, to be finished in 2011. Thus for the first time, Russian and Chinese interests in Central Asian gas could be in direct competition.

Conclusion

China's economic presence in Central Asia is very multi-faceted. Beijing seeks to establish itself in as many sectors as possible with an eye to occupying the many economic vacuums left by the collapse of the Soviet Union. In the sphere of hydrocarbons, it is improbable that China will completely make up for lost time. Despite its political purchases of fields, it cannot become one of the major players on the Kazakh oil market with neither Tengiz nor Kashagan under its control. It has succeeded, however, in several years, in implanting itself on numerous onshore sites. Today, more than twenty per cent of Kazakh oil production is Chinese.

It also demonstrated its tenacity in constructing the Atyrau-Alanshankou pipeline, which many observers dismissed as too costly and too complex to finish, and will benefit in a few years from a direct liaison with the Caspian Sea. Though late in its arrival in the Central Asia energy market, China proves that it has the capacity to become an important regional actor, and it now seems poised to capture large parts of the Uzbek and Turkmen markets, which are less competitive and more neglected by large Western companies compared to Kazakh markets.

China's increasing presence in the Central Asian energy market could gradually set the stage for an energy rivalry between Asia and Europe. The European Union, the United States, large Western oil companies, and China have increasingly conflicting interests in Central Asian hydrocarbons. Asia's booming economy will likely pull energy flows from the center of the continent toward Asia, even if such a result remains, for the moment, still virtual and late in its arrival on the Western radar.

For the time-being, China finds itself more or less in agreement with Russian firms. The two powers are not in concurrence with one another, each having its own sphere of activity, but this situation could rapidly evolve in years to come. Both have a paradoxical vision of the Central Asian energy market: it is important for them politically and commercially, but it does not affect their vital economic and strategic interests. Indeed, China will not be able to eliminate its dependence on the Middle East through Central Asian oil and gas, and Moscow has its own hydrocarbon riches, which it seeks to preserve by controlling Central Asian exports.

However, Moscow and Beijing are on the same page when it comes to gaining economic and political influence. Both pragmatically try to reinforce their political leverage over weak Central Asian states through their growing economic presence. Such a strategy is made easier by the two countries' large, state-run energy companies, which are an extension of official political interests. Russia remains, for the moment, more present in Central Asia than China is, but this domination has been somewhat reduced. Thus, if China is not destined to become the premier actor on the Central Asian hydrocarbon market, it will soon, if not already, have more influence than Moscow in other crucial sectors, such as trade.

With the Sino-Central Asian trade boom over the last years, China is now second only to Russia among Central Asia's trading partners—well ahead of Iran and Turkey. In fact, in the three countries with which it shares borders, the volume of trade is already equal to that of Russia, and even superior when taking into account the importance of border trade and contraband. Recent developments, which are bound to increase in magnitude in the coming years, entail numerous changes for Central Asian societies. They will benefit from consumer products that are more fitting to the low standard of living of their populations, but which are also capable of satisfying the growing technological consumption needs of the middle classes, in particular in Kazakhstan. The massive influx of Chinese products will give the peoples of Central Asia the opportunity to reassume their traditional role as a transit culture by exporting goods as far away as Russia, as the Kyrgyz and Uzbek migrants situated in Russia are already starting to do.

The long-term implications of China's engagement for landlocked Central Asia in terms of transit and transport will partially determine the future of the region. Chinese investments in infrastructure like hydroelectricity, transport, and telecommunications will enable all the Central Asian states to escape from the increased isolation that they have experienced after the disappearance of infrastructure networks dating from the Soviet era. In the development and opening of Central Asia, China seems destined to play the same major role in the South of Central Asia in the 21st century that Russia played in the North in the 19th and 20th centuries.

In terms of geopolitics, China may also rapidly replace Russia in its role as the dominant regional power facing the West. Thus, pipeline projects running westward to Europe, like the Transcaspian, could be considered as a threat by Beijing, as they are today by Moscow. The increased presence of China in Central Asia would also probably undermine several goals that the United States and the European Union have set themselves concerning energy security (oil, gas, and uranium), international stability, and democratisation.

In addition, Russia's and China's refusal to liberalise civil society could have a fundamental impact in Central Asia, meaning a strengthening of Islamism. The spreading of Islamist messages in Muslim societies since the Iraq war and the chronic instability of neighboring Afghanistan make already weak and corrupt Central Asian states, which enjoy little support from their societies, particularly vulnerable. The absence of a strong Western presence in the region, which both Moscow and Beijing refuse, could thus contribute to the heightening of regional instability.

Furthermore, the development of Sino-Central Asian relations, such as it is now taking shape, also entails the possibility that the economies of Central Asia will be encouraged into restrictive specialisations: by being nearly exclusively exporters of raw materials, the new states run the risk of having their last processing industries disappear. Such a limited specialisation coupled with the continued de-industrialisation of the area could be factors of social destabilisation, since they may well accelerate the rapid pauperisation of the lower strata of the population.

It, therefore, remains to be studied how the Central Asian societies will manage, in the years to come, the everincreasing Chinese presence and evolutions in ways of life, economic development, and political and cultural influence that Beijing will exert over Central Asia. In all the cases, whatever the negative or positive consequences, with this massive economic presence of China in Central Asia, Beijing now represents the most credible economic alternative for the states of Central Asia to free themselves from Russian tutelage.[00]

NOTES AND REFERENCES

1. D. Satpaev. "Kitai na provode. K kazhdoi strane TsentrAzii u Pekina svoi podkhod," [China on the way. Beijing has a specific approach to each Central Asian country], *CentrAsia,* January 22, 2007, <www.centrasia.ru/newsA.php4?st=1169450220> (April 11 2007).
2. V. Paramonov, A. Strokov. *Economic Involvment of Russia and China in Central Asia,* Central Asian Series, Conflict Studies Research Center, Defence Academy of the United Kingdom, 7/12 (2007), p. 2.

3. The Kyrgyz populations of the Murghab region confirm that they traded with the Kyrgyz in the PRC and in Afghanistan during the Soviet era and have regularly organised barter trade through family networks.
4. The Institute of Uighur Studies (Institute of Oriental Studies, Academy of Sciences, Almaty), March 2005.
5. G. Raballand, A. Andrésy. "Why should trade between Central Asia and China continue to expand?," *Asia-Europe Journal*, to be published.
6. G. Raballand, A. Andrésy. "Why should trade between Central Asia and China continue to expand?"
7. V. Paramonov, A. Strokov. *Economic Involvment of Russia and China in Central Asia*, p. 6.
8. Hsiu-Ling Wu, Chien-Hsun Chen. "The Prospects for Regional Economic Integration Between China and the Five Central Asian Countries," *Europe-Asia Studies*, 56, 7 (2004), pp. 1059-1080.
9. For a break-down by product, *Ibid.*, pp. 1069-1070.
10. *Ibid.* p. 1069-1070.
11. G. Raballand, A. Andrésy. "Why should trade between Central Asia and China continue to expand?"
12. V. Shevchenko. "Sindrom Khorgosa?," [The Khorgos syndrome?], *Kazakhstanskaia pravda*, May 27, 2005, <http://www.nomad.su/?a=13-200605290119> (April 19 2005).
13. "MinProm o razvitii ekonomicheskikh otnoshenii mezhdu Kyrgyzstanom i Kitaem," [Minister of Industry's statement on the development of the economic relations between Kyrgyzstan and China], *AKI-Press*, June 23, 2006, <http://www.akipress.org/news/29316> (March 14 2007).
14. V. Paramonov, A. Strokov. *Economic Involvment of Russia and China in Central Asia, op. cit.*, p. 8.
15. "Xianjiang's border trade to Kazakhstan on the fast track," *The Government of the Xinjiang* Uygur Autonomous Region web site, January 2006, <http://www.xinjiang.gov.cn/1$002/1$002$013/352.jsp?articleid=2006-1-3-0003> (March 12 2007).
16. Central Asia Human Development Report. Bringing Down Barriers: Regional Cooperation for Human Development And Human Security, UNDP, 2005, p. 189.
17. D. Satpaev. "Ten' 'kitaiskogo dragona' zhestkie storony miagkoi ekspansii," [The Shadow of the "Chinese Dragon" or The Hard

Realities of a Soft Expansion] Evraziiskii dom, January 18, 2007, <http://www.eurasianhome.org/xml/t/digest.xml?lang=ru&nic=digest&pid=1816> (March 12 2007).

18. G. Raballand, B. Kaminski. "La déferlante économique chinoise et ses conséquences en Asie centrale," *Monde chinois*, no. 4, 2007, to be published.
19. G. Raballand, A. Andrésy. "Why should trade between Central Asia and China continue to expand?"
20. A. Umarov, D. Pashkhun. *Tensions in Sino-Central-Asian Relations and their Implications for Regional Security*, Central Asian Series, Conflict Studies Research Center, Defence Academy of the United Kingdom, 06/02 (2006).
21. *Ibid.*
22. V. Paramonov, A. Strokov. *Economic Involvment of Russia and China in Central Asia*, p. 4.
23. "Sotrudnichestvo v oblasti sudokhodstva dlia Kitaia i Kazakhstana mozhet byt' vzaimovygodnym," [Cooperation on river navigation could be advantageous for China and Kazakhstan], *Professional*, 97, November 2005, <http://www.inform.kz/showarticle.php?lang=rus&id=140231> (April 11 2007).
24. Precursor Control on Central Asia's Border with China, United Nations, Office on Drugs and Crime, Regional Office for Central Asia, p. 9.
25. "Prigranichnye ambitsii," [Borders Ambitions], *Ekspert Kazakhstan*, 18 (120), May 14, 2007, <http://www.expert.ru/printissues/kazakhstan/2007/18/news_ekonomicheskaya_zona_dostyk/> (June 03 2007).
26. S. Bel'gibaev. "Otkrytie zonovoi dyry: SEZ na granitse s Kitaem mogut stat' 'vostochnym vorotami' dlia deshevoi rabochei sily," [Opening breaches: the free trade zones on the border with China may become the 'oriental doors' to a cheap labour force], *Gazeta.kz*, 42, March 14, 2006.
27. N. Swanström, N. Norling, Zhang Li. "China," in F. Starr (ed.) *The New Silk Roads. Transport and Trade in Greater Central Asia*, Central Asia-Caucasus Institute & Silk Road Studies Program, Johns Hopkins University-SAIS, 2007, p. 406.
28. Z. Bakhautdinova. "Dostyk-Alashan'kou, stantsiia budushchego," [Dostyk-Alashan'kou, the train station of the future], *Izvestia.kz*, July 9, 2006, <http://www.izvestia.kz/news.php?date=07-09-06&number=4> (April 15 2007).

29. "Prem'er Kazakhstana odobril programmu razvitiia pogranichnogo perekhoda Dostyk na granitse s Kitaem i zheleznodorozhnogo uchastka Aktogai-Dostyk na 2006-20011 g.," [The Kazakhstan Prime Minister validated the projects for the development of the Dostyk Border Post on the Border with China and of the Aktogai-Dostyk railway link for 2006-2011], *ITLS* web site, April 18, 2004, <http://www.itls.kz/index.php?p=news_more&id=11> (March 19 2007).
30. "New railway linking China, Europe to be built," *People's Daily,* March 18, 2004, <www.chinadaily.com.cn/english/doc/2004-03/18/content_315973.htm> (April 15 2007).
31. "Voprosy razvitiia tsentra Khorgos i zheleznodorozhnogo perekhoda Dostyk-Alashan'kou obsuzhdeny v pravitel'stve RK," [Kazakhstan Government studies questions concerning the development of the Khorgos center and the Dostyk-Alashan'kou railway link], *KazInform,* May 4, 2007, <http://www.nomad.su/?a=3-200705070234> (June 05 2007).
32. "Work on free trade zone on the agenda," *People's Daily,* November 2, 2004, <http://english.peopledaily.com.cn/200411/02/eng20041102_162447.html> (March 06 2007).
33. "China, Kazakhstan sign agreement to strengthen railway transport cooperation," *People's Daily,* May 18, 2004, <http://english.people.com.cn/200405/18/eng20040518_143586.html> (April 05 2007).
34. "Zheleznye dorogi ozabotilis' tranzitom," [Railways are kept busy with Transit Issues], *Blotter,* March 14, 2006, <http://blotter.ru/news/article089A0/default.asp> (April 15 2007).
35. "Kazakhstan protiv dorogi Khorgos-Sary-Ozek," [Kazakhstan is opposed to the Khorgos- Sary-Ozek railway], *KazInform,* May 31, 2005, <www.apnkz. ru/?chapter_name=events&data_id=3399&do =view_single> (April 11 2007).
36. "Propusknaia sposobnost' zheleznodorozhnykh perekhodov mezhdu Kazakhstanom i Kitaem budet uvelichena vdvoe," [The transit capacity of railways between Kazakhstan and China will double], *KazInform,* December 13, 2005, <http://www.apkinform.com/showart.php?id=31764> (April 1 2007).
37. "Kazakhstan, China Plan Additional Border Railroad-Link in 2009," *Almaty Region web site,* <http://www.almaty-reg.kz/almaty/investeng.phtml> (May 28 2007).
38. M. Junussova. *Global Market Needs New Cities or Development of Border Trade Ports of Kazakhstan,* REAL CORP 007 Proceedings, Vienna, May 20-23, 2007.

39. "China Opens New Transport Links to Kazakhstan," *RFE/RL,* September 1, 2006, <http://www.rferl.org/featuresarticle/2006/09/220f685e-15cc-4019-a042-87471f670071.html> (April 05 2007).

40. "Stroitel'stvo i rekonstruktsiia avtodorogi Aksai-Chundzha-Kolzhat nachalis' v Almatinskoi oblasti," [The building and reconstruction of the Aksai-Chundzha-Kolzhat road began in Almaty region], *Professional,* 121, April 24, 2006, <http://www.professional.kz/?mod=text&tx=067075> (April 15 2007).

41. Xinjiang's Land Port and Border web site, <http://www.china.org.cn/english/features/Xinjiang/114781.htm> (May 28 2007).

42. "China Boosts Trade Ties with Kazakhstan," *Washington Profile,* February 2, 2006, <http://www.washprofile.org/en/node/4593> (March 06 2007).

43. "Kitaiskaia kompaniia budet reabilitirovat' trassu Osh-Sarytash-Irkeshtam," [A Chinese Company will rehabilitate the Osh-Sarytash-Irkeshtam road], *Informatsionno-analiticheskii portal pr.kg,* March 13, 2007, <http://www.pr.kg/n/detail.php?id=15431> (April 15 2007).

44. T. Maekawa. "Silk Road Opens Up New Routes to Prosperity in Central Asia," *Asian Development Bank,* November 2006, <http://www.adb.org/Media/Articles/2006/11091-Central-Asia-Silk-Road/default.asp> (March 06 2007).

45. "Bumpy Road to the People's Republic of China,"*ADB Review,* October 2005, <http://www.adb.org/Documents/Periodicals/ADB_Review/2005/vol37-5/bumpy-road.asp> (April 04 2007).

46. J. W. Garver. "Development of China's Overland Transportation Links with Central, South-West and South Asia," *The China Quaterly,* 185 (2006), p. 3.

47. "Azië: Regional Road Corridor Improvement Project (PRC/KGZ/TAJ)," <http://www.evd.nl/info/zoeken/ShowBouwsteen.asp?bstnum=186966&location=> (May 28 2007).

48. V. Dubovitsky. "The Tajik-Chinese relations: the period of wariness over, the era of cooperation begins," *Ferghana.ru,* January 30, 2007, <http://enews.ferghana.ru/article.php?id=1810> (February 06 2007).

49. S. Aksakalov. "A New Silk Road? Tajikistan-China Border Crossing Opens," *Central Asia-Caucasus Analyst,* June 2, 2004, <http://www.cacianalyst.org/view_article.php?articleid=2417> (April 15 2007).

50. F. Starr. "Central Asia's Reemerging Transport Network: Promise and Perils for Mountainous Regions," Paper for the International

Workshop Strategies for Development and Food Security in Mountainous Areas of Central Asia," Dushanbe, June 6-10, 2005.

51. "Kitai gotov investirovat' 900 millionov dollarov v Kyrgyzstane v obmen na resursy i stroitel'stvo zh.d.," [China wants to invest 900 million dollars in Kyrgyzstan in exchange for resources and the construction of a railway], *CentrAsia,* January 29, 2005, <http://www.centrasia.ru/newsA.php4?st=1106979480> (March 06 2007).

52. "China Offers Assets-for-Investment Deal," *IWPR web site,* November 13, 2006, <http://iwpr.net/?p=bkg&s=b&o=325357&apc_state=henbbkgdate200611> (March 05 2007).

53. "Tadzhikistan i Kitai sozdaiut novye sovmestnye predpriiatiia po razrabotke mestorozhdenii zolota," [Tajikistan and China create new joint-ventures for the extraction of gold desposits], *Mineral.ru,* December 2005, <http://www.mineral.ru/Chapters/News/20700.html> (March 24 2007).

54. "Kitaiskaia i kazakhstanskaia kompanii sozdali SP po dobyche zolota v Kazakhstane," [Chinese and Kazakh companies create a joint-venture for the extraction of gold in Kazakhstan], *RosInvest,* September 7, 2005, <http://www.rosinvest.com/news/126039/> (April 15 2007).

55. "Kazatomprom vedet peregovory o prodazhe Kitaiu urana," [Kazatomprom holds negotiations over the sale of uranium to China], *BusinessPress,* August 24, 2001, <http://www.businesspress.ru/newspaper/article_mId_21960_aId_80147.html> (March 24 2007).

56. "Ul'binskii metallurgicheskii zavod zaregistriroval predpriiatie v Kitae," [The Ulbinsk metallurgic complex opens an office in China], *Infogeo.ru,* August 30, 2004, <http://www.infogeo.ru/metalls/news/?act=show&news=5432> (March 29 2007).

57. "Iadernomu Kitaiu nuzhen importnyi uran," [A Nuclear China needs to import uranium], *Iranatom.ru,* September 2005, <http://www.iranatom.ru/news/media/year05/september/chiur.htm> (April 19 2007).

58. T. Tashimov. "Kazatomprom propishetsia na kitaiskom rynke," [Kazatomprom is registered on the Chinese market], *Ekspert Kazakhstan,* 21, 123 (2007) <http://www.expert.ru/printissues/kazakhstan/2007/21/atomnaya_energetika/> (April 25 2007).

59. "Kitai budet dobyvat' olovo v Kirgizii," [China will extract tin in Kyrgyzstan], *apn.kz,* June 30, 2005, <www.apn-kz.ru/?chapter_name=events_print&data_id=3389&do=view_single> (April 19 2007).

60. "Almazek Atambaev izbran predsedatelem Soveta direktorov ZAO Sarydzhaz Energo," [Almazek Atambaev elected president of the ZAO Sarydzhaz Energy director's council], *Tatar.kg*, July 6, 2006, <http://www.tazar.kg/news.php?i=1230> (April 19 2007).

61. V. Dubovitsky. "The Tajik-Chinese relations: the period of wariness over, the era of cooperation begins," *Ferghana.ru*, January 30, 2007, <http://enews.ferghana.ru/article.php?id=1810> (February 25 2007).

62. "Kitai postroit v Turkmenii stekol'nyi kombinat – krupneishii v Tsentral'noi Azii," [China is constructing a glass factory in Turkmenistan, the largest in Central Asia], *Ferghana.ru*, January 31, 2007, <www.ferghana.ru/news.php?id=4948&mode=snews> (February 25 2007).

63. This section on hydroelectricity is taken from S. Peyrouse. "The Hydroelectric Sector in Central Asia and the Growing Role of China," *The China and Eurasia Forum Quarterly*, 5, 2 (2007), pp. 131-148. For further details, consult the article.

64. R. Dwivedi. "China's Central Asia Policy in Recent Times," *The China and Eurasia Forum Quarterly* 4, 4 (2006), p. 158.

65. "Kazakhstan, China to jointly build large-scale power plant," *People's Daily Online*, April 1, 2006 <http://english.people.com.cn/200604/01/eng20060401_255104.html> (May 25 2007).

66. "Kazakhstano-kitaiskuiu granitsu razmyvaet. Na Khorgose budut stroit' damby," [Eroding the Kazakhstan-Chinese frontier. Dams will be built on Khorgos] *CentrAsia*, August 11, 2003, <http://www.centrasia.ru/newsA.php4?st=1060553880> (March 05 2007).

67. G.D. Bessarabov, A. D. Sobianin. "Vodnye problemy KNP: kazakhskii i rossiiskii aspekty," [PRC Hydraulic problems: Kazakh and Russian Aspects], *China databases web site*, <http://www.chinadata.ru/china_water.htm> (May 03 2007).

68. G. Feller. "Central Asian Power Rapid Development of Coal And Hydroelectric Power For Export - Financed by Russia, Iran & China," *Eco World*, September 25, 2006, <http://www.ecoworld.com/home/articles2.cfm?tid=403> (May 03 2007).

69. "Po itogam peregovorov liderov Kazakhstana i Kitaia v Shankhae podpisan riad dvukhstoronnikh soglashenii," [Several bilateral agreements signed following Kazakhstan and Chinese leaders talks in Shanghai], *KazKommertsbank news*, June 14, 2006, <http://news.kkb.kz/news/show.asp?no=447469> (March 15 2007).

70. "China, Tajikistan Set to Strengthen Economic Cooperation," *New Eurasia*, January 19, 2007, <http://tajikistan.neweurasia.net/?p=155> (April 04 2007).

71. "Chinese to Build Tajik Hydroelectric Plant," *RFE/RL*, January 18, 2007, <http://www.rferl.org/featuresarticle/2007/01/C7ECA5D9-67F9-4659-88F9- 696875AC873E.html> (April 25 2007).
72. "K Rossii i Iranu, stroiashchim krupnye GES v Tadzhikistane, prisoedinilsia novyi investor," [A new investor joined Russia and Iran to build the large hydroelectric stations in Tajikistan], *Varorud*, August 20, 2007, <http://www.tajinfo.ru/news/1153973007/pindex.shtml> (April 25 2007).
73. "'South-North' Electric Main to be Key Link in Tajikistan's Electric System, Says President Rahmonov," *The Times of Central Asia*, September 18, 2006.
74. "Pravitel'stvo Kitaia vydelit Tadzhikistanu v seredine iunia bolee 603 millionov dollarov," [The Chinese government will give Tajikistan, in mid-June, more than 603 million dollars], *SNG News*, June 5, 2006, <http://www.cawater-info.net/news/06-2006/05.htm> (April 25 2007).
75. T. Kellner. *La République populaire de Chine et l'Asie centrale post-soviétique : étude de politique étrangère* (Ph.D., Institut Universitaire de Hautes Études Internationales, Genève, 2004), p. 462.
76. "Kirgiziia predlagaet Kitaiu sovmestno dostroit' kaskad Narynskikh GES," [Kyrgyzstan proposes to China joint construction of Naryn Hydroelectric Cascad] *CentrAsia*, September 22, 2004, <http://www.centrasia.ru/newsA.php4?st=1095883140> (April 11 2007).
77. "Almazek Atambaev izbran predsedatelem Soveta direktorov ZAO Sarydzhaz Energo," [Almazek Atambaev elected president of the ZAO Sarydzhaz Energo director's council], *tatar.kg*, July 6, 2006, <http://www.tazar.kg/news.php?i=1230> (March 20 2007).
78. "MInProm o razvitii ekonomicheskikh otnoshenii mezhdu Kyrgyzstanom i Kitaem," [Minister of Industry's statement on the development of the economic relations between Kyrgyzstan and China], *AKI-Press*, June 23, 2006, <http://www.akipress.org/news/29316> (April 15 2007).
79. "Kitai osnachshaet Turkmeniiu novymi passazhirskimi vagonami i teplovozami," [China supplies Turkmenistan with new carriages and locomotives], *CentrAsia*, August 11, 2006, <http://www.centrasia.ru/newsA.php4?st=1155278340> (April 15 2007).
80. "Rukovoditeli KNP i RK podpisali soglasheniia o rasshirenii investitsii KNP v neftegazovuiu otrasl'," [The Leaders of the PRC and of Kazakhstan have signed agreements to increase Chinese investments in the hydrocarbon sector], *Kazakhstan Today*, June 3, 2003, <http://www.gazeta.kz/art.asp?aid=29631> (March 24 2007).

81. "Peregovory o priobretenii kitaiskikh passazhirskikh vagonov vedet Kazakhstan," [Kazakhstan holding discussions about the purchase of Chinese passenger carriages], *Professional*, 93, October 9, 2005, <http://www.pr.kg/n/detail.php?id=15431> (April 15 2007).
82. A. Ismagulova. "Defitsit passazhirskikh vagonov v Kazakhstane v 2010 g. sostavit bolee 1200 edinits," [The shortage of passenger carriages in Kazakhstan will exceed 1,200 units by 2010], *RDZ-Partner*, April 20, 2007, <http://www.rzd-partner.ru/news/2007/04/20/303219.html> (May 28 2007).
83. "Po itogam peregovorov liderov Kazakhstana i Kitaia v Shankhae podpisan riad dvukhstoronnykh soglashenii," [Several bilateral agreements signed following Kazakh and Chinese leaders' talks in Shanghai], *KazKommertsbank news*, June 14, 2006, <http://news.kkb.kz/news/show.asp?no=447469> (March 06 2007).
84. "Kazakhstan rassmatrivaet vozmozhnost' priobreteniia 38 passazhirskikh vagonov u kitaiskoi kompanii," [Kazakhstan studies the possibility of purchasing 38 passenger carriages from a Chinese firm], *Kazakhstan Today*, January 14, 2006, <http://www.gazeta.kz/art.asp?aid=69950> (March 06 2007).
85. "Kitaiskaia kompaniia vyigrala tender po stroitel'stvu avtotrassy Dushanbe-Osh," [A Chinese company wins the tender for the construction of the Dushanbe-Osh road], *SNG News*, November 26, 2006, <http://sngnews.ru/articles/5/55549.html> (April 05 2007).
86. "Kitaitsy postroiat v Tadzhikistane dva strategicheski vazhnykh tonnelia," [China to construct two strategically important tunnels in Tajikistan], *SNG News*, <http://www.sngnews.ru/frame_article/5/66196.html> (April 05 2007).
87. "Kitai vydelil tri kreditnye linii dlia Tadzhikistana," [China extends three lines of credit to Tajikistan], *Regnum*, April 10, 2006, <http://www.regnum.ru/news/620951.html> (April 05 2007).
88. "Kitaiskaia kompaniia ECI namerena uchastvovat' v rekonstruktsii TadAza," [Chinese company ECI has decided to participate in reconstructing TadAz], *SNG News*, May 11, 2006, <www.sngnews.ru/archive/2006/05/11/63362.html> (April 05 2007).
89. "Rostelekom prinial uchastie vo vstreche operatorov stran ChOS Regional Carrier Meeting," [Rostelecom participated to the Regional Carrier Meeting of the SCO members operators], *Rostelecom web site*, August 25, 2005, <http://www.rt.ru/press/news/detail.php?ID=35207> (March 24 2007).
90. "Kazakhstan zakupaet deshevyi Internet v Kitae," [Kazakhstan buys cheap Internet from China], *Netoscope*, January 8, 2001, <http://www.netoscope.ru/news/2001/08/01/3052.html> (March 06 2007).

91. "ZTE budet vypuskat' apparaturu CDMA-450 v Kazakhstane," [ZTE will set up CDMA-450 system in Kazakhstan], *Onliner*, June 21, 2004, <http://www.onliner.ru/news/21.05.2004/20.25n/> (March 06 2007).
92. "A Grand Opening of Middle Asia Representative Office of China Telecom (HK) International Ltd.," *China Telecom web site*, June 2006, <http://www.chinatelecom.com.hk/en/newshow.jsp?id=43> (April 15 2007).
93. "V TUIT otkroetsia uchebnyi tsentr Huawei Technologies," [A Huawei Technologies formation center to open at TUIT], *Security.uz*, June 15, 2005, <http://www.security.uz/news/default.asp?id=10667 &do=print> (April 15 2007).
94. "China Mobile eyes expansion to Uzbekistan," *People's Daily*, August 2005, <http://english.people.com.cn/200508/10/eng20050810_201431. html> (April 24 2007).
95. "Huawei Technologies i Perfectum Mobile uspeshno zapustili set' CDMA v Uzbekistane," [Huawei Technologies and Perfectum Mobile successfully established CDMA system in Uzbekistan], *HTCom.ru*, June 27, 2006, <http://www.htcom.ru/news-pc/newsd-19193/> (April 15 2007).
96. "Privatizatsiia nedoprivatizirovannogo. Kirgizskii parlament odobril prodazhu Kyrgyztelecom," [A privatisation not followed through on. The Kyrgyz Parliament enables the sale of Kyrgyztelecom], *ComNews.ru*, June 6, 2006, <www.comnews.ru/ index.cfm?id=22902&caid=print> (April 17 2007).
97. "V Pekine Prezident Kurmanbek Bakiyev oznakomilsia s rabotoi krupnoi kompanii Huawei Technologies," [In Beijing, President Kurmanbek Bakiyev gets familiarised with the work of Huawei Technologies], *Kyrgyz Presidential Administration web site*, June 10, 2006, <www.president.kg/press/news/1222/> (April 17 2007).
98. "Dochka ZTE stala piatym operatorom mobil'noi sviazi v Tadzhikistane," [A TZE branch is now the fifth largest operator of mobile communications in Tajikistan], *3Gnews.ru*, June 7, 2004, <http://www.3gnews.ru/news/200406/07/1518/index.html?r= calendar_day> (April 15 2007).
99. "Vympelkom i Huawei zapustili set' HSDPA v Tadzhikistane," [Vympelkom and Huawei set up HSDPA system in Tajikistan], *ITNews*, April 2, 2007, <http://itnews.com.ua/31585.html> (June 05 2007).
100. "Kompaniia ZTE namerena vlozhit' v kommunikatsii Tadzhikistana eshche 70 millionov dollarov," [ZTE intends to invest $70 million

in the communication system in Tajikistan], *SNG News*, June 20, 2006, <http://www.sngnews.ru/archive/2006/06/20/64820.html> (April 15 2007).

101. "ZTE nadvigaetsia," [ZTE approachs], ComNews.ru, December 21, 2003, <www.comnews.ru/index.cfm?id=9119&caid=print> (March 24 2007).

102. "Kompanii iz Germanii i Kitaia pomogut Turkmenistanu modernizirovat' sistemy sviazi," [German and Chinese companies help Turkmenistan to modernise its communication system], *Turkmenistan.ru*, July 6, 2004, <www.turkmenistan.ru/?page_id=3&lang_id=ru&elem_id=2993&type=event&layout=pri> (March 05 2007).

103. "Kitai predostavil Turkmenistanu l'gotnyi kredit v razmere 200 millionov iuanei na razvitie sviazi i telekommunikatsii," [China offers Turkmenistan a low-interest loan of 200 million yuans to develop its connections and telecommunications], *Market.ru*, December 17, 2006, <http://www.finmarket.ru/z/nws/news.asp?id=555517&rid=1> (April 11 2007).

104. M. B. Olcott. "Is China A Reliable Stakeholder in Central Asia?," Testimony before the U.S.-China Economic and Security Review Commission, August 4, 2006, <http://www.carnegieendowment.org/publications/index.cfm?fa=view&id=18606&prog=zr> (April 15, 2007).

105. N. Swanstrom. "China and Central Asia: a new Great Game or traditional vassal relations?," *Journal of Contemporary China*, 14 (2005), pp. 569-584.

106. G. Raballand, R. Gente. "Oil in the Caspian Basin: Facts and Figures," in B. Najman, R. Pomfret, G. Raballand. (ed.), *The Economics and Politics of Oil in the Caspian Basin. The Redistribution of Oil Revenues in Azerbaijan and Central Asia*, London, Routledge, 2007.

107. Sh. Shuja. "China's Energy Needs and Central Asia," *National Observer*, Council for the National Interest, Melbourne, 67 (2006), pp. 56-65.

108. T. Kellner. "La politique pétrolière de la RPC : stratégies et conséquences internationales," *Puissance Chine ? Outre-terre. Revue de géopolitique*, 15 (2006), pp. 425-469.

109. P. Andrews-Speed, S. Vinogradov. "China's Involvement in Central Asian Petroleum: Convergent or Divergent Interests?," *Asian Survey*, 40, 2 (2000), pp. 377-397.

110. Xiaojie Xu. "The Oil and Gas links between Central Asia and China: a Geopolitical Perspective," *OPEC Review*, March (1999), pp. 33-54.

111. M. Kielmas. "China's Foreign Energy Asset Acquisitions: From Shopping Spree to Fire Sale?," *The China and Eurasian Forum Quarterly*, 3, 3, (2005), pp. 27-30. *The Economic Aspects of the Chinese-Central Asia Rapprochement* 49 America. However, these new markets cannot replace the dominance of the Middle East.112

112. B. M. Frolic, G. T. Chin. "The Challenge of Energy Security in Northeast Asia: China's Rising Energy Needs and Northeast Asian Cooperation," *North Pacific Region Advanced Research Center Publications*, 2000, <http://www.norpac.or.jp/main2/follow/1999-4.pdf> (May 10 2007).

113. C. E. Ziegler. "The Energy Factor in China's Foreign Policy," *Journal of Chinese Political Science*, 11, 1 (2006), pp. 1-23.

114. K. Esimova. "Kazakhstan-Chinese Cooperation in the Energy Sphere," *Central Asia and the Caucasus*, 1 (2005), pp. 146-152.

115. E. Watkins. "CNPC becomes sole owner of Kazakh-Chinese development JV," *Oil and Gas Journal Online*, June 6, 2003.

116. M. Barbasov. "An Oil Pipeline to China: An Element of Struggle for Caspian Resources," *Central Asia and the Caucasus*, 4, (2004), pp. 105-116.

117. Xiaojie Xu. "Oil and Gas Linkages between Central Asia and China," James A. Baker Institute for Public Policy, July 18, 2000, <http://riceinfo.rice.edu/projects/baker/publications/xuchina/xuchina.html> (March 20 2007).

118. A. Chebotarev. "Kazakhstan: Priority Oil Routes," *Central Asia and the Caucasus*, 9, 3 (2001), pp. 29-30.

119. "Kazakhstan: Major Oil and Natural Gas Projects," US Energy Information Administration, <http://www.eia.doe.gov/emeu/cabs/Kazakhstan/kazaproj.html> (May 15 2007).

120. P. Wonacott. "Western consortium shuts CNOOC out of oil project," *The Asian Wall Street Journal*, May 12, 2003.

121. F. William Engdahl. "China lays down gauntlet in energy war," *Asia Times*, December 21, 2005, <http://www.atimes.com/atimes/China/GL21Ad01.html> (April 14 2007).

122. "Chinese Company Takes Over Kazakh Oil Field," *Interfax-Kazakhstan*, October 21, 2003.

123. B. Khusainov. "Severobuzachinskaia intriga," [The North Buzachi intrigue], *Ekspert Kazakhstan*, 1, January 19, 2004, <http://www.expert.ru/printissues/kazakhstan/2004/01/01kaknelson/> (March 01 2007).

124. "Chinese oil giant goes on offensive as Kazakh energy assets battle hots up," *University of Alberta China Institute News*, October 29, 2005, <http://www.uofaweb.ualberta.ca/chinainstitute/nav03.cfm?nav03=44364&nav02=43876&nav0 1=43092> (March 05 2007).

125. V. Socor. "Implications of China's Takeover of Petrokazakhstan," *Eurasia Daily Monitor*, 2, 165, 2005, <http://www.jamestown.org/edm/article.php?article_id=2370186> (April 14 2007).

126. S. Blank. "China, Kazakh Energy, and Russia: An Unlikely Ménage à Trois," *The China and Eurasian Forum Quarterly*, 3, 3 (2005), pp. 99-109.

127. M. Yermukanov. "Russian Lukoil Plans to Dig Deep for Kazakh Oil," *Eurasia Daily Monitor*, 2, 189 2005, <http://www.jamestown.org/edm/article.php?article_id=2370326> (April 21 2007).

128. M. Yakovleva. "China Thirsts for Kazakh Oil," *Russian Petroleum Investor*, June 2005, <http://www.wtexecutive.com/cms/content.jsp?id=com.tms.cms.article.Article_rpi_article_1> (March 28 2007).

129. "KazMunaiGaz, CNPC to Jointly Develop Darkhan Field," *Interfax Information Services*, October 5, 2005, <http://www.uofaweb.ualberta.ca/chinainstitute/nav03.cfm?nav03=44401&nav02=43876&nav01=43092> (April 15 2007).

130. "CITIC to buy Kazakhstan oil assets," *Beijing Invest*, October 2006, <http://www.bjinvest.gov.cn/english/bn/200610/t141833.htm> (May 03 2007).

131. G. Christoffersen. "China's Intention for Russian and Central Asian Oil and Gas," *NRB Analysis*, The National Bureau of Asian Research, 9, 2 (1998).

132. M. Barbasov. "An Oil Pipeline to China: An Element of Struggle for Caspian Resources".

133. Xuanli Liao. "Central Asia and China's Energy Security," *The China and Eurasia Forum Quarterly*, 4, 4 (2006), pp. 61-69.

134. "The 'Great Game' goes on," *Petroleum Review*, February 26, 2007, <http://www.uofaweb.ualberta.ca/chinainstitute/nav03.cfm?nav03=57276&nav02=57275&nav01 =57272> (April 14 2007).

135. "Kazakhstan-China oil pipeline opens to commercial operation," *People's Daily Online*, July 12, 2006, <http://english.people.com.cn/200607/12/eng20060712_282194.html> (March 28 2007).

136. M. Yakovleva. "China Thirsts for Kazakh Oil".

137. M. Yermukanov. "Chinese Need Russian Oil to Fill Pipeline from Kazakhstan," *Eurasia Daily Monitor*, 2, 216, 2005, <http://

jamestown.org/edm/article.php?volume_id=407&issue_id=3532&article_id=2370494> (May 03 2007).

138. S. Smirnov. "The Chinese Dragon is Thirsty for Oil and Gas," *Central Asia and the Caucasus*, 6 (2004), pp. 67-76.

139. Guo Xuetang. "The Energy Security in Central Eurasia: the Geopolitical Implications to China's Energy Strategy," *The China and Eurasia Forum Quarterly*, 4, 4 (2006), pp. 117-137.

140. "Kitaem vedetsia bol'shaia rabota po priobreteniu riada neftianykh kompanii, rabotaiushchikh v Kazakhstane," [China tries to acquire several oil companies working in Kazakhstan], *Nomad.su*, November 2, 2006, <http://www.nomad.su/?a=3-200611020217> (April 17 2007).

141. E. Djantureyeva. "Oil and Gas Producers Sum up the Results," *Kazakhstan International Business Magazine*, 1 (2006), <http://www.investkz.com/en/journals/46/70.html> (April 17 2007).

142. "Natsional'naia neftianaia korporatsiia Kitaia i AO Kyrgyzneftegaz zakliuchili soglashenie o dobyche nefti na iuge Kirgizii," [The CNPC and Kyrgyzneftegaz signed a contract on extraction of oil in the South of Kirghizia], *Mineral.ru*, July 2002, <www.mineral.ru/Chapters/News/3593.html> (March 27 2007).

143. "China emerges as a major energy player," *Alexander's Oil and Gas Connections*, 9, 17 (2004), <http://www.gasandoil.com/goc/news/nts43583.htm> (April 04 2007).

144. "Kazakhstan-China gas pipeline study to be ready in 2004," *Interfax Kazakhstan*, October 10, 2003.

145. "China, Kazakhstan mulling gas pipeline construction," *China Daily*, April 14, 2006, <http://www.chinadaily.com.cn/china/2006-04/14/content_567792.htm> (March 28 2007).

146. T. Kellner, "La Chine et la nouvelle Asie centrale," Bruxelles, Groupe de recherche et d'information sur la paix et la sécurité (GRIP) (2002), p. 26.

147. "China launches massive gas pipeline campaign," *Oil and Gas Journal Online*, June 5, 2000.

148. "China emerges as a major energy player".

149. "Turkmenistan: gas pipeline to China is ready," *Asia News*, August 22, 2006, <http://www.asianews.it/index.php?l=en&art=6997> (April 17 2007).

150. V. Socor. "Turkmenistan-China Gas Agreement Unrealistically Ambitious," *Eurasia Daily Monitor*, 3, 69, 2006, <http://jamestown.org/edm/article.php?article_id=2370964> (April 17 2007).

151. S. Blagov. "Itera Suggests Reviving Zarit Consortium for Caspian Exploration," *Eurasia Daily Monitor*, 4, 51, 2007, <http://www.jamestown.org/publications_details.php?volume_id=420&issue_id=4035&article_i d=2372001> (May 05 2007).

152. T. Niazi. "The Ecology of Strategic Interests: China's Quest for Energy Security from the Indian Ocean and the South China Sea to the Caspian Sea Basin," *The China and Eurasia Forum Quarterly*, 4, 4 (2006), pp. 97-116.

153. Huasheng Zhao. "Central Asia in China's Diplomacy," in E. Rumer (ed.), *Central Asia. Views from Washington, Moscow and Beijing* (London/ New York, M. E. Sharpe, 2007), p. 168.

154. "Kitaiskii neftedobychik otkazalsia ot proekta v Uzbekistan," [A Chinese oil company refuses a project in Uzbekistan], *Ferghana.ru*, April 19, 2007, <http://www.ferghana.ru/news.php?id=5806&mode=snews> (May 05 2007).

155. "CNPC to Tap Oil and Natural Gas in Uzbekistan," *Xinhua News Agency*, September 3, 2006, <http://www.china.org.cn/english/2006/Sep/179963.htm> (May 05 2007).

156. A. Krasinskaia. "Vse gazoprovody vedut v Kitai," [All gas pipelines lead to China], *CentrAsia*, June 4, 2007, <http://www.centrasia.ru/newsA.php4?st=1178259540> (June 09 2007).

157. "Novyi uzbeksko-kitaiskii gazoprovod budet prednaznachen dlia tranzita turkmenskogo gaza," [The new Uzbek-Chinese gas pipeline is intended to transport Turkmen gas], *Ferghana.ru*, June 7, 2007, <http://www.ferghana.ru/news.php?id=5988&mode=snews> (June 09 2007).

BIBLIOGRAPHY

Adshead, Samuel Adrian M. *Central Asia in World History*. New York: St. Martin's Press, 1993.

Ahrari, M. E., *The New Great Game in Muslim Central Asia*, McNair Paper 47, National Defense University Press, Washington, DC, January 1996.

Akiner, Shirin, ed. *Central Asia: 130 Years of Russian Dominance, an Historical Overview*. Durham: Duke University Press, 1994.

Akiner, Shirin, ed. *Economic and Political Trends in Central Asia*. New York: Routledge & Kegan Paul, 1992.

Akiner, Shirin. *Islamic Peoples of the Soviet Union: An Historical and Statistical Handbook*. New York: Routledge, 1986.

Alden, C. (2006): "Leveraging the dragon: Towards an Africa That Can say No". *EAfrica, Electronic Journal of Governance and Innovation*, February 2005.

Allworth, Edward, ed. *Central Asia: 120 Years of Russian Rule*. Durham: Duke University Press, 1989.

Alptekin, Erkin. "Chinese Policy in Eastern Turkestan," *Institute of Muslim Minority Affairs Journal*, 13, January 1992, 185-95.

Andreyev, Nikolai. "Central Asia: From Marx to Mohammed," *New Times International* [Moscow], No. 39, 1992, 19-22.

Andreyev, Nikolai. "What Future for Uzbekistan, Kirgizia, Turkmenia?" *Current Digest of the Post-Soviet Press*, 44, July 22, 1992, 8-11.

Anjaparidze, Zaal, "Negotiability Versus Negotiations: Georgia and the Abhaz Question," *Jamestown Prism*, Vol. 4, No. 6, Part 4, March 20, 1998.

Anshan, Li (2007): China's *Engagement in Africa: Singular Interest or Mutual Benefit.* Conference Paper, Resource Governance in Africa in the 21st Century, Heinrich Böll Foundation, Berlin. www.boell.de/downloads/intlpolitics/China_Li_Anshan.pdf

Arvanitopoulos, Constantine, "The Geopolitics of Oil in Central Asia," *Thesis*, Vol. 1, Issue No. 4, Winter 1997–1998, pp. 18–27.
"Azerbaijan Accuses China of Selling Secrets to Armenia," *Radio Free Europe/Radio Liberty Newsline*, Vol. 3, No. 97, Part I, May 19, 1999.

Aziz, Sartaj, "The Rediscovery of Central Asia," *Economics Review* [Karachi], 23, June 1992, 15-17.

Baldick, Julian. *Imaginary Muslims: The Uwaysi Sufis of Central Asia.* Irvington: New York University Press, 1994.

Banuazizi, Ali, and Myron Weiner (eds.), *The New Geopolitics of Central Asia and Its Borderlands*, I. B. Tauris, London and New York, 1994.

Banuazizi, Ali, and Myron Weiner, eds. *The New Geopolitics of Central Asia and Its Borderlands.* Bloomington: Indiana University Press, 1994.

Baumann, Robert F. *Russian-Soviet Unconventional Wars in the Caucasus, Central Asia, and Afghanistan.* Fort Leavenworth, Kansas: Combat Studies Institute, 1993.

Becker, Abraham S., "Russia and the Caucasus-Central Asia States: Why is Moscow Floundering?" paper prepared for the RAND Conference on Security Dynamics in Central Asia and the Caucasus, March 1998.

Berger, B. (2006): *"China's engagement in Africa – Can the EU sit back?"*, *South African Journal for International Affairs* 13(1), SAIIA, South Africa

Berger, B.; Wissenbach, U. (2007a): *EU-China-Africa Trilateral Development Cooperation: Common challenges and new directions.* Discussion Paper, Deutsches Institut für Entwicklungspolitik, Bonn. www.ec-an.eu/files/bergerweissenbach_0.pdf

Blandy, C. W., *Oil is Not the Only Stake*, Conflict Studies Research Center, Report S28, Camberley, Surrey, February 1997.

Blank, Stephen J., *Energy, Economics, and Security in Central Asia: Russia and Its Rivals,* Strategic Studies Institute, U.S. Army War College, Carlisle Barracks, PA, 1995.

Bourdeaux, Michael, ed. *The Politics of Religion in Russia and the New States of Eurasia.* Armonk, New York: M.E. Sharpe, 1995.

Bremmer, Ian, and Ray Taras (eds.), *Nations and Politics in the Soviet Successor States,* Cambridge University Press, New York, 1992.

Brown, Bess A., "Security Concerns of the Central Asian States," in Jed C. Snyder (ed.), *After Empire: The Emerging Geopolitics of Central Asia,* NDU Press, Washington, DC, 1995.

Brown, Bess. "Central Asia: The First Year of Unexpected Statehood," *RFE/RL Research Report* [Munich], 2, No. 1, January 1, 1993, 25-36.

Brown, Bess. "Three Central Asian States Form Economic Union," *RFE/RL Research Report* [Munich], 3, No. 11, April 1, 1994, 33-35.

Brzezinski, Zbigniew, "The Eurasian Balkans," in *The Grand Chessboard,* Basic Books, New York, 1997.

Clark, Susan L. *Security in Russia and Eurasia: The New National Militaries and Emerging Defense Policies.* Boulder, Colorado: Westview Press, 1995.

Clark, Susan, "The Central Asian States: Defining Security Priorities and Developing Military Forces," in Michael Mandelbaum (ed.), *Central Asia and the World,* Council on Foreign Relations, New York, 1994.

Clawson, Patrick, "The Former Soviet South and the Muslim World," in Jed C. Snyder (ed.), *After Empire: The Emerging Geopolitics of Central Asia,* NDU Press, Washington, DC, 1995.

Cohen, Ariel, *The New 'Great Game': Oil Politics in the Caucasus and Central Asia,* The Heritage Foundation Backgrounder No. 1065, Washington, DC, January 25, 1996.

Coker, C. (2007): "Strangers at the Gates: Africa, the challenge of China and the Eclipse of the West", *Estratégia e Segurança na África Austral,* FLAD e IPRI-UNL, Julho 2007. www.ipri.pt/publicacoes/working_paper/pdf/2-coker.pdf

Council of the European Union (2007): *The Africa-EU Strategic Partnership . Joint Africa-EU Strategy and its First Action Plan (2008-2010)*, December 2007.

Dani, A.H. and V.M. Masson (eds.), *UNESCO History of Civilisations of Central Asia*. Paris: UNESCO, 1992.

Davies, P. (2007): *China and the End of Poverty in Africa – toward Mutual Benefit?*

Davis, Christopher M. "Health Care Crisis: The Former Soviet Union," *RFE/RL Research Report* [Munich], 2, No. 40, October 8, 1993, 35-43.

Dawisha, A.I., and Karen Dawisha, eds. *The Foreign Policy Interests of Russia and the New States of Eurasia*. Armonk, New York: M.E. Sharpe, 1995.

Dawisha, Karen, and Bruce Parrott. *Russia and the New States of Eurasia: The Politics of Upheaval*. Port Chester, New York: Cambridge University Press, 1994.

Deweese, Devin. *Islamisation and Native Religion in the Golden Horde*. University Park: Pennsylvania State University Press, 1994.

Dienes, Leslie. "Economic Geographic Relations in the Post-Soviet Republics," *Post-Soviet Geography*, 34, October 1993, 497-529.

Diller, Daniel C., ed. *Russia and the Independent States*. Washington: Congressional Quarterly, 1993.

Doolotaliyev, S. "Some Issues in the Development of the Sary-Dzhaz Mining Industrial Center, Kirghiz SSR," *Sovetskaya Geografiya*, 30, May 1989, 371-4.

EC (2008): *The EU, Africa and China: Towards trilateral dialogue and cooperation.*

ECDPM (2007): *EU, China and Africa: A trilateral partnership in theory, a bilateral one in practice?* Editorial, ECDPM, Maastricht www.ecdpm.org

Eickelman, Dale F., ed. *Russia's Muslim Frontiers: New Directions in Cross-Cultural Analysis*. Bloomington: Indiana University Press, 1993.

Eisenman, J.; Kurlantzick, J. (2006): *China's Africa Strategy*. American Foreign Policy Council www.afpc.org/china-africa.shtml

Elebayeva, Aynur B. "The Osh Incident: Problems for Research," *Post-Soviet Geography*, 33, February 1992, 78-86.

Ellison, Herbert J., and Bruce A. Acker, "Azerbaijan: U.S. Policy Options," National Bureau of Asian Research Briefing, June 1997, pp. 1–9.

Emerson, Sarah A., "The Relevance of Caspian Oil for the World," paper prepared for the Fourth Annual Energy Conference on Caspian Resources, The Emirates Center for Strategic Studies and Research, October 1998.

Evans, John L. *Russia and the Khanates of Central Asia to 1865*. New York: Associated Faculty Press, 1982.

Ferdinand, Peter. *The New States of Central Asia and Their Neighbors*. New York: Council on Foreign Relations Press, 1994.

Fierman, William, ed. *Soviet Central Asia: The Failed Transformation*. Boulder, Colorado: Westview Press, 1991.

Finberg, Jared, "GUAM's Potential Outside of the CIS," *Weekly Defense Monitor*, Center for Defense Information, May 24–31, 1997.

Fues, T.; Grimm, S.; Laufer, D. (2006): *China's Africa Policy: Opportunity and Challenge for European Development Policy*, German Development Institute, Bonn.

Fuller, Graham. *Central Asia: The New Geopolitics*. Santa Monica, California: Rand, 1992.

Furtado, Charles F., and Henry R. Huttenback, eds. "The Ex-Soviet Nationalities Without Gorbachev," *Nationalities Papers*, 20, Fall 1992, 1-124.

Gleason, Gregory. "The Political Economy of Dependency under Socialism: The Asian Republics in the USSR," *Studies in Comparative Communism*, 24, December 1991, 335-53.

Goldstein, A. et al. (2006): *The Rise of China and India: What's in it for Africa?* Summary, OECD, Paris.

Goron, Leonard, and Alex Pravda, eds. *Who's Who in Russia and the New States*. London: I.B. Tauris, 1993.

Grimm, S. (2008): *Africa-China-Europe trilateral co-operation: Is Europe naïve?* Opinion, EDC2020, Nov.08.

Gross, Jo-Ann, ed. *Muslims in Central Asia: Expressions of Identity and Change*. Durham: Duke University Press, 1992.

Haghayeghi, Mehrdad. *Islam and Politics in Central Asia*. New York: St. Martin's Press, 1995.

Henze, Paul B. *Whither Turkestan?* Santa Monica, California: Rand, 1992.

Holstag, J. (2006): "The European Union and China: The Great Disillusion". *European Foreign Affairs Review*, Vol 11(4). www.ec-an.eu/node/149

Holstag, J. (2007): *Friendly Giant? China's Evolving Africa Policy*. Asia Paper vol. 2 (5), BICCS Background Paper, 24 August 2007.

Holstag, J. (2008): *A paper tiger for Africa*. BICCS Asia Briefing, August, Brussels Institute of Contemporary China Studies, Brussels.

Hostler, Charles Warren. *The Turks of Central Asia*. Westport, Connecticut: Praeger, 1993.

Humphrey, J. (2007): *Research in Europe and Africa-China Relationships*. A Report for the Rockefeller Foundation, Institute of Development Studies, Brighton, UK.

Kaiser, Robert J. *The Geography of Nationalism in Russia and the USSR*. Princeton: Princeton University Press, 1994.

Kangas, Roger, "With an Eye on Russia, Central Asian Militaries Practice Cooperation," *Transition*, Vol. 2, No. 16, August 9, 1996.

Karasik, Theodore. *Azerbaijan, Central Asia, and Future Persian Gulf Security*. Santa Monica, California: Rand, 1993.

Kedzie, Christopher R. *Stumbling Blocks and Stepping Stones: The Crossing from Soviet Domination to Self Rule in the Republics of Central Asia*. Santa Monica, California: Rand, 1994.

Kellett, N. A., *Russian Peacekeeping Part II: The Strategic Context*, Canadian Department of National Defense, Research Note 96/08, Ottawa, Canada, December 1996.

Kurlantzick, J. (2006): *Beijing's Safari – China's move into Africa and its implications for aid, development and governance*. Policy Outlook, Carnegie Endowment for International Peace, Washington.

Landau, Jacob M. *Pan-Turkism: From Irredentism to Cooperation.* Bloomington: Indiana University Press, 1995.

Lipski, Andrei. "The Community of Central Asia: Inside or Outside the CIS?" *International Affairs* [Moscow], October 1993, 51-5.

Maier, Frith. *Trekking in Russia and Central Asia: A Traveler's Guide.* Seattle: Mountaineers Books, 1994.

Malik, Hafeez, ed. *Central Asia: Its Strategic Importance and Future Prospects.* New York: St. Martin's Press, 1994.

Mandelbaum, Michael, ed. *Central Asia and the World: Kazakhstan, Uzbekistan, Tajikistan, Kyrgyzstan, and Turkmenistan.* New York: Council on Foreign Relations Press, 1994.

Manning, Richard (2006): "Will Emerging Donors Change the Face of International Cooperation?" in *Development Policy Review* 24:4: 371-385

Manz, Beatrice F., ed. *Central Asia in Historical Perspective.* Boulder, Colorado: Westview Press, 1994.

Martin, Keith. "Environment: Central Asia's Forgotten Tragedy," *RFE/RL Research Report* [Munich], 3, No. 29, July 29, 1994, 35-48.

Menon, Rajan, "Central Asia's Foreign Policy and Security Challenges: Implications for the United States," *National Bureau of Asian Research Analysis,* Vol. 6, No. 4, December 1995.

Menon, Rajan, "In the Shadow of the Bear: Security in Post-Soviet Central Asia," *International Security,* Vol. 20, No. 1 Summer 1995, pp. 149–181.

Mesbahi, Mohiaddin, ed. *Central Asia and the Caucasus after the Soviet Union: Domestic and International Dynamics.* Gainesville: University Press of Florida, 1994.

Michel, L. (2007): *UE–Chine-Afrique: d'une relation de concurrence à un partenariat triangulaire pour le développement de l'Afrique.* Conference "EU-China-Africa", EC, Brussels 28/06/07.

Migranyan, Andranik. "Russia and the Near Abroad," *Current Digest of the Post-Soviet Press,* 47, March 9, 1994, 1-4 and March 16, 1994, 6-11.

Munro, Ross, "Central Asia and China," in Michael Mandelbaum (ed.), *Central Asia and the World,* Council on Foreign Relations, New York, 1994.

Nascimento, L. et al (2007): *Competition or Partnership? China, United States and Africa–An African View.* Discussion Paper 2/2007, Brenthurst Foundation, Johannesburg.

Naumkin, Vitaly. *State, Religion, and Society in Central Asia: A Post-Soviet Critique.* London: Ithaca Press, 1993.

Neves, Miguel Santos (2007): *Recent Trends in EU-China Relations and future prospects: partners or competitors in the context of glocalisation?* IEEI, 2007.

Olcott, Martha Brill, "Central Asia's Post-Empire Politics," *Orbis,* Spring 1992, pp. 253–268.

Olcott, Martha Brill. *Central Asia's New States: Independence, Foreign Policy, and Regional Security.* Washington: United States Institute of Peace Press, 1996.

Paksoy, G.B., ed. *Central Asia Reader: The Rediscovery of History.* Armonk, New York: M.E. Sharpe, 1994.

Partridge, Ben, "Caucasus/Central Asia: Region Relies Too Much on Oil and Gas," *Radio Free Europe/Radio Liberty Daily Report,* April 14, 1998.

Pilkington, John. "Kyrgyzstan: A Tale of Two Journeys," *Geographical Magazine,* 65, April 1993, 8-12.

Pipes, Daniel. "The Politics of the 'Rip Van Winkel' States: The Southern Tier States of the Ex-Soviet Union Have Moved the Borders of the Middle East North," *Middle East Insight,* 10, November-December 1993, 30-40.

Potter, William C., *Nuclear Profiles of the Soviet Successor States,* Monterey Institute of International Studies, Monterey, CA, May 1993.

Pryde, Ian. "Kyrgyzstan: Secularism vs. Islam," *World Today,* 48, November 1992, 208-11.

Pryde, Ian. "Kyrgyzstan: The Trials of Independence," *Journal of Democracy,* 5, January 1994, 109-20.

Rashid, Ahmed. *The Resurgence of Central Asia: Islam or Nationalism?* Karachi: Oxford University Press, 1994.

Ro'i, Yaacov, ed. *Muslim Eurasia: Conflicting Legacies.* London: Frank Cass, 1995.

Rotor, Igor. "Kyrgyzstan: Capitalist Experiment in Central Asia," *Current Digest of the Post-Soviet Press*, 44, April 8, 1992, 4-5.

Rumer, Boris Z. *Soviet Central Asia: "A Tragic Experiment."* Winchester, Massachusetts: Unwin Hyman, 1990.

Shlapentokh, Vladimir, Munir Sendich, and Emil Payin, eds. *The New Russian Diaspora: Russian Minorities in the Former Soviet Republics*. Armonk, New York: M.E. Sharpe, 1994.

Shome, Parthasarathi, and Julio Escolano. "The State of Tax Policy in the Central Asian and Transcaucasian Newly Independent States," *Bulletin of International Fiscal Documentation*, 48, April 1994, 159-66.

Shukurov, E., ed. *Discovery of Kyrghyzstan*. Bishkek: International Foundation "A Discovery of Kyrghyzstan," 1993.

Solana, Javier (2007): "Challenges for EU-China Cooperation in Africa". *China Daily*, 7 February 2007.

Sparks, John. *Realms of the Russian Bear: A Natural History of Russia and the Central Asian Republics*. Waltham, Massachusetts: Little Brown, 1992.

Starr, S. Frederick, ed. *The Legacy of History in Russia and the New States of Eurasia*. Armonk, New York: M.E. Sharpe, 1994.

Szporluk, Roman, ed. *National Identity and Ethnicity in Russia and the New States of Eurasia*. Armonk, New York: M.E. Sharpe, 1994.

The Europa World Year Book 1994, 2. London: Europa, 1994.

The Europa World Year Book 1995, 2. London: Europa, 1995.

The Europa World Year Book 1996, 2. London: Europa, 1996.

The Military Balance 1993-1994. London: International Institute for Strategic Studies, 1993.

The Military Balance 1994-1995. London: International Institute for Strategic Studies, 1994.

The Military Balance 1995-1996. London: International Institute for Strategic Studies, 1995.

The Statesman's Year-Book 1993-1994. Ed., Brian Hunter. New York: St. Martin's Press, 1993.

The Statesman's Year-Book 1994-1995. Ed., Brian Hunter. New York: St. Martin's Press, 1994.

The Statesman's Year-Book 1995-1996. Ed., Brian Hunter. New York: St. Martin's Press, 1995.

Thomas, Paul. *The Central Asian States: Tajikistan, Uzbekistan, Kyrgyzstan, Turkmenistan.* Brookfield, Connecticut: Millbrook Press, 1992.

Thompson, D. (2005): "China's Emerging Interests in Africa: Opportunities and Challenges for Africa and the United States", in *African Renaissance,* Vol.2 No.4, July-August 2005. wwwcsis.org/media/csis/press/0508china african interests.pdf

United Nations. Department for Economic and Social Information and Policy Analysis. *Demographic Yearbook 1994.* New York: 1996.

United States. Central Intelligence Agency. *The World Factbook 1994.* Washington: GPO, 1994.

United States. Central Intelligence Agency. *Handbook of International Economic Statistics 1995.* Washington: GPO, 1995.

United States. Department of State. Bureau of International Narcotics Matters. *International Narcotics Strategy Report March 1996.* Washington: GPO, 1996.

WEFA Group. *Eurasia Economic Outlook February 1996.* Eddystone, Pennsylvania: 1996.

Wheatcroft, Stephen G., "Revisiting the Crisis Zones of Euro-Asia, Part Two: The Crisis Zones in 1997," *Russian and Euro-Asian Bulletin,* April 1997, pp. 1–4.

Wild, L.; Mepham, D. (eds) (2006): *The New Sinosphere – China in Africa.* Institute for Public Policy Research www.ippr.org/articles/index.asp?id=2419

Wimbush, S. Enders, "Central Asia and the Caucasus: Key Emerging Issues and U.S. Interests," unpublished paper prepared for the RAND Conference on Security Dynamics in Central Asia and the Caucasus, March 1998.

Winrow, Gareth, *Turkey in Post-Soviet Central Asia,* Royal Institute of International Affairs, London, 1995.

Wissenbach, U. (2007): *Partners in Competition? The EU, Africa and China*. Conference Summary Proceedings, 28/06/2007.

Wixman, Ronald. *Peoples of the USSR: An Ethnographic Handbook*. Armonk, New York: M.E. Sharpe, 1984.

World Bank. *Kyrgyz Republic: Agricultural Sector Review*. Washington: 1995.

World Bank. *Kyrgyz Republic: Economic Report*. Washington: 1994.

World Bank. *Kyrgyz Republic: Energy Sector Review*. Washington: 1995.

World Bank. *Kyrgyz Republic: National Environmental Action Plan*. Washington: 1995.

World Bank. *Kyrgyz Republic: Poverty Assessment and Strategy*. Washington: 1995.

World Bank. *Kyrgyzstan: Social Protection in a Reforming Economy*. Washington: 1993.

World Bank. *Kyrgyzstan: The Transition to a Market Economy*. Washington: 1993.

World Bank. *Statistical Handbook 1995: States of the Former USSR*. Washington: 1995.

Yadav, Surya Narain (2006). Shanghai Fire: Issues, Achievements and Prospects, Seminar Paper, Presented to the Institute of Chinese Studies, New Delhi.

Zviagelskaia, Irina, *The Russian Policy Debate on Central Asia*, Royal Institute of International Affairs, London, 1995.

INDEX

A

B

C

I

J

K

L

M

N

O

P

Q

R

S

T

U

W

X

Y

Z